Evangelism and Social Concern in the Theology of Carl F. H. Henry

Evangelism and Social Concern in the Theology of Carl F. H. Henry

Jerry M. Ireland

Foreword by
Edward L. Smither

◆PICKWICK *Publications* • Eugene, Oregon

EVANGELISM AND SOCIAL CONCERN IN THE THEOLOGY OF
CARL F. H. HENRY

Copyright © 2015 Jerry M. Ireland. All rights reserved. Except for brief quotations in critical publications or reviews, no part of this book may be reproduced in any manner without prior written permission from the publisher. Write: Permissions. Wipf and Stock Publishers, 199 W. 8th Ave., Suite 3, Eugene, OR 97401.

Pickwick Publications
An Imprint of Wipf and Stock Publishers
199 W. 8th Ave., Suite 3
Eugene, OR 97401

www.wipfandstock.com

ISBN 13: 978-1-4982-0950-2

Cataloguing-in-Publication Data

Ireland, Jerry M.

    Evangelism and social concern in the theology of Carl F. H. Henry / Jerry M. Ireland ; foreword by Edward L. Smither.

    xviii + 238 p. ; 23 cm. Includes bibliographical references.

    ISBN 13: 978-1-4982-0950-2

    1. Henry, Carl F. H. (Carl Ferdinand Howard), 1913–2003. 2. Church and social problems. 3. Evangelicalism. I. Smither, Edward L. II. Title.

BV3793 .I74 2015

Manufactured in the U.S.A.   05/20/2015

Scripture quotations marked *KJV* are from The Authorized (King James) Version. Rights in the Authorized Version in the United Kingdom are vested in the Crown. Reproduced by permission of the Crown's patentee, Cambridge University Press.

Scripture quotations marked *NASB* are taken from the New American Standard Bible®, Copyright © 1960, 1962, 1963, 1968, 1971, 1972, 1973, 1975, 1977, 1995 by The Lockman Foundation. Used by permission.

Scripture quotations marked *NEB* are taken from the New English Bible, copyright © Cambridge University Press and Oxford University Press 1961, 1970. All rights reserved.

Scripture quotations marked (NIV) are taken from the Holy Bible, New International Version®, NIV®. Copyright © 1973, 1978, 1984, 2011 by Biblica, Inc.™ Used by permission of Zondervan. All rights reserved worldwide. www.zondervan.com The "NIV" and "New International Version" are trademarks registered in the United States Patent and Trademark Office by Biblica, Inc.™

Scripture quoatations marked *RSV* are taken from the Revised Standard Version of the Bible, copyright 1952 [2nd edition, 1971] by the Division of Christian Education of the National Council of the Churches of Christ in the United States of America. Used by permission. All rights reserved.

To my wife, Paula, and daughter, Charis

Contents

Foreword by Edward L. Smither | ix
Preface | xi
Acknowledgments | xv
Abbreviations | xvi

1. Evangelism and Social Concern | 1
2. Henry's Life and Impact | 36
3. Henry's Theological Method | 61
4. Henry and Evangelism | 101
5. Henry and Social Concern | 153
6. Conclusion | 219

Bibliography | 223

Foreword

IT IS ALWAYS EXCITING when someone is writing from the context of Christian mission. Theological reflection in the midst of engaging in the *missio Dei* is a challenging but ultimately rewarding endeavor that will surely benefit the church. Jerry Ireland is a missionary and theologian burdened with mission and its activities—evangelism, church planting, and humanitarian aid among others—on the continent of Africa. Historic Christian mission has always been in Word (proclaiming the death, burial, and resurrection of our Lord, discipling, church planting) and deed (compassionate service) and for centuries the relationship was a rather intuitive one. Basil of Caesarea (329–79), Ephrem of Syria (306–73), and Columbanus (543–615) acted in a manner that said, "of course we preach the gospel; of course we feed the poor." Yet, in the last century, the church has pondered more deeply the relationship between Word and deed ministry. What takes precedence? What is ultimately the most important? This question has been bugging evangelicals in particular since the 1974 Lausanne Congress on World Evangelization as the literature attests.

In this book, Ireland has taken a wise approach to resolving the question by conversing with Carl F. H. Henry, the leading voice of new evangelicalism in the latter half of the twentieth century and the one who helped evangelicals to think best about appropriate cultural engagement, including evangelism in the modern world. As the reader will see, Ireland has adequately raised the Word vs. deed issue, narrated Henry's own spiritual journey, and navigated Henry's thought to offer us wisdom for our times on this important question. Though Henry was not a cross-cultural missionary himself, his theology is certainly valuable to the evangelical missionary movement. Thankfully, Ireland, who is a cross-cultural missionary has immersed himself in the storehouse of Henry's thought and emerged with an accessible argument to aid those pondering mission in

Word and deed. In short, this is a careful study that is sure to help us be better equipped as the people of God participating in the mission of God.

—Edward L. Smither, PhD

Professor of Intercultural Studies
Columbia International University

Preface

I BECAME A CHRISTIAN through the compassionate outreach of the church. It was through the ministry of Teen Challenge, started by David Wilkerson in the late 1950s, that I was able to leave behind a ten year drug addiction and discover the abundant life that Christ promises. Because of this, I've always had strong feelings about the importance of these types of ministries. As one might imagine, then, when I became a missionary with the Assemblies of God in 2007, I was shocked to discover that some of my colleagues were highly skeptical of compassionate ministries, and in some cases, saw them as a dire threat to the true mission of the church.

As I began reading widely on this topic, I found myself, at first, somewhat taken in with the holistic mission/mission as transformation movement. It seemed that these were the only folks giving sufficient attention especially to the Old Testament (OT) emphasis on caring for the least well-off. In fact, it seemed as though some of the priority advocates were ready to excise the entire OT because it went against their perspective. But, over time, the more I read, the more I began to notice some excesses by those in the holism camp, and began to see that some, not all, but some, of the suspicions regarding holism were justified. Increasingly, I noticed a general tendency within the holism camp to overstate their argument, and at times, to misrepresent the meaning of certain crucial passages of Scripture.

Then I came across the writings of Carl F. H. Henry. When I first read Henry, I suspected that he was inconsistent because he seemed to speak the language of both holism and prioritism. He frequently spoke of evangelism as the church's top priority, and yet, no one who has read Henry can miss his strong and thorough emphasis on the necessity of compassion and social action. I wondered if perhaps he was addressing himself differently to different groups, trying to "be all things to all people," as it were. But the more I read of Carl Henry, the more I discovered that he was anything but inconsistent. What I discovered instead, was that Henry had more than any other writer faithfully balanced the evangelistic and cultural mandates of the church. He had indeed appreciated what the OT prophets so frequently emphasized about social holiness, and understood how this was implicit in much of the New Testament's reference to care for the poor and needy. Furthermore, in advocating for evangelical social concern he labored more extensively than others to preserve the ancient Christian doctrine of individual repentance and salvation, and keep the verbal proclamation of God's Word as the central feature of Evangelical identity. A favorite phrase of his, "The God of the Bible is the God of justice and justification," perfectly encapsulates this Henrian perspective.

I would like to take a moment to address some potential criticisms of this work. For example, I suspect that some may charge me with letting Henry do all (or most) the heavy lifting, since the bulk of this project is given to presenting Henry's thoughts in some detail. On this, I plead guilty as charged. One of the primary goals of this work is to present in an accessible form the bulk of Henry's thoughts as they relate to evangelism and social concern. This is because Henry's contribution to this debate has not been fully appreciated and the only way to correct this is to show what Henry said and why. Beyond that, when I disagree with Henry I have said so. It just so happens that I find many of his arguments convincing. Second, some may want to fault my approach for not setting Henry in contrast to another writer on this topic. Yet, this assumes that there is someone out there who is Henry's equal in this debate. Such an assumption is simply misguided. Of course, others have written on this subject from a number of theological perspectives. But no one has produced works comparable to Henry's either in sheer volume, or in depth of thought. It is simply a historical fact that on this topic, Carl Henry has no equal. By that I do not mean to say that Carl Henry is always right, but only that no one else has worked out the theological foundations to the degree that Henry has.

As I have already indicated, I don't agree with everything that Carl Henry has said. He was a Reformed Baptist and I am an Arminian Pentecostal. We have our differences. But herein lies the value of Carl Henry. In 2009, a panel discussion at the annual meeting of the *Evangelical Theological Society*, consisting of Russell D. Moore, Richard Mouw, Craig Mitchell, and Peter Hetzel, all reflecting on the life and legacy of Carl F. H. Henry, agreed that Henry probably died a disappointed man. And the primary reason given for Henry's disappointment was the fact of an increasingly divided and fractured Evangelicalism. Yet, Russell Moore has shown in his excellent book *The Kingdom of Christ*, how Henry played a pivotal role in advocating an evangelical consensus on inaugurated eschatology. My belief is that Henry may yet play a similar role on the issue of evangelism and social concern. I have written this work with that very hope in mind, for I too share Henry's dream of seeing Evangelicals find more ways to come together. I only hope the pages that follow shed some light on Henry's expansive efforts in this area, and move this discussion in that direction.

Acknowledgments

MANY PEOPLE DESERVE THANKS for the genesis of this book. First, I would like to thank those with whom I had sometimes heated discussions on this topic. Those conversations stirred in me a passion to pursue this further in search of a biblical solution.

Second, the faculty and staff of Liberty Baptist Theological Seminary deserve special mention, as this project has emerged from my dissertation done through this fine institution. Especially influential in the production of this work were the members of my PhD committee, Drs. Kevin King Sr., Ed L. Smither, and Daniel R. Mitchell. These, along with Dr. Leo Percer, were instrumental in helping me to think through some of these issues. Their critical reflections on this work have made it better than it would have otherwise been.

Third, thanks also is owed to Assemblies of God World Missions, for giving the freedom to pursue this project and seeing it as a valuable asset to our work in Africa. I pray that this work honors the trust they have bestowed on me.

Fourth, I want to thank the fine folks at Wipf and Stock for seeing promise in this project and agreeing to publish this work. Especially helpful have been Laura Poncy, Matt Wimer, and Dr. Charlie Collier. Finally, much thanks is owed to my sweet wife, Paula, and precious daughter, Charis, who have without complaint endured and supported my academic pursuits and writing projects.

Abbreviations

AG	Assemblies of God
BGEA	Billy Graham Evangelistic Association
CD	*Church Dogmatics* (Barth)
CP	Conservative-Propositional [approach to theology]
CT	*Christianity Today*
CRESR	Consultation on the Relationship between Evangelism and Social Responsibility
ETS	Evangelical Theological Society
GRA	*God, Revelation, and Authority*
JETS	Journal of the Evangelical Theological Society
LCWE	Lausanne Congress on World Evangelism
LXX	Septuagint
NAE	National Association of Evangelicals
NICNT	New International Commentary on the New Testament
NICOT	New International Commentary on the Old Testament
NCC	National Council of Churches
NIDNTT	Brown, Colin, ed. *New International Dictionary of New Testament Theology*. 4 vols. Grand Rapids, MI: Zondervan, 1975–1985. Accordance.

NIDOTTE	VanGemeren, Willem, ed. *New International Dictionary of Old Testament Theology & Exegesis*. Grand Rapids, MI: Zondervan, 1997. Accordance.
NT	New Testament
OT	Old Testament
SOM	Sermon on the Mount
SWJT	*Southwestern Journal of Theology*
TDNT	Kittel, Gerhard and Gerhard Friedrich, eds. *Theological Dictionary of the New Testament*. Grand Rapids: Eerdmans, 1967.
WCC	World Council of Churches

— 1 —

Evangelism and Social Concern

CARL F. H. HENRY's legacy, at least in part, centers on his efforts to promote a balanced view of evangelism and social concern.[1] In one of his earliest works, in fact, the one that gained him widespread recognition as an important emerging twentieth-century theologian, *The Uneasy Conscience of Modern Fundamentalism,* Henry especially tackled the issue of social malaise among Fundamentalists.[2] Beyond that, though, Henry unapologetically called the church to uphold the "most urgent task" of world evangelism.[3] In both, Henry demonstrates a keen ability to study and evaluate both current trends and future horizons.[4] As Carl Trueman has said, "indeed, Henry's unerring ability to see the big picture, to focus

---

1. His evangelical defense of the authority and inerrancy of Scripture, rooted in a revelational epistemology is his greatest single contribution, especially in his six-volume *God, Revelation, and Authority* published variously between 1976 and 1983 (hereafter, *GRA*). As Carl R. Trueman, says, "without a doubt it is the most exhaustive evangelical statement on these issues to have been produced in the twentieth century"; "Admiring the Sistine Chapel," 48. Yet, as Cerillo and Dempster observe, Henry, "more than any other individual, led the way in formulating the apologetic for a socially relevant evangelicalism"; Cerillo, and Dempster, "Carl F. H. Henry's Early Apologetic," 366.

2. While Henry upheld the Fundamentalist assessment that sin constituted humanities greatest problem, he also noted that Christianity is ill-served by uncritically jettisoning the social relevance of the Gospel in reaction to liberal theology; Henry, *The Uneasy Conscience,* 16.

3. Henry, *Evangelicals at the Brink of Crisis,* 2; see also *GRA,* 2:22, wherein Henry says, "the unmistakable priority of God's people, the church in the world, is to proclaim God's revealed Word."

4. This is evident for example, in a number of Henry's works, including *The Uneasy Conscience of Modern Fundamentalism; Remaking the Modern Mind; Faith at the Frontiers;* and *A Plea for Evangelical Demonstration.*

on issues of real substance, and to communicate the significance of these issues to the theological public is not open to debate."[5]

One finds in examining Henry's writings on the subject of evangelism and social concern a multi-layered, revelation-centered approach that carefully and biblically seeks to balance these two mandates of the church. Henry skillfully navigates the opposite extremes of cultural retreat, and, the more pressing danger of losing evangelistic fervor. One must read Henry with care, though. There are points when he seems not far from the Fundamentalist paradigm he sought to challenge.

For instance, he says in *The Uneasy Conscience*, "the evangelical task *primarily* is the preaching of the Gospel in the interest of individual regeneration by the supernatural grace of God, in such a way that divine redemption can be recognized as the best solution of our problems, individual and social."[6] Yet, in the very next breath, Henry calls for Evangelicals to "outlive" their pagan neighbors as part of their evangelistic outreach.[7]

The relationship between evangelism and social concern continues to divide Evangelicals.[8] In light of this, few in recent history have more to offer this debate than Carl Henry. A full study of Henry's writings

---

5. Trueman, "Admiring the Sistine Chapel," 48–49.

6. Henry, *The Uneasy Conscience*, 88, (emphasis added). It is a well-known hallmark of Fundamentalism to withdraw from social concern altogether in the interest of individual regeneration. As Ro observes, this derived from the belief that, (1) regenerate humanity would naturally change social norms, and (2) social concern specifically constituted a deviation from the church's primary mandate of saving souls; Bong Rin Ro, "The Perspective of Church History," 32. Also, as Dollar observes, social gospel advocates such as Washington Gladden called for the Christianizing of society "at a time when Fundamentalists saw society as doomed and were busy in the task of winning individual souls out of the wickedness around them"; Dollar, *A History of Fundamentalism*, 69. This, however, as Henry himself observes, is not to say that Fundamentalism was unilaterally without a social program, or that liberalism always embodied a social consciousness; see *Uneasy Conscience*, 4.

7. Henry, *Uneasy Conscience*, 89. Throughout this work, terms such as "Evangelical" and "Fundamentalist" will be capitalized when used as nouns, but "evangelical" or "fundamentalist" when used as adjectives.

8. A divided and disjointed Evangelicalism was a chief concern of Henry's; c.f. Moore, *The Kingdom of Christ*, 31, 178. As to the diversity of views among evangelicals, David Hesselgrave identifies three broad approaches to the issue, (1) Liberation Theology, (2) Holism Theology, and (3) Prioritism Theology. Evangelicals mostly fall into the one of the latter two categories, which Hesselgrave, as we shall discuss in this chapter, even further divides; see Hesselgrave, *Paradigms in Conflict*, 117–40. Henry outlines his prospectus for evangelical ecumenism in Henry, *Faith at the Frontiers*, 92–103.

demonstrates that Henry sought to move past fruitless debates over minor points of Christian doctrine and focus instead on broad themes capable of uniting a fractured Evangelicalism. For Henry, that meant first, humanity's greatest need was for supernatural regeneration by the Holy Spirit. Second, it also meant that social concern was not optional.[9] Regarding the latter, he says, "the temptation to stress evangelism only as 'the Christian answer' and to withdraw from social confrontation is dangerous and one that Protestant orthodoxy best avoid."[10] He also describes the "evangelistic mandate" broadly in some of his later works. For example, he describes the early church's mission "to recall men to their created dignity, to rescue them from sin's hell and death, to renew them in salvation's grace and power, to awaken their sense of eternal destiny, and to renew them in the image of God," as all part of the Great Commission and the church's "Number One task in the world."[11] That is, here the "number one task" sounds like more than simply preaching, with the diverse concepts of "recalling," "rescuing," and "renewing." Elsewhere he states, "the church of Christ *must in life and word* be the global echo of the Risen Christ's invitation to turn from judgment to joy. This address to the world is not only in audible words, but also in compassionate demonstration of the gospel truth."[12] Clearly, Henry believes that evangelism and social concern constitute vital components of biblical Christianity. But precisely how do they fit together, and how should they be defined both individually, and in relation to one another? What theological considerations prove crucial in the pursuit of these answers? The answer to these questions will emerge from this study, described more precisely below.

Key Questions

Though Henry's impact on Evangelical social concern has been well noted and lauded, his theological foundations for both evangelism and social concern have not to date been sufficiently examined. Frequently, references to Henry's contribution to an evangelical social agenda tend to

---

9. Cf. Henry, *The Uneasy Conscience*, 39; also Henry, *Remaking the Modern Mind*, 307.

10. Henry, *A Plea for Evangelical*, 43.

11. Ibid., 64–65.

12. Ibid., 88. Similarly, in *Aspects of Christian Social Ethics*, Henry says the church's task is "essentially redemptive *and* benevolent, alert to man's spiritual needs"; Henry, *Aspects of Christian Social Ethics*, 47 (emphasis added).

focus primarily on his early work, *The Uneasy Conscience of Modern Fundamentalism*.[13] This study, as a corrective to that lacuna, examines Carl Henry's theological foundations and numerous writings as they relate to evangelism and social concern, with a goal of answering the following questions:

1. What are the foundations and key features of Carl F. H. Henry's theology of evangelism and social concern?

2. How precisely does Henry relate evangelism and social concern to one another in the mission of the church, and on what basis does he prioritize evangelism?

3. How might Henry's theology of evangelism and social concern contribute to the ongoing evangelical debate on this topic?

Though Carl Henry never wrote a systematic theology, he did write a great deal on the foundations of Evangelical theology, especially in *God, Revelation, and Authority (GRA)*. The goal of this study is to better understand Henry's view of those foundations for his theology of evangelism and social concern and to shed light on the current debate, as it continues to occupy evangelical theologians, and often gets bogged down in polemics and caricature.[14]

This study presents a three-fold thesis: First, Henry's theological foundations for social concern ultimately present an integrated relationship between evangelism and social concern that maintains the priority of evangelism. This is especially significant since most discussions on this

---

13. For instance, Budziszewski observes, "The influence of Uneasy Conscience can hardly be overstated; it has become an epitome of the evangelical social ethos"; *Evangelicals in the Public Square*, 44; see also Charles, *The Unformed Conscience of Evangelicalism*, 57–60; Collins, *The Evangelical Moment*, 37; Bosch, *Transforming Mission*, 405; Tizon, *Transformation after Lausanne*, 28–29. The point here is not that each of these writers are unaware of Henry's more in-depth works, but that their discussion of his contribution to social concern almost always begin and end with the publication of *Uneasy Conscience*. Given that history has proven Henry somewhat prophetic on this issue in that the Kingdom consensus he sought after has become reality, it seems axiomatic that a fuller, more robust discussion of Henry's contribution is in order. Two important works, however, do address this topic indirectly: Miroslav Kis's 1983 PhD dissertation entitled "Revelation and Ethics: Dependence, Interdependence, Independence: A Comparative Study of Reinhold Niebuhr and Carl Henry," (McGill University), and Russell D. Moore's 2002 PhD dissertation entitled, "Kingdom Theology and the American Evangelical Consensus: Emerging Implications for Sociopolitical Engagement," (The Southern Baptist Theological Seminary).

14. Cf. Little, *Polemic Missiology*, Kindle edition, chapter 1.

topic stress that integration and priority are mutually exclusive.¹⁵ Henry though shows that one can prioritize evangelism and proclamation, without sacrificing the integrated nature of social concern. Second, Henry's contribution to this debate have been under appreciated and largely overlooked. Many studies of Henry have often focused on his revelational epistemology or solely on his social concern, but none have yet appeared that address this specific aspect of Henry's theology.¹⁶ Third, and most crucially, Carl F. H. Henry may offer a way past this time-consuming debate that tends to pit Evangelical against Evangelical and distracts from more pressing issues by his focus on core theological foundations capable of bringing about Evangelical unity (such as the doctrine of revelation, the biblical concept of the Kingdom of God, and a redemptively-focused ecclesiology). Henry's model can best be described as "a regeneration model" in that it underscores the unique role of the church in God's plan to offer the gift of salvation to sinful humanity.

A Settled Matter?

David Moberg once observed that, "some Christians may see the issue of the relationship between evangelism and social concern . . . as an old and settled matter." However, Moberg adds, "the minister who is caught in the crossfire of the conflict on the subject will certainly not agree with them."¹⁷ Indeed, this controversy took center stage at a fairly recent General Council of one of America's largest Pentecostal denominations. At the 53rd General Council of the Assemblies of God (AG), U.S. (Orlando, Florida, 2009), a resolution was put forth to add to the Assemblies of God constitution a fourth reason for being. The existing reasons for being prior to this council were: to (1) glorify God, (2) seek and save the lost, and (3) make disciples. The suggested change would add: (4)

---

15. For evidence, see latter part of this chapter, under "Priorism-Holism Debate."

16. For studies of Henry's epistemology, see especially Carswell, "A Comparative Study of the Religious Epistemology of Carl F. H. Henry and Alvin Plantiga"; Jones, "Revelation and Reason in the Theology of Carl F. H. Henry, James I. Packer, and Ronald H. Nash"; Thornbury, "Carl F. H. Henry: Heir of Reformation Epistemology,"*Southern Baptist Journal of Theology*; Thornbury, *Recovering Classic Evangelicalism*; Wagner, "The Revelational Epistemology of Carl F.H. Henry"; Waita, "Carl F. H. Henry and the Metaphysical Foundations of Epistemology";; King Sr., "The Crisis of Truth and Word in the Revelational Epistemology of Carl F. H. Henry"; Dempster, "The Role of Scripture in the Social Ethical Writings of Carl F.H. Henry."

17. Moberg, *The Great Reversal*, 11.

demonstrate [God's] love and compassion for the world. The purpose of adding this fourth reason was to "align our mission more exactly with that of our Lord while also accurately reflecting what the Assemblies of God is presently engaged in." Though the resolution eventually passed, some who feared it would place the AG on the "slippery slope" toward a social gospel nearly derailed the resolution.[18] Thus, as Henry himself once observed, "Perhaps no problem has distressed the modern churches more than determining the legitimacy of claims made upon Christian loyalties by champions of personal evangelism on the one hand and by those who call the church to social involvement on the other. These tensions now vex the church as never before in recent history."[19]

Few people have played a more crucial role in advancing this discussion in recent times than Carl Henry, and yet the full weight of his contribution remains largely unappreciated.[20] The re-awakening of the modern evangelical social conscience can especially be traced to Henry, who following WWII challenged the Fundamentalist community for its turn away from social concern.[21] In fact, Henry stands as *the* pivotal figure in the development of modern evangelical social thought.[22] Henry, more than any other theologian of his day, challenged the Fundamentalist retreat from social engagement and called the church back to an active role in society. Yet, Henry did so from a purely bibliocentric perspective. He achieved this by keeping Scripture and its teachings central to his views regarding the church's role in society and in understanding its task in effecting social change. Plus, he did so without ever minimizing or diminishing the need for individual regeneration and the necessity of evangelism. Henry never divorced his call to social ethics from the reality of sin and judgment, and the attenuating need of personal salvation. Thus,

---

18. See Assemblies of God, "Resolution 1, Reason for Being" http://ag.org/top/ Events/ General_Council_ 2009/Business/index.cfm (accessed March 10, 2011).

19. Henry, "The Tensions between Evangelism and the Christian Demand for Social Justice," 3.

20. Cf. King Sr., who observes, "the formal historical study of Carl Henry, his methodology, and its role in the rise and development of evangelicalism has a remarkable dearth of attention given the magnitude of his contributions"; "The Crisis of Truth and Word," 8; also, as Doyle points out regarding *GRA*, "this [work] is a major contribution to Christian theology, covering a broad range of subjects, but hardly anyone reads it"; Doyle, *Carl Henry*, xi.

21. Cerillo and Dempster, "Carl F. H. Henry's Early Apologetic," 369.

22. Cf. Tizon, *Transformation*, 29.

Henry's thoughts on the subject prove highly instructive for Evangelicals searching for a sound footing on this issue.[23]

At the heart of this study is the issue of precisely how the church frames its doctrinal positions.[24] Some claim that the language of priority, especially as it concerns evangelism, is necessary in order to keep the church from losing its focus on the Great Commission (Matt 28:18–20). Others have pointed out that the very notion of priority opens the door for a dichotomized and one-sided approach to making disciples. For example, the late South African missiologist David Bosch, who applauds Henry's contribution to the evangelical awakening to social needs, makes the following observation regarding the notion of priority:

> The moment one regards mission as consisting of two separate components, one has, in principle, conceded that each has a life of its own. One is then by implication saying that it is possible to have evangelism without a social dimension and Christian social involvement without an evangelistic dimension. What is more, if one suggests that one component is primary and the other secondary, one implies that one is essential, the other optional.[25]

Whether Bosch is correct or not on the issue of priority, his observation raises an important point: namely, when it comes to the formulation of doctrinal statements (and the relationship between evangelism and social concern is surely that), individual words prove extremely important. The difference between heresy and orthodoxy is often a matter of degree.[26] History abounds with evidence demonstrating that the way in which the church states and thereby understands its mission and objectives has

---

23. For instance, Richard Mouw, in his forward to the 2003 edition of Henry's *The Uneasy Conscience of Modern Fundamentalism* (Grand Rapids: Eerdmans), notes that even though "the notion of a socially active evangelicalism is taken for granted . . . Bible-believing Christianity still suffers to some degree from an uneasy conscience." His point here is that the issue of Christian social concern continues to be a point of debate; Kindle edition, under "Foreword."

24. I use the word "doctrine" here to refer to the exposition of Scripture in the life of the church, and distinguished from Dogma, as the officially endorsed ecclesiastical statements of faith, especially as they relate to the ecumenical councils of the early church.

25. Bosch, *Transforming Missions*, 405.

26. For example, in the early church's christological controversies, the difference between the positions of Leo I and Nestorius highlight the reality that orthodoxy and heresy can be separated by the slightest nuance.

profound implications regarding the way in which it functions—or does not function—in the world. Therefore, how one both defines and states the relationship between evangelism and social concern often determines the importance given to each in the mission of the church.[27]

The Approach of This Text

This study begins with an in-depth analysis of Henry's own writings on the subject of evangelism and social concern. Topically, this study will examine Henry's work first in relation to his views on evangelism and second with regard to his thoughts on social concern. In this, the focus will be on major works wherein Henry addresses these issues. In stating Henry's position, effort will be made whenever possible to set Henry's position alongside alternative evangelical positions. Since much of Henry's writing was directed at opposing approaches, which he often deemed problematic, at times these opposing views will be critiqued by Henry himself. Where that is not the case, secondary sources will be introduced to elucidate various options. Before unfolding the rest of the methodology in this study, a brief word is in order about the potential bias of the author.

A Note About the Author

No one comes to the study of theology from a purely objective position. All have some prior theological commitments. By stating and thereby recognizing these commitments though, one can minimize the degree to which those commitments hinder objectivity. First, I am an Evangelical in the Pentecostal tradition, ordained in the Assemblies of God, USA. I am theologically conservative, and the more I study theology the more I am convinced that it will be this form that endures.[28] Second, my work centers on equipping churches in Africa for compassionate outreach. Thus, Evangelical social concern constitutes the bulk of my daily work and livelihood. Third, and this may seem odd given my differences with

---

27. Cf. Adeyemo, "A Critical Evaluation," 48–59.

28. By "conservative" I mean to refer to Evangelical Christianity that upholds the fundamental doctrines of classic orthodoxy, especially the Trinity, virgin birth, substitutionary atoning death of Christ, the inspiration and inerrancy of Scripture, and the necessity of all persons to repent and trust Jesus for salvation, made available through his historical death and bodily resurrection, and realized through the work of the Spirit in the lives of individuals.

Henry on some important theological issues, but I find myself increasingly convinced that Carl Henry needs to be heard again.

The following is a historical-theological study. A chief objective of this study will be to allow Henry to speak for Henry. That is, before asking if Henry was right or wrong about this or that argument, we shall first endeavor simply to understand "why he says what he says."[29] There are a few reasons for this. First, as we shall see, Henry has been frequently misinterpreted and misrepresented. It seems therefore that the surest way to overcome this is to whenever possible let Henry speak for himself. Plus, Henry's theology of evangelism and social concern is rather unique in its thoroughness. In this arena, he simply has no equal. No one has spilt more ink, or devoted more of their scholarly reputation to the task of working out this issue than has Carl Henry. Because of this, his arguments are worthy of some in-depth exploration. Second, Henry's work relevant to this topic alone spans well over a dozen books and nearly half a century. This fact alone makes the Henry corpus inaccessible to nearly all but those with ample time to tackle so ominous a mountain of work. That said, one of the goals of this project is the dissemination of Henry's thoughts on this topic into a more manageable form, while at the same time presenting the most important features of his arguments. This constitutes the historical part of this study.[30] Third, Henry's theology of evangelism and social concern holds forth promise for an evangelical consensus, and the evaluation of his theology will focus especially on this issue. Henry was right when it came to advocating a consensus on the Kingdom of God, and he may be proved right again.[31] This is the theological part of this study.

Chapter Summaries

Chapter 1 will set the stage by describing the research problem and goals. Then, prior to examining Henry's work, attention will be given to his historical setting. An understanding of the fundamentalist-modernist

---

29. Cf. Bradley and Muller, *Church History*, 50.

30. As Trueman observes, because of his chosen interlocutors, such as the sixties counter culture, the Jesus Movement, and the logical positivism of A. J. Ayer, all of which are now defunct, even though in some cases their effects remain, Henry's *GRA* is now interesting primarily, though not exclusively, for its historical importance; Trueman, "Admiring the Sistine Chapel," 52.

31. Moore, *The Kingdom of Christ*, 31.

controversy, featuring so prominently in Henry's writings will prove crucial to giving Henry a fair hearing, as will various conferences that addressed evangelism and social concern in which Henry participated, such as the Berlin Congress in 1966, and various Lausanne World Congresses on Evangelism.[32] Henry, like all persons, was a product of his time. In other ways, however, he also appears as something of an evangelical prophet, seeing clearly the disasters that lay ahead for the church if she fails to correct her course. In order to fully appreciate both the times that shaped the man and the man who shaped the times, a survey of the major events that defined Henry's life will be necessary. This will be the topic of chapter 2.

Chapter 3 will focus on Henry's epistemological and methodological assumptions as a necessary first step in evaluating and exploring Henry's thoughts. Here the goal will be to pursue the way in which Henry's revelational epistemology figures into his approach to Scripture and thereby into his formulation of doctrine. This proves most helpful, in that Henry carefully articulates his own theological method, especially in volume one of his magnum opus, *God, Revelation, and Authority*. Henry's articulation of his methodology aids not only in the evaluation of his work, but also importantly distinguishes Henry among Evangelical theologians, who have at times been (rightly) accused of bypassing methodological questions.[33]

Chapter 4 discusses Henry's views on evangelism. This section will draw heavily on *GRA*, wherein Henry outlays much of his theological foundations as well as the evangelical impetus derived from them. Other key works in this section will include Henry's commentary on the 1966 World Congress on Evangelism in Berlin, *Evangelicals at the Brink of Crisis*. Also, one is hard pressed to find a work of Henry's that never gets around to the topic of evangelism, and thus, many other works will be included here as well. Especially important here will be the links that Henry establishes between the doctrine of revelation and the task of evangelism.

Chapter 5 examines Henry's views on evangelical social concern and how it relates to the mission of the church. What biblical foundations

---

32. Cf. Bradley and Muller's observation that "without a grasp of [the relevant] context, the contents of the document will either remain utterly puzzling to us or they will be assimilated to, and therefore misinterpreted by, our own cultural and intellectual milieu." Bradley and Muller, *Church History*, 59.

33. Franke, *The Character of Theology*, 88; see also, McGrath, "Evangelical Theological Method," 15–16. Other works in which Henry deals with method will also be considered, including *Frontiers in Modern Theology*.

support this type of work in the church? Furthermore, should the church as a whole engage in social concern or only some individual Christians? Is social concern secondary to evangelism, or an integral but separate part? How do these two functions of the church stand in relation to one another, and on what grounds? What theological foundations might keep evangelicals from drifting toward a social gospel? Key works here will be *GRA* (especially volumes three and four), *Aspects of Christian Social Ethics, Christian Personal Ethics, The God Who Shows Himself, A Plea for Evangelical Demonstration,* and *The Ministry of Development in Evangelical Perspective*, and others.

Finally, chapter 6 will offer an assessment and conclusion in light of ongoing discussions relating to this topic among Evangelicals. This will include a synthesis of Henry's main thoughts on how evangelism and social concern relate to one another, and then briefly, how these views might be helpfully applied in a twenty-first century context.

In the study of Henry's work, each of the areas relevant to this study will be examined across the corpus of Henry's writings. What did Henry have to say about the nature, function and place of both evangelism and social concern in the church's mission, and how did he defend those statements theologically?

Also, the following items will be particularly watched for. First, does there exist internal consistency in Henry's writings on these topics? Or, does Henry demonstrate a development or nuancing in his description of the relationship between evangelism and social concern? Second, does Henry's work display logical consistency?[34] Does he contradict himself? Do his theological foundations support his conclusions? Third, are his theological foundations sound? Do they faithfully represent the teachings of Scripture, or are they dependent upon *a priori* philosophical or other assumptions? The study concludes with an evaluation of Henry's total argument regarding the relationship between evangelism and social concern and its application to the contemporary church.

---

34. As we shall see in chapter 3, these are criteria Henry himself considered fundamental to true knowledge.

Definitions and Key Terms

Definitions prove to be a key issue in the debate over evangelism and social concern.[35] While this study will focus on Henry's articulation and definition of the various terms relevant to this study (especially *Evangelicalism*, *evangelism*, and *social concern*) it is necessary at the outset to define the key concepts. This will of course not be a comprehensive study of every relevant term, but only those most crucial for understanding the present topics.[36]

What Is an Evangelical?

Carl Henry defined Evangelicals as those "to be known in the world as the bearers of good news in message and life—the good news that God offers new life on the ground of Christ's death and resurrection in the context of a biblically controlled message."[37] Others have defined the Evangelical movement as one in "modern Christianity, transcending denominational and confessional boundaries that emphasizes conformity to the basic tenets of the faith and a missionary outreach of compassion and urgency."[38] As such, this movement is both a historical and a theological movement. It is thus impossible to define this term without at least a brief discussion of these two facets.

Historically, during the Reformation the term was used first for Lutherans, and later Calvinists as well, who sought to refocus the church on the Gospel and its message. This same desire to recapture biblically faithful and culturally relevant Christianity also became a hallmark of

---

35. This is evident for example, in the tendency among members of the World Council of Churches (WCC) to equate social action with proclamation of the Gospel, and thereby say that social concern *is* evangelism; cf. Pickard, "Evangelism and the Character of Christian Theology," 140.

36. The terms defined here are selected on two criteria. First, they are endemic to the topics of evangelism and social concern. That is, the terms "evangelism" and "social concern" cannot be understood without some understanding of how these specific terms (and closely related ideas) function in Scripture. Second, these also prove fundamental to Henry's writings on these topics, as shall be evident in the course of this study. The goal here will be to, at least minimally, understand these concepts in their biblical context. Where there is major disagreement among scholars on how to best understand these terms, those disagreements will be addressed.

37. Henry, *Conversations with Carl Henry*, 8.

38. Pierard, "Evangelicalism," 379–82.

renewal and revival movements across the globe, including German Pietism, Methodism, and the Great Awakening.³⁹ In all of this, evangelicalism was seen as a return to the practices and beliefs of the apostolic church. Through missionary outreach evangelical Christianity spread from Europe (back) to the global south and other places, especially during the missionary fervor of the nineteenth and twentieth centuries. In America too, Evangelicalism took hold through revivalist movements led by men such as Charles Finney and D. L. Moody. However, in the early twentieth century, owing to challenges from modernity, Evangelicals began to withdraw from cultural engagement into fundamentalist enclaves.⁴⁰ Following WWII, a new breed of Evangelicals emerged, led by individuals such as Carl F. H. Henry and Harold Ockenga, who sought to renew Evangelical passion for social concern and cultural relevancy.⁴¹

David W. Bebbington, who understands Evangelicalism as originating with Wesley, Whitfield, and the Enlightenment, and not as representing classic orthodoxy, describes Evangelicalism according to his now famous quadrilateral: (1) biblicism—giving preeminent place to the Bible, (2) crucicentrism—making central the atoning work of Christ on the cross, (3) conversionism—emphasizing that all humanity needs conversion from being in sin and rebellion against God, and (4) activism—wherein the Gospel demands human effort in its expression.⁴² Similarly, Alister McGrath defines Evangelicalism according to the following six "fundamental convictions:"

1. The supreme authority of Scripture as a source of knowledge of God and a guide to Christian living.

---

39. Ibid., 380.

40. Marsden, *Reforming Fundamentalism*, 4. This historical development will be more fully discussed in subsequent chapters, especially two, four, and five. It will also suffice to note here that Fundamentalism can be defined as a militant opposition to modernity and liberal theology, coupled with a pessimistic view of the world that generally manifested itself in a neglect of social concern; ibid., 10.

41. A fuller discussion of Henry's pivotal role in the emergence of neo-Evangelicalism will take place in chapter two.

42. Bebbington, *Evangelicalism in Modern Britain*, 2–17; see also Bloesch, who explores the question of "how distinctive is evangelicalism?", Bloesch, *Essentials of Evangelical Theology* vol. 2, 235–59. For responses to Bebbington's claim regarding the Enlightenment origins of Evangelicalism, see Haykin and Steward, *The Advent of Evangelicalism*.

2. The majesty of Jesus Christ, both as incarnate God and Lord and as the Savior of sinful humanity.

3. The lordship of the Holy Spirit.

4. The need for personal conversion.

5. The priority of evangelism for both individual Christians and the church as a whole.

6. The importance of the Christian community for spiritual nourishment, fellowship and growth.[43]

Yet, we might rightly wonder how a movement that includes Charismatics and Pentecostals, Calvinists and Arminians, dispensationalists and covenant theologians, high church and house church believers, can possibly be grouped together in any legitimate way?[44] Does not this vast diversity seem to strain the possibility of definition beyond credulity? To answer this, George Marsden offers "three distinct, overlapping senses in which evangelicalism may be thought of as a unity." First, it is a "conceptual unity" encompassing a group of Christians that "fit a certain definition." Second, Evangelicalism can be thought of as a broad organic unity that, despite some significant differences, tend to move in "a common direction." And third, within these broader understandings, there exists a core group that self-identify as Evangelical. These include both individuals and institutions that tend to think of themselves as a transdenominational community.[45]

What Is Evangelism?

Evangelism in this study relates to the witness of the church in society.[46] Some see this as an entirely, or mostly, verbal activity, while others

---

43. McGrath, *Evangelicalism and the Future of Christianity*, 55–56.

44. Cf. Marsden, *Evangelicalism and Modern America*, viii.

45. Ibid., ix; see also Ellingsen, who takes a sociological approach to identifying Evangelicalism, first looking at those who self identify as Evangelicals, and the secondarily looking at the various theological distinctives of those who make up the movement; Ellingsen, *The Evangelical Movement*; 46–48. For a helpful discussion of the "nature and method of evangelical theology, see Davis, *Foundations of Evangelical Theology*, 43–72.

46. See Acts 1:8, 22; 2:32; 3:15; 5:32; 10:39.

prefer to define it more broadly.[47] Roger Olson has minimally defined evangelism as "the proclamation of the gospel of Jesus Christ in order to facilitate conversions to Jesus Christ and to Christianity."[48] At times, one finds evangelism described in terms of a broader scope of activities. As Warner says, "although verbal proclamation of Jesus' message of salvation remains at the heart of evangelism, throughout the Gospels the ministry of evangelism is consistently embodied."[49] Even in Henry's day some advocated the idea that evangelism included the concept of witness, and that witness went beyond what the church says to include what the church does.[50]

At the very least though, it may be said that evangelism is the effort by which the church seeks to invite others to come to faith in Christ. "Motivated by an overwhelming spirit of thankfulness and gratitude, evangelicals are eager to proclaim the good news of the gospel, what God, through Christ and by means of the Holy Spirit, has done for their bodies and souls."[51] Evangelism, therefore, especially refers to the outward reaching efforts of the church to share its faith and thereby lead others to a saving knowledge of Jesus. Or, as Quebedeaux observes, "evangelical is something you are, evangelism is something you do."[52]

NT Terms for Evangelism

To aid in our evaluation of evangelism, and in our understanding of the term, a look back at the key terms that the first-century church used for this practice will prove helpful. That is, how did the first believers understand the task of evangelism, and what terms especially defined the practice? In answering this question, we will look at a whole complex

---

47. For example, Flemming says, "Evangelism means the invitation through word, deed and example, for people to follow Christ with their whole lives as part of the Christian community"; Flemming, *Recovering the Full Mission of God*, 18.

48. Olson, *The Westminster Handbook to Evangelical Theology*, 175; see also the discussions on the relationship between proclamation and evangelism in Litfin, *Word Versus Deed: Resetting the Scales to a Biblical Balance*, especially chapter 2.

49. Warner, "Evangelism," 288.

50. See Pierce, who observes "we are deluding ourselves if we think that witness is all talk," "Commissioned to Communicate"; Pierce, *One Race, One Gospel, One Task*, 20–21.

51. Collins, *The Evangelical Moment*, 57.

52. Quebedeaux, *The Worldly Evangelical*, 52; cited in Collins, *The Evangelial Movement*, 57.

of terms related to preaching and evangelism. In doing so we will see that though preaching and evangelism *per se* are in some ways unique to Christianity, the term "gospel" was used in the Greco-Roman world prior to it being coopted by Jesus' followers. And so, we will briefly examine the non-Christian notion of "gospel" and then look at how Christianity transformed the term.

The Gospel

Carl Henry famously remarked on several occasions that "the Gospel is only Good news if it gets there on time."[53] The terms "good news" and "gospel" come from the Greek word *euaggelion*. This was an important word among Greeks prior to the advent of Christ.[54] The "good news" referred to everything from the emperor's birthday to his coming of age, and often these events were spoken of in salvific terms. The empire itself was believed to bestow a kind of salvation upon its citizens in providing them with security and the benefits of civilization. Christianity though took over this term and transformed it by applying it uniquely to Christ.[55]

Several NT writers make use of the term "good news" or "Gospel," though at times with slightly different emphases. Importantly though, the good news came to refer both to the events of Jesus' life and ministry, but especially to the proclamation of those events. For example, Mark 1:1 refers to "the Gospel (*euaggelion*) of Jesus Christ," denoting the whole of Jesus' life and ministry. Later, Jesus himself refers to the Gospel (*euaggelion*) as the message that must be preached to the whole world (Mark 13:10). Paul uses some form of the word over seventy times in his thirteen epistles.[56] In light of these different emphases, Michael F. Bird helpfully

---

53. Cf. Thornbury, *Recovering Classic Evangelicalism*, 175.

54. Green, *Evangelism in the Early Church*, 87. In order to maintain consistency throughout this study and with Henry's own approach, Greek and Hebrew terms will be expressed as transliterations rather than in original languages in the main body of this study, although biblical languages will occasionally be used in the notes. Concerning the Gospel, "εὐαγγέλιον" is most frequently used by Paul (over sixty times), and it is likely that Paul took over the term from its common usage and employed it to especially define the Christian message; see "εὐαγγέλιον" in *NIDNTT*.

55. Ibid.

56. Plummer, "Paul's Gospel," 45; NT references to *euaggelion* (or some form of) include—Matt 4:23; 9:35; 11:5; 24:14; 26:13; Mark 1:1, 14–15; 8:35; 10:29; 13:10; 14:9; 16:15; Luke 3:18; 4:18; 7:22; 9:6; 16:16; 20:1; Acts 8:25, 40; 14:7, 15, 21; 15:7; 16:10; 20:24; Rom 1:1, 9, 15–16; 2:16; 11:28; 15:16, 19–20; 16:25; 1 Cor 1:17; 4:15; 9:12, 14,

describes six aspects of the biblical Gospel that prove fundamental to the NT understanding:

1. The Gospel is the message of the Kingdom of God (Isa 52:7; Matt 4:23).
2. The Gospel includes the story of Jesus' life, death, resurrection, and exaltation (Mark 1:1; Luke 24:26)
3. The Gospel announces the status of Jesus as Son of David, Son of God, and Lord (Acts 2:36; Rom 1:2-4; 2 Tim 2:8)
4. The Gospel proclaimed by the apostles is intimated in the OT (1 Cor 15:3-4; Rom 1:2-3).
5. The response that the Gospel calls for is faith and repentance (Mark 1:15; Acts 20:21).
6. Salvation is the chief benefit of the Gospel (Rom 1:16; Eph 1:13).[57]

Related to this notion of proclamation, two other terms found in the NT are important. The words *kērussō* and *kērygma* both relate to the concept of proclamation and to heralding the good news. *Kērussō* means to proclaim as a herald, and *kērygma* as a noun refers to the precise message. Both terms share a semantic affinity with *euaggelion*. Thus one encounters phrases such as *kērussein to euaggelion*, or "preach the good news," as well as *euaggelizesthai ton Iēsoun*, or "telling the good news of Jesus." Because Jesus both proclaimed the good news of God's deliverance and salvation (Luke 4:18–19), and was himself the source of good news, the content of the Gospel and the preaching of the Gospel became inseparable concepts.[58]

16, 18, 23; 15:1; 2 Cor 2:12; 4:3-4; 8:18; 9:13; 10:14, 16; 11:4, 7; Gal 1:6-9, 11; 2:2, 5, 7, 14; 3:8; 4:13; Eph 1:13; 3:6; 6:15, 19; Phil 1:5, 7, 12, 16, 27; 2:22; 4:3, 15; Col 1:5, 23; 1 Thess 1:5; 2:2, 4, 8-9; 3:2; 2 Thess 1:8; 2:14; 1 Tim 1:11; 2 Tim 1:8, 10; 2:8; Phlm 1:13; 1 Pet 1:12; 4:6, 17; Rev 14:6.

57. Bird, *Evangelical Theology*, 47–52. As concerning point number six, Bird defines "salvation" further as "sharing in the new heaven and new earth, which awaits God's people." Thus, salvation is not here defined narrowly as merely escaping the coming judgment, but rather rings aloud with present tense implications. Yet, Bird also cautions against preaching "another gospel" (2 Cor. 11:4; Gal 1:6), and cites an imbalanced approach to social concern as a real danger. However, "this is not to say that pursuing justice and helping the poor is not an important task for God's people; it is part of our mission to be salt and light"; ibid., 53.

58. Green, *Evangelism*, 91–92. The NT uses *kērygma* infrequently, but importantly in Paul, especially Rom. 16:25; 1 Cor. 2:4; 15:14; et al. The verb form, *kērussōis* the more common term, occuring over sixty times; cf. "κήρυγμα" in *NICNTT*.

Crucial to understanding the essence of the *kērygma* of the early church is that it centered especially on Jesus' ushering in the new messianic age, the promised coming Kingdom. This is evident in that at several points the NT writers also explicitly link the Gospel to the Kingdom of God, as in "the Gospel of the Kingdom" (Matt 4:23; 9:25; 24:14; Luke 16:16; cf. Mark 1:15). The NT pictures Jesus not only as preaching, but more precisely preaching that the Kingdom of God has come/is coming/will come in full.[59]

Finally, a third word proves crucial in understanding proclamation in the early church. The term "witness" (Gr. *marturēo*) in the NT derives much of its impetus from usage in the LXX, wherein, first, God is the main referent to the verb form of the word, as Scripture records God's self-witness and revelatory acts. "Accordingly, the NT frequently speaks of God or the Spirit or the Scriptures bearing witness. Without this witness there would be no revelation."[60] Second, though, not only does God graciously and sovereignly provide witness of himself, but God also calls his people to be his witnesses, especially in Isaiah (43:10-12; 44:8). Jesus likewise calls his followers to be his witnesses (Luke 24:48; Acts 1:8). "Supremely, it is witness to Jesus which is required, and this includes his earthly life, his cross, and particularly his resurrection."[61] So complete was the early church's dedication to this concept of witnessing to Christ that many of Jesus' disciples would follow Him in paying with their very lives to make known the hope of the Gospel. Scripture itself records the deaths of Stephen and James in this regard, and it is widely attested by the early church fathers that the other disciples as well died a martyr's death.

Conversion/Repentance

Repentance (Heb. *šûb*) is one of most dominant themes of OT prophets (Isa 31:6; 44:22; Jer 3:14; 18:11; 25:5; Ezek 18:30, 32; Hos 3:5; Zech 1:3;

---

59. cf. Matt 4:17, 23; 9:35; 24:14; Luke 4:43; 9:2; Acts 8:12; 28:31; Batson, *The Treasure Chest of the Early Christians*, 29.

60. Green, *Evangelism in the Early Church*, 106; also, as Snyder points out, the words *marturēo* and *euaggelizesthai* (or some form of), appear over twenty times in Acts; thus, "the great concern and dynamic of the early church was to tell the good news about Jesus and the resurrection; to bear witness to what had been seen, heard, and experienced"; *The Community of the King*, Kindle edition, under chapter six, "The Evangelistic Mandate."

61. Green, *Evangelism*, 106-108.

et. al.). "In the OT this term designates both a movement away from and a turning toward."[62] This idea is furthermore carried over into the NT, where the primary words are *metanoia* ("repentance") and its cognates, and *epistrophē* ("a turning around").[63] As Erickson points out, there are therefore two aspects of conversion, repentance and faith. "Repentance is the unbelievers turning away from sin, and faith is his or her turning toward Christ."[64] Also, "conversion in the NT often entails recognition of and participation in the Kingdom of God."[65]

What Is Social Concern?

Social concern in this study refers to those aspects of the Christian faith variously referred to as compassionate ministry, Christian ethics, and/or social justice. It encompasses personal ethics, ethics for the community of God's people, and the church and individual Christians in relation to justice issues and human rights.[66] It relates primarily to how believers relate to and serve the poor and needy. Social concern can then be said to be the *diaconal* function of the church, as it seeks to love God and neighbor.[67] As defined in the Lausanne Covenant, social concern then is based on the following affirmation:

62. Markham, "Conversion," 176.

63. For *metanoia* see for example Matt 3:8, 11; 9:13; Mark 1:4; 2:17; Luke 3:3, 8; 5:32; 15:7; 17:4; 24:47; Acts 5:31; 11:18; 13:24; 19:4; 20:21; 26:20; Rom. 2:4; 2 Cor 7:9–10; 2 Tim 2:25; Heb 6:1, 6; 12:17; 2 Pet 3:9; for *epistrophē*, see, for example, Acts 15:3.

64. Ibid.; Erickson, *Christian Theology*, 946; cf. Ezek 18:30–32; 33:7–11; also, in some instances in Scripture conversion seems to be instantaneous (e.g., Lydia; Acts 16:14), and for others more of a process, as seems the case with Nicodemus (John 19:39); ibid. 946–47.

65. Markham, *Dictionary of Scripture and Ethics*, 176. Also, as Markham says, in Luke-Acts especially, "conversion is cast in the form of a 'journey'"; cf. Luke 1:79; Acts 9:2; 16:17; 19:9, 23; 22:4; et al.; see also Kirk, *The Good News of the Kingdom Coming*, 31.

66. Though some writers may distinguish between "social action," defined generally as compassionate ministry or development-type work, and "social justice" which directs its efforts towards political structures, such a distinction is unnecessary at this point in this study, as both can be included in the broader category of "social concern." For an excellent and accessible discussion on defining the term "rights," see Wolterstorff, *Journey toward Justice*, 42–56.

67. See Luke 10:27 (and parallels); Acts 6. Though not found in the Gospels, *diakoneō* and its cognates features prominently in Acts, but even more so in the

We affirm that God is both the Creator and the Judge of all. We therefore, should share his concern for justice and reconciliation through out human society and for the liberation of men and women from every kind of oppression. Because men and women are made in the image of God, every person, regardless of race, religion, color, culture, class, sex, or age, has an intrinsic dignity because of which he or she should be respected and served, not exploited.[68]

The Lausanne Covenant also helpfully distinguished between social concern and evangelism and warns against confusing the two. "Although reconciliation with other people is not reconciliation with God, nor is social action evangelism, nor is political liberation salvation, nevertheless we affirm that that evangelism and socio-political involvement are both our Christian duty."[69] Often social concern is described as part of the church's cultural, or creation mandate, in contrast to her evangelistic mandate.[70] Within the broad theme of the biblical Kingdom of God, these two mandates are generally seen as in someway intertwined.[71] Ott and Strauss helpfully delineate the church's mission in the world by distin-

---

Pauline corpus, and generally means "to serve," "to wait on", "to take care of." It is also used for the proclamation of the Gospel and for Christian mission (Acts 6:4; 20:24; 2 Tim 4:11); NT references include: Matt 20:26; 23:11; Mark 9:35; 10:43; Luke 22:26–27; John 12:26; Acts 6:1, 4; Rom 12:7; 13:4; 15:8, 25, 31; 16:1; 2 Cor 3:7–9; 6:3; 9:12; Gal 2:17; Eph 3:7; 6:21; Col 1:7, 23, 25; 4:7; 1 Thess 3:2; 1 Tim 4:6.

68. See Lausanne Covenant, Article 5, "Christian Social Responsibility," Lausanne Covenant. http://www.lausanne.org/en/ documents/lausanne-covenant.html (accessed Sept. 11, 2013).

69. Ibid.

70. Ott and Strauss, *Encountering Theology of Mission*, 159; Miles, *Evangelism and Social Involvment*, 27; DeYoung and Gilbert, *What is the Mission of the Church*, 208.; cf. Snyder, who says "there is a cultural mandate for the Christian as well as an evangelistic mandate"; *The Community of the King*, chapter one, "Kingdom Consciousness."

71. As Moore explains, in Jesus the incarnate King, "the purposes of creation, redemption, and consummation are seen holistically as God's purpose to glorify Christ by fulfilling the Adamic creation mandate, the universal Noahic promise, the patriarchal covenants, and the Israelite monarchy in Him, thus exalting Jesus as preeminent over the entire cosmos as the agent of creation, the true *imago Dei*, the Davidic subjugator of all rival powers, the firstborn of the eschatological resurrection from the dead, and the atonement through whom final cosmic peace is found at last (Col 1:15–23)"; *The Kingdom of Christ*, 108; also, as Miles explains, the cultural mandate comes especially from Gen 1:26–31, "be fruitful and multiply, and fill the earth and subdue it; and have dominion over . . . every living thing"; the evangelistic mandate is based especially on Matt 28:16–20, the Great Commission; Miles, *Evangelism and Social Involvement*, 27.

guishing its three-fold nature: Doxology—the Great Calling; Evangelism and Discipleship—the Great Commission; and Compassion and Social Concern—the Great Commandment.[72] The primary NT term for social ministry is *diakonia*, or service.[73]

Who Are the Poor?

Christian social concern may be described as endeavoring to understand and practice what God commands regarding the poor and needy. One of the primary areas of debate when it comes to social concern centers around how the term "poor" should be understood in Scripture. Is this primarily a spiritual designation, or primarily a physical one, or both? To answer this we will look briefly at how these terms are used in the OT and NT.

Concerning the OT, a few important things emerge in looking at references to poverty in the Hebrew Scriptures. First, there are several terms used for poor/poverty, and the meaning can be either spiritual poverty or physical lack. Often there is at least a tangential connection between the two. As H. Kvalbein points out:

> Hebrew has many terms for "poor": *anî* (76 times, 29 in Ps), *ebyôn* (61 times, 23 in Ps), *dal* (48 times) *rwš* (21 times, 14 in Prov), *miskēn* (4 times, only in Eccles., but common in the Talmud and Midrash). The word *anî* has a broad meaning, including "weak," "miserable," "helpless," and "suffering." It can refer to the socially and materially poor who are dependent on support from other people (Exod 22:21–27; Lev 19:10; Isa 3:14–15; Hab 3:14). But in the psalms of lament, where a common self-designation is "I

---

72. Ott and Strauss, *Encountering Theology of Mission*, 157; Miles too equates the cultural mandate with the Great Commandment to love one's neighbor (Matt 22:37–40); Miles, 28; similarly, also, John Stott, too, distinguishes the various elements of the church's mission according to the Great Commission of Matt 28:18–20, and the Great Commandment; see Stott, *Christian Mission*, 45–48. Importantly, also, Ott and Strauss's discussion centers especially on mission, and this is, therefore, not to suggest that mission and evangelism are synonymous. For helpful surveys on the relationship and differences between mission and evangelism, see Guder, *The Continuing Conversion of the Church*, 3–27; Chilicote, *The Study of Evangelism*, 6–17.

73. Iosso, "Social Service, Social Ministry," 739. Iosso describes NT dimensions of ministry according to four themes, *kerygma* (proclamation), *leitourgia* (worship), *konōnia* (community), and *diakonia* (service); ibid. As already noted, *diakonia* is also used to refer to evangelistic activity, as in Acts 6:4 and the reference there to "the ministry (*diakonia*) of the word" (NASB95).

am poor and needy," the "need" is never material poverty, *e.g.* lack of food or clothing or other necessities for life; it is persecution by enemies, illness and bodily weakness, or guilt. The supplicants present themselves as helpless beggars before God. In some contexts the *anî* is contrasted with the "proud"; "humility" is presented as a positive moral quality (Prov 3:34; Ps 18:27; Zech 9:9; Zeph 2:3).[74]

The physical aspect is evident in numerous texts, including those that commend having an "open hand" toward the poor (Deut 15:11), and the more explicit command to leave the corners of the fields from which the poor may glean (Lev 19:9–10; Deut 24:17–22). In addition it was forbidden that Israelites should take advantages of the poor through unfair loans (Exod 22:25–27; Deut 24:12–13). Also, the OT prophets frequently denounced injustice against the poor,[75] indicating that they especially suffer at the hands of others. Also, widows, orphans, the handicapped (or "afflicted"), and strangers are often identified as victims and in need of special provision or protection.[76]

That the term "poor" has spiritual/religious conations is evident in several passages, especially those wherein the writer self-identifies as the poor (Ps 35:10) and in other places where the poor are equivocated with the righteous (Ps 18:27; Zeph 3:12). Plus, the poor are often contrasted with those whose confidence is in themselves, or even with the wicked (Prov 15:16; 30:11–14).[77] Also, the OT links true religion with an active concern for the poor (Isa 58:5–10).

In the NT, *ptochos* is the primary term used for "poor," and it too caries both senses of material and spiritual deprivation. According to Craig Blomberg, NT scholars have, since about 1980, generally tended away from a strictly materialistic meaning of "poor," in Luke's Gospel especially, and a new consensus has emerged defining the "poor" as "those

---

74. Kvalbein, "Poor/Poverty," Accordance electronic ed., n.p.

75. Amos 8:4–6; Is. 10:1–4; 32:6–7; Mic 3:1–4; Jer 5:26–29; Ezek 18:12–13.

76. Exod 22:22; Deut 10:18; 14:29; 16:11, 14; 24:17, 19–21; 26:12–13; 27:19; Job 22:9; 24:3; Ps 94:6; Isa 1:17, 23; 9:17; 10:2; Jer 7:6; 22:3; 49:11; Lam 5:3; Zech 7:10; Mal 3:5; see also Hoppe, "Poverty and the Poor," 608–11.

77. Cf. Harrison, "Poor. "Harrison observes regarding the "non-economic meaning" of "poor" that within national Israel "the faithful minority . . . regarded themselves rather introspectively as the poor, harassed remnant of spiritual fidelity in a vast morass of Hellenistic paganism. Thus the 'poor' also meant 'the faithful;'" ibid., 515.

who are both pious and disenfranchised."[78] NT passages that do support the material sense include warnings in James against exploitation of the poor.[79] As with the OT, James singles out the vulnerability of orphans and widows, and relates true religion to concern for the these groups.[80] Also, Jesus, John the Baptist, and the disciples embraced a lifestyle of poverty.[81]

Jesus' inaugural sermon in Luke 4:18 and its reflection of Isa 61:1, referring to the Gospel being preached to the poor, is also cited in reply to John the Baptist's question from prison (Luke 7:22). In Isaiah 61 the context is the salvation of Israel, and this must therefore inform the Lukan usage. As Kvalbein says:

> In Nazareth it is applied to the congregation in the synagogue; in the answer to the Baptist it concludes a list of Jesus' healing miracles which includes terms used in Isaiah to refer to the salvation of Israel. The 'poor' are the people of Israel. In Isaiah 61:1 and in later texts alluding to it the meaning cannot be narrowed to people in social and economic need; the term denotes the whole people of Israel, in need of God's acts of mercy.[82]

In the Gospels Jesus and his disciples gave to the poor (John 12:5; 13:29) and encouraged almsgiving (Matt 6:1–4). Jesus' reference to the poor in spirit in the Beatitudes (Matt 5:3) focuses on "human distress and the need for God," and not so much on economic poverty, though the two can be and often are related.[83] In the Lukan parallel (Luke 6:20), the emphasis is not on the poor in general but on Jesus' disciples.[84]

78. Blomberg, *Neither Poverty nor Riches*, 222.

79. Jas 1:27; 2:1–7; 4:13–17.

80. Hoppe points out that James especially reiterates in the NT the OT prophetic concern for the poor, denouncing any injustice toward the poor by inveighing against the excesses of the rich (James 5:1–6); *Dictionary of Scripture and Ethics*, 610.

81. Mark 1:6, 18, 20; 38-39; 2:23–25; 11:12.

82. Kvalbein, "Poor/Poverty," n.p. Also, Green observes, that although economic depravity is not entirely out of view, the broader meaning of diminished status "is paramount"; Green, *The Gospel of Luke*, n.p.; see also Hesselgrave, *Paradigms in Conflict*, 128–135. Plus, as Leon Morris observes, the focus on the year of the Lord indicates the coming of God's salvation; Morris, *Luke*, n.p; cf. Flemming, *Recovering the Full Mission of God*, 103.

83. As France observes, reference to the poor in Matt. 5:3 recalls the poor of the Psalms and OT prophetic books, where the term includes economic poverty but especially focuses on spiritual poverty and the need of God. This is evident in Isa. 66:2, wherein the poor are those who "tremble" at God's word; France, *Matthew*, n.p; cf. Kvalbein, "Poor/Poverty," n.p.

84. See "πτωχός" *NIDNTT*. This is evident in Luke's usage of the second person

Other important NT references include Paul's concern for the poor expressed in his collection for the famine afflicted in Jerusalem (Gal 2:10; Rom 15:26), and by encouraging the wealthy to be exceedingly generous (2 Cor 8–9). From these, it becomes apparent that the poor in the OT and NT are both the economically poor, but also those who recognize their need of God and look to Him for salvation. In conclusion:

> In God's sight all people share equally in the image of God, but some people, on account of their physical, psychological, or socioeconomic situation, are singled out for an extra measure of the protection of God. They are those whom society has undervalued, ostracized, and often rendered powerless. They are the victims of oppression, discrimination, and exploitation. The rich and strong are often able to silence them, to make them weak, and to banish them to obscurity. The God of the Bible, however, sees all things and hears even the voice of the poor and the oppressed. Following the paradigm of the Exodus, God acts to set oppressed people free, both spiritually and physically. The task facing the church today is to locate itself within God's initiative, to protect those who have no protector, to feed those who have no breadwinner, to abolish oppression and discrimination, and, in turn, to allow the poor to evangelize the church with a full message of spiritual and physical redemption.[85]

---

plural. As Kvalbein says, the message of the Lukan beatitudes "is not that everybody who is poor is blessed, but that the disciples, in spite of their suffering now, are blessed because they are the recipients of the Kingdom of God. Matthew's general blessing of the metaphorically 'poor' ('poor in spirit') is here applied to the disciples as a word of comfort in their sufferings or literal 'poverty'"; *New Dictionary of Biblical Theology*, n.p. There is some disagreement though as to the precise identity of the poor in this passage in Luke. For example, Green argues that the focus of Jesus' discourse, even though he turns to his disciples in v. 20, is directed toward the larger gathered crowd. This is because no textual markers differentiate the "you" in v. 20 from the "you" in v. 24, directed toward the rich. Thus, it seems best to understand that those who choose to follow Jesus find comfort from their marginalized status, whatever that may include; Green, *The Gospel of Luke*, n.p.

85. Domiers, *'ebyôn*, NIDOTTE. On the issue of whether the Jerusalem collection (referenced above) evidenced a general concern for the poor by Paul, or if by contrast, Paul demonstrates no significant interest in caring for the poor, as some would claim, see Longenecker, who concludes that Paul's understanding of the Jesus movement was that it was marked by a constant regard for the poor, rooted in a crucicentric understanding of grace and love. As Longenecker says, concern for the poor then "lies at the very core of the Judeo-Christian tradition, having been showcased in Israel's scriptures, in Jesus' proclamation and ministry, and in the best practices of the early Jesus-movement—including those Jesus-followers whose corporate life had been nurtured by Paul"; Longenecker, *Remember the Poor*, 205.

The Kingdom of God

Another key concept in understanding both social concern and evangelism is that of the biblical Kingdom of God.[86] Though this has not always been true, there exists today a broad consensus among Evangelicals regarding the nature of the Kingdom of God and its importance to understanding Jesus' message and ministry.

For example, as George Eldon Ladd said several decades ago, "Modern scholarship is quite unanimous in the opinion that the Kingdom of God was the central message of Jesus."[87] Scholars continue to affirm that the Kingdom of God constitutes the focal point of Jesus' ministry.[88] This theme unites the messages of both the OT and the NT.[89] Furthermore, it encompasses both the evangelistic and social mandates of the church.[90] Thus, the reign of God especially informs both Jesus' ministry and the purpose of the church (see Matt 4:17; Mark 1:15; Luke 4:43; 8:1; Acts 8:12; 28:31).[91] The scholarly consensus on the meaning of the Kingdom can be defined as inaugurated eschatology, or, the Kingdom as partially but not fully present. The best is yet to come. As Grenz observes, "Recent theological discussions have been fruitful in that most scholars now agree that eschatology focuses primarily on the Kingdom of God. They also speak of this kingdom as in some sense both a present and a future reality, so that ours is the time of the already and the not yet."[92]

Justice, Righteousness, and Peace

The key biblical terms for understanding social justice are the Hebrew terms, *mišpāt*, *sedāqâ*, and *šālôm*. The most common of these terms is *mišpāt* and most often refers to some aspect of justice. In this, two usages dominate. The first reflects a judicial or legal understanding of the term

---

86. For example, see Snyder, *The Community of the King*; Stassen and Gushee, *Kingdom Ethics*; Dempster, "Evangelism, Social Concern, and the Kingdom of God," 22–43; Glasser, *Announcing the Kingdom*.

87. Ladd, *A Theology of the New Testament*, 57.

88. Fee, "The Kingdom of God," 8.

89. Glasser, *Announcing the Kingdom*, 20.

90. Mott, *Biblical Ethics and Social Change*, 82.

91. Chilton and McDonald, *Jesus and the Ethics of the Kingdom*, 3.

92. Grenz, "The Deeper Significance of the Millenium Debate," 20; also cited in Moore, *The Kingdom of Christ*, 36.

and is often related to those in power or authority. Often this concept carries the connotation of certain rights.[93] The second sense though refers to moral principles and ethical ideals. This sense pervades the Psalms and prophetic books.[94]

An important development in the OT concept of justice is the coupling of *mišpāt* with *sedāqâ* ("righteousness"). These two words appear together thirty-nine times, again especially in the Psalms and prophetic literature. Especially important, is the use of this coupling to describe the essence of God's reign, as these qualities describe the foundation of his throne (Ps 89:14; 97:2). Thus, "throughout the OT, it is clear that the foundation for any human exercise of justice is the understanding that the identity and the action of God are characterized by justice."[95] The presence of *šālôm* then evidences God's own justice realized in human social relationships and in every area of life. "Although never fully realized, *šālôm* is made visible to the degree that justice is done, righteousness shown, faithfulness demonstrated, and steadfast love returned in response to God."[96]

The Prioritism-Holism Debate

In order to understand and evaluate Henry's priority model, it will be helpful to set it in the context of the controversy surrounding evangelism and social concern among Evangelicals. Most evangelicals do not deny that Christian social engagement and demonstrations of compassion are part of the biblical mandate for the church. Where the differences lie, however, is in precisely defining social concern in relation to evangelism. For example, David Hesselgrave has identified three primary positions

---

93. Exod 15:25; Lev 5:10; Deut 5:1; concerning rights, see Deut 18:3–5; 24:17; concerning power and authority, see 1 Sam. 8:11–18; Birch, "Justice," 434–435.

94. For example, Ps 9:7–12; 10:17–18; 82:3–4; 106:3; Isa 1:11–17; 5:7; 10:2; Jer 22:3, 15–16; Amos 5:7; Micah 6:6–8; ibid., 435.

95. Birsch, "Justice," 435; cf. McGrath, who points out, "It is virtually impossible to read the Old Testament without being aware of the social dimensions of the faith. The Old Testament prophets in particular stress that the privilege of being the people of God carries with it social responsibility—such as demands for social justice"; McGrath, *Evangelicalism and the Future of Christianity*, 165. Also, as Seifrid points out, "in biblical thought, 'righteousness' is simultaneously moral and creational, having to do with God's re-establishing 'right order' in the fallen world which he has made"; "Righteousness, Justice, and Justification," 741.

96. Birsch, *Dictionary of Scripture and Ethics*, 435.

that might be applied in describing evangelical alternatives. Those positions are "revisionist holism," "restrained holism," and "traditional prioritism."[97] The revisionist perspective emphasizes ministry to both society and individuals and rejects as false and unbiblical any dichotomies between the physical and spiritual needs or between body and soul. Bryant Myers serves as an example of this approach.[98] The second position, restrained holism, characterizes the approach of John Stott and, in this writer's view, Carl Henry as well. This view emphasizes the necessity of social responsibility but upholds the priority of evangelism. Finally, traditional prioritism gives strict priority to evangelism, and holds social action to be a secondary task of the church.[99]

Hesselgrave's options are also similar to the proposal made by the Grand Rapids Consultation on the Relationship between Evangelism and Social Responsibility (CRESR) in 1982, which sought to resolve ambiguities in the 1974 Lausanne Covenant, and which ultimately declared that there are three viable options for biblically faithful Christians. Specifically, social action can be seen either as: "(1) A consequence of evangelism—one of the principle aims of a changed life is to serve others; (2) A bridge to evangelism—with no need of manipulation, good deeds naturally create opportunities to share the Gospel; (3) Partner with evangelism—the church must witness Christ in the world by both word and deed."[100]

That fact that this consultation did not arrive at a consensus, but deemed several options as legitimate solutions, attests to the complexity of the issue. Indeed, in many ways, the current debate on this topic can be traced by looking at the issue within the context of the Lausanne Congresses on World Evangelism and its various ensuing Consultations. Few individuals figure more prominently in the Lausanne Congresses as it concerns evangelism and social concern than John Stott. First published

---

97. Hesselgrave, *Pardigms in Confict*, 118–38.

98. Cf. Myers, *Walking With the Poor*.

99. Though by and large helpful and accurate, Hesselgrave's ensuing critique seems problematic, especially his implication that holism (of any sort) is less biblical. The problem with this assertion becomes obvious when one notices that Hesselgrave's critiques in favor of prioritism in no way mitigate against a restrained holism (which again gives priority to evangelism) more than they do against traditional prioritism; see Hesselgrave, *Paradigms in Conflict*, 135–38; cf. Tizon, *Transformation after Lausanne*, 38; Stott, *The Lausanne Covenant*, 5.

100. Tizon, *Transformation After Lausanne*, 49; Stott, *Making Christ Known*, 181–82.

in 1975, following Lausanne I, Stott's *Christian Mission in the Modern World* addressed this issue.[101]

Stott, who underwent a transformation in how he understands this,[102] believes that the way forward to a more biblical approach begins with a biblical understanding of the Great Commission. Specifically, he says that social responsibility is not only a consequence of the Great Commission, but that the commission itself "must be understood to include social as well as evangelistic responsibility, unless we are to be guilty of distorting the words of Jesus."[103] What he means by this is the most general way of stating Jesus' purpose is to say, in accord with Jesus himself, that he came to serve (Mark 10:45; Luke 22:27). This, then, ought to generally characterize our understanding of what it means to make disciples. In other words, everything that Jesus did can be understood as service, whether it was healing the sick or preaching a sermon. Therefore, "our mission, like his, is to be one of service."[104] Stott goes on to define the precise relationship between evangelism and social concern as "partnership:"

> As partners the two belong to each other and yet are independent of each other. Each stands on its own feet in its own right alongside the other. Neither is a means to the other, or even a manifestation of the other. For each is an end in itself. Both are expressions of unfeigned love.[105]

Stott argues that the Great Commission, despite its importance, is not all that Jesus commanded of his followers. One must also consider the Great Commandment to love one's neighbor (Matt. 22:39), which Jesus expressly declared to be second in importance only to loving God.[106] Stott observes regarding one's neighbor:

> Our neighbor is neither a bodiless soul that we should love only his soul, nor a soulless body that we should care for its welfare

---

101. Stott, *Christian Mission in the Modern World*. The Lausanne/1974 International Congress on World Evangelization was the vision of Billy Graham, who enlisted Carl Henry and Christianity Today to join as the primary sponsors. As Henry observes, this event included over 2700 representatives from over one hundred countries, with the main plenary sessions translated into five languages; Henry, *Confessions of a Theologian*, 349.

102. Cf. Little, "What Makes Mission Christian," 67–69.

103. Stott, *Christian Mission*, 37.

104. Ibid., 39.

105. Ibid., 43.

106. Ibid., 46.

alone, nor even a body-soul isolated from society. God created man, who is my neighbor, a body-soul-in-community. Therefore, if we love our neighbor as God made him, we must inevitably be concerned for his total welfare, the good of his soul, his body, and his community.[107]

Stott does believe that evangelism is the church's top priority. Despite the sorrow we may feel over social inequality or oppression, Stott rhetorically asks, "is anything so destructive of human dignity as alienation from God through ignorance or rejection of the gospel?"[108]

Stott was instrumental in drafting the Lausanne documents relating to the relationship between evangelism and social concern. In *Making Christ Known*, Stott provides the text of the Lausanne Covenant of 1974, plus later documents, along with commentary. Section 5 of the original covenant, titled "Christian Social Responsibility," does not explicitly mention the priority of evangelism, although the later (1982) CRESR chaired by Stott, does make that assertion. But the framers of the original 1974 document express repentance for having neglected social concerns, and "for having sometimes regarded evangelism and social concern as mutually exclusive."[109] Stott's commentary, however, notes that "a large group at Lausanne, concerned to develop a radical Christian discipleship, expressed themselves more strongly, 'We must repudiate as demonic the attempt to drive a wedge between evangelism and social action.'" Stott also points out that the Covenant bases social concern on four main doctrines: the doctrine of God, the doctrine of man, the doctrine of salvation, and the doctrine of the Kingdom of God.[110]

Christopher R. Little more recently has strongly defended the priority model and criticized the idea of holism. First, he says the idea that evangelism and social responsibility are inseparable cannot be sustained by the primary "missional models" in the NT, namely Jesus and Paul. As to Jesus, Little says he refused to allow followers to persist in following him without first submitting to his Kingship (cf. John 6:1ff). That is, Jesus explicitly made the issue of salvation, not justice, preeminent. Plus, though mission may include word and deed, deed needs an explanatory word, whereas the opposite is not true. Second, Paul, like Jesus, focused

---

107. Ibid., 47.

108. Ibid, 57.

109. Stott, *Making Christ Known*, 24.

110. Ibid.; cf. Tizon's discussion of the "radical discipleship" element from the Global South at Lausanne I; Tizon, *Transformation after Lausanne*, 40–43; ibid. 25.

far more on evangelism than on social justice (Acts 11:26). Little also notes that compassionate outreach is not unique to Christianity, and therefore in itself offers nothing that cannot be found outside Christianity. As to the holistic emphasis on the Kingdom of God, Little, following Köstenberger, argues that Jesus' disciples do not model their ministry on his, as his is that of the unique Son of God. As such, Little completely downplays any identification of Kingdom qualities with the people of God, except as "a spiritual experience."[111]

A Modern Debate?

While some would claim that the discussion regarding the relationship between evangelism and social concern is an entirely modern one and solely the product of the fundamentalist-modernist controversy,[112] there is evidence that even the early church was also aware of the dangers of de-emphasizing evangelism in favor of social action, even while upholding and advocating for a socially relevant faith. For example, in his third homily on 1 Corinthians, John Chrysostom argues for the weightiness of

111. Little, "What Makes Mission Christian," 207–17; several prominent scholars have criticized Little's approach on numerous accounts, but especially (1) Robert McQuilkin's reply that Little has not given adequate attention to justice and compassion as they relate to the church's mission, (2) Paul McKaughen's reply that Little has wrongly understood the impetus for holistic mission as not Liberation Theology, but that the poor are the largest demographic of the lost, (3) Steven Hawthorne's response, noting Little's fairly tenuous support for his arguments, while ignoring other Scriptures that would contradict, but especially Little's option for denying the importance of the Kingdom of God to understanding the church's mission, as though the Kingdom of God were not a genuinely prominent biblical theme, (4) Ron Sider's critique emphasizing that Paul's role as evangelist and missionary cannot be said to solely define the mission of the church, as Little suggests, (5) René Padilla's point that no advocate of holistic mission holds to Little's description of it, thus amounting to a straw man argument, (6) Ralph Winter's observation that Little's citation of Jesus feeding the five thousand confuses missionary deeds with the expectation of deeds by the hearer, and that words also need deeds, as much as deeds need words (that is, words refer to reality—here Winter gives the example of healing a withered hand, noting that if one says this tells us about God, it means nothing without the act of healing); plus Little's statement that "before there can be a Wilberforce there must be a Wesley," apparently ignores the vast amount of time and effort Wesley gave to social concern; see "Responses to Christopher Little's 'What Makes Mission Christian,'" 75–85. Plus, it would seem from Little's argument that he is unaware of either Henry, Stott, or Hesselgrave's restrained holism category since he attributes to holism the inherent neglect of evangelism; Little, "Christian Mission Today," 88.

112. Heldt, "Revisiting the 'Whole Gospel,'" 151.

eternal matters and simultaneously understands that one's actions make a forceful argument in leading others to Christ. He says, "Let us win them therefore by our life." Adding, however, "there is nothing to weigh against a soul, not even the whole world. So that although you give countless treasure unto the poor, you will do no such work as he who converted one soul."[113]

Long before Chrysostom, the church evidenced passion for both evangelism and social concern. For example, in perhaps the church's earliest document on discipleship, *The Didache*, there exists an emphasis on both evangelism and compassion, especially in the area of peacemaking.[114] This is especially important given this document's believed connection to the Twelve. Though a full discussion of social justice and evangelism in the early church lies beyond the scope of this study, this brief reference helps to show that the need to clarify how these issues relate to one another has long occupied the church's thinking.[115] Without a doubt the fundamentalist-modernist controversy sharpened the divisions over this issue. But the issue cannot be said to be entirely recent. As Henry, too, observes, "it may be well to remind ourselves that the ancient biblical writers also had to wrestle with the tensions between personal evangelism and social justice."[116]

---

113. Chrysostom, "Homily 3 on 1 Corinthians," 136. John Chrysostom was born in the middle of the fourth century in Antioch, in Syria. He first served as a priest in Antioch and later became bishop of Constantinople in 397. His eloquence as a preacher earned him the nickname, "Golden Mouth." He was also a strong advocate for social reform.

114. Batson, *The Treasure Chest of Early Christians*, 50. Batson points out that *The Didache* refers to both evangelistic, itinerate missionaries, and an emphasis on compassion; for a translation of the text of *The Didache*, see http://www.earlychristianwritings.com/didache.html.

115. Cf. Clement of Rome, *Epistle to Corinthians*; Polycarp, *Epistle to the Philippians*; Justin Martyr, *First Apology*; Irenaeus, *The Demonstration of Apostolic Preaching*; Hippolytus, *On the Apostolic Preaching*; Clement of Alexandria, "Who is the Rich Man that Shall be Saved?"; Cyprian, *On the Unity of the Church*; Basil, "In the Time of Famine and Drought"; Basil, "Against Those Who Lend at Interest"; Augustine, Sermon 56, et al.; the point here is that all of these ancient texts in some significant way connect evangelism or word ministry to either charity or some other specific act of social concern, or deed ministry.

116. Henry, "The Tension Between Evangelism and the Christian Demand for Social Justice," 5.

The Revolt against Prioritism

Those who reject any notion of priority are uneasy with separating the two because they feel it opens the door for the neglect of social concern. This fear has led to a revolt among many Evangelicals against the very notion of establishing hierarchical priorities. For example, we have already noted David Bosch's critique, wherein he claims that the very notion of priority inherently makes one thing necessary and the other optional. Andrew Kirk, a British Evangelical with an admitted appreciation for liberation theology, agrees. He says, "some Christians establish a list of priorities for the church as if by paying attention to the top of the chart one could justify the neglect of items further down."[117] Kirk is especially concerned about attempts by the original Lausanne Congress on World Evangelism (LCWE) in 1974 and its subsequent ad hoc committees. As Kirk points out, the 1974 Lausanne Covenant declared, "In the church's mission of sacrificial service, evangelism is primary."[118] Yet, the covenant went on to affirm the necessity of social concern. However, the follow up Consultation to this in Pattaya, Thailand (1980), was, in Kirk's view, hijacked by church growth advocates from North America who too narrowly defined evangelism as a strictly verbal task.[119] Thus, in an effort to overcome any confusion, and to mollify participants from the global south who were unhappy with the 1980 statement, yet another Consultation was convened, this time in Grand Rapids in 1982. The Grand Rapids Report articulated two main ideas:

> First, evangelism comes logically first, for 'Christian social responsibility presupposes socially responsible Christians, and it can only be by evangelism and discipling that they have become such.' Secondly, 'evangelism relates to people's eternal destiny'. This means that if ever one was obliged to chose 'between satisfying physical and spiritual hunger, between healing bodies and saving souls' one would have to opt for evangelism, for 'a person's eternal, spiritual salvation is of greater importance than his or her temporal and material well-being.[120]

---

117. Kirk, *The Good News of the Coming Kingdom*, 57; cf. Kirk, *Liberation Theology*; also for a summary of the development of integral mission, essentially another term for holism, see Padilla, "Integral Mission and Its Historical Development," 42–58.

118. Ibid., 90.

119. Ibid., 15; cf. Henry, *Confessions of a Theologian*, 350.

120. Ibid., 90–91.

In his response to this, Kirk proves especially useful for providing context to our topic, as he articulates what are probably the most common responses to the priority position. First, Kirk argues that the first claim rests on a too narrow definition of evangelism as strictly verbal. Second, he argues that there are indeed eternal consequences for neglecting social concern, at least for the person who fails to do it. He rests this latter argument on Matt 25:31–46, and the separation of the sheep and goats, and argues that Jesus is here making the point that a failure to care for the poor will lead to judgment.[121]

Similarly, Delos Miles describes evangelism and social concern as "two wings of the same gospel bird," as well as "two sides of the same coin."[122] Miles understands the relationship between the two to be that of "partnership." He denies social concern by the church should ever cease, at least prior to the return of Jesus. Nor does he see social concern as a distraction from evangelism, or as equivalent to evangelism. Rather, he advocates an approach modeled on Jesus, whose ministry was characterized by both proclamation (*kērugma*) and service (*diaconia*).[123] Scott J. Jones goes further and minimizes the differences between evangelism and social concern, implying that both are equally important in the church's mission. In this, he claims that liberation theologies from Latin America have helpfully contributed to a broadened understanding of evangelism to include "politics, social justice, and economics."[124]

More recently, Duane Litfin, President Emeritus of Wheaton College, has written on this topic in his text, *Word Vs. Deed: Resetting the Scales to a biblical Balance*. Here he argues first, that evangelism is a verbal task, and second, that compassionate deeds are primary means by which we "enact the gospel." He also argues that determining which is

---

121. Kirk, *The Good News of the Kingdom Coming*, 91–92. However, as many commentators have pointed out, this passage almost certainly refers not to the poor in general, but rather, Jesus' reference to "the least of these" is directed toward his disciples; cf. Morris, *The Gospel According to Matthew*, n.p.; Blomberg, *Christians in an Age of Wealth*, Kindle ed., under chapter four, "Jesus and the Gospels," n.p.; Morris adds that Jesus' reference to the disicples specifically, of course, does not give believers license to neglect the poor, as this is abudantly commanded elsewhere in Scripture; also, as Keener observes, the "popular view that this text refers to the treatment of the poor or those in need," is not exegetically compelling, even though such an interpretation would be consistent with other teachings in Scripture and with biblical ethics in general; cf. Keener, *Matthew*, 361.

122. Miles, *Evangelism and Social Involvement*, under "preface," n.p.

123. Ibid., 22.

124. Jones, *The Evangelistic Love of God and Neighbor*, 60.

most important, word or deed, ultimately depends on circumstances. His primary concern may be described, though, as warning against confusing evangelism with social action or vice versa.[125]

With a more robust emphasis on biblical foundations than Litfin's text, Dean Flemming's *Recovering the Full Mission of God* also addresses the relationship between word and deed. Flemming says of his approach, "Instead of contrasting word and deed, therefore, I prefer to talk about the connection between *telling* and *living* the good news."[126] Flemming defines evangelism as both proclamation and living authentically as the people of God. He argues that in both the OT and NT witness as word and witness as lifestyle go together. Similarly to Litfin, he too argues that in the church's mission, the issue of priority is determined by the realities one is confronted with.[127]

Flemming addresses the priority issue at some length and makes several points that will aid in our study of Henry. Though he affirms that the term "gospel" centers on a "message to be told and heard," he nonetheless finds the language of priority problematic. Like Bosch and Kirk, he too fears that priority language will lead to considering social concern as optional. He further argues that Jesus' mission for his disciples included both word and deed as means of evidencing the Kingdom (Acts 10:36-38). Second, he argues that the notion of priority places the work of the church in a hierarchical order, even before one becomes aware of the real life situation to which one must respond. That is, could not circumstances dictate that at times social concern should come first? Yet, would not giving unequivocal priority to evangelism preclude this? Third, Flemming argues that the issue of priority must also take into account individual callings and gifts. To prioritize evangelism is to force some into a paradigm that is out of line with their particular gifts. Finally, Flemming argues, following Christopher Wright, that more important than priority

---

125. Litfin, *Word versus Deed*, Kindle edition, especially chapters three, six, and the conclusion. Though a valuable text in many ways, Litfin's lengthy discussion of abstractions will seem tedious to those mostly concerned with ascertaining the scriptural foundations.

126. Flemming, *Recovering the Full Mission of God*, 14.

127. Cf., Flemming's comment that "this does not mean, however, that speaking, practicing, and embodying the gospel always function in equal balance. At times, due to the needs of the context, one takes a leading, and another a supporting role"; ibid., 256.

is "ultimacy." This means to place evangelism as the ultimate goal, even if it cannot always take priority in everyday practice.[128]

Conclusion

In this chapter we have seen that Carl F. H. Henry's statements on evangelism and social concern deserve further investigation. Second, we have shown that to be an Evangelical is to give primary place in the theological task to Scripture, and to uphold the necessity of conversion and the importance of a faith actively lived out in the world. The NT terms for evangelism especially highlight that God has revealed a verbal message for human redemption that stands in constant need of proclamation. Yet, this Good News must also accompany a transformed life exhibiting full commitment to Christ. Third, Christian social concern must balance biblical references to the material poor with those that equate poverty with spiritual need. Furthermore, God's ethical demands can be located in God's own character and reign as King. It is the biblical Kingdom of God that especially informs the ministry of Jesus and the purpose of the church.

The debate over prioritism or holism has at times set these two options against one another as mutually exclusive. Hesselgrave's descriptions, though, are helpful in understanding evangelical options: traditional prioritism, restrained holism, and revisionist holism. Support for all three can be found among contemporary theologians. Finally, the primary criticism against the priority model has been that it inevitably leads to the neglect of social concern. Our ensuing study of Henry, which will begin in the next chapter, will examine the degree to which Henry agreed with, challenged, or modified these points.

---

128. Flemming, *Recovering the Full Mission of God*, 264–69.

— 2 —

Henry's Life and Impact

WHEN CARL F. H. Henry died in 2003, he had firmly established himself as one of the great leaders of modern Evangelicalism. He had been hailed as both an evangelical prophet and crowned dean of evangelical theology. Along with a handful of others, he had helped birth the neo-Evangelical movement.[1] Henry's 1947 booklet, *The Uneasy Conscience,* published when Henry was only thirty-four years old, helped launch and define the effort to reform Fundamentalism.[2] Plus, his defense of the authority of Scripture in his six-volume *God, Revelation, and Authority* established Henry as perhaps the preeminent evangelical theologian of the twentieth century.[3] But who is this man who so effectively spoke for, guided, and shaped an entire movement?

---

1. Richard John Neuhaus ascribes to Henry the role of prophet, see Neuhaus, "A Prophetic Jeremiad," 30. For the designation, "dean of evangelical theology," see Henry's obituary in *Baptist Press News* (http://www.bpnews.net/bpnews.asp?id=17234); also, see George, "The Man Who Birthed Evangelicalism"; Kantzer, "The Carl Henry That Might Have Been," 15.

2. As Mohler observes, this text became a manifesto for the burgeoning movement; Mohler, "Carl F. H. Henry," Kindle edition, under "Carl Henry and the Evangelical Movement." The term "neo-evangelical" is usually attributed to Harold J. Ockenga, though Henry observes that he himself had used the term "new Evangelical" in writings around that same time; see Henry, *Confessions of a Theologian*, 117.

3. Henry notes glowing reviews of *GRA*, by such prominent scholars as Bernard Ramm and Ronald Nash, plus a review in the New York Times that called it "the most important work of evangelical theology in recent times"; Henry, *Confessions of a Theologian*, 366; see also George, "Inventing Evangelicalism," 48–51.

Humble Beginnings

Born January 22, 1913 in New York City's Manhattan to German immigrants, Carl Ferdinand Howard Heinrich was the first of eight children, each given two middle names. His father was a Lutheran and his mother a Catholic. In Carl's words, they were "Christmas and Easter Christians." He adds, "we had no family prayers, no grace at table, no Bible in our home."[4] The family would change its last name to Henry at the outbreak of WWI, as did many New Yorkers of German descent at that time, for fear of persecution. Even with the name change, Henry's father experienced harassment owing to his being an immigrant with a job, when many of America's young men were being sent off to fight a war.[5]

Hard work was endemic to the Henry household, his father putting in six days a week at a mid-city bakery, and his mother tirelessly taking care of the children and home. One can only speculate that this environment shaped Henry's views of work, which would figure prominently in his later writings on Evangelical social responsibility. Though a hard worker, Henry's father was also occasionally given to drunkenness and a violent temper.[6]

Henry showed academic prowess early, skipping three grades. After the family moved to Long Island in 1920, the children began attending Sunday school at a local Episcopal church, avoiding "conflict over Catholic or Lutheran alternatives."[7] Henry entered high school in 1925 "with a solid academic record" but beset by physical ailments.[8] Until an uncle helped him identify his problem as fallen arches, Henry wondered if he would live to be thirty-five.

Henry was baptized and confirmed by the Episcopal Church in 1926. As he recalls his life until that point, "I was born at the juncture of the Protestant Reformation—Mother a Catholic and Father a Lutheran; I had faithfully attended Sunday school, and as a most courteous participant at that; within two weeks I had been baptized and confirmed in the faith."[9]

---

4. Henry, *Confessions*, 17–18.
5. Ibid., 15–16.
6. Ibid., 18, 24.
7. Ibid., 21.
8. Ibid., 26.
9. Ibid.

Henry the Newspaper Man

In high school, during his junior year, Henry had to choose between either a college prep track or business secretarial route. He chose the latter and soon was typing eighty-five words a minute. In the fall of 1928 Henry began reporting high school sporting events for the Republican owned *The Islip Press*, as well as its Democratic oriented competition, the *Islip Messenger*.[10]

Henry's only religious experience during this period of his life, following his confirmation in 1926, came after he nearly ran down two women pedestrians in the midst of a heavy rainstorm. Another driver who witnessed the incident stopped and put the women into his car, offering to take them to the hospital. The driver told Henry to follow him. Unable to see well because of the storm, Henry lost sight of the car and never made it to the hospital. That night, Henry reports, "I prayed desperately to God as if he were an ambulance or fire department poised to give emergency rescue. I spent more time on my knees and shed more tears than I had ever done in my life. I tried to strike a deal with God, but I had nothing to offer. My only plea was, "I'm sorry . . . Please, God, help me."[11]

In his senior year of high school, Henry experienced what he suspected was class prejudice. He had submitted an essay to the annual contest sponsored by the Daughters of the American Revolution, and had won with his work that began, "Abraham Lincoln was a common man." The contest had promised a new watch to the winner, but instead gave Henry a bronze medallion, leaving Henry, as he described the incident sixty years later, to ponder, "whether the preannounced award would have been bestowed instead had I come from the other side of the tracks, rather than from Lincoln's side."[12] Thus, Henry knew what it was to experience injustice owing to his social status. The extent to which these experiences, though, shaped Henry's later advocacy of Christian social concern can only be the subject of speculation. It is difficult, however, to imagine that they did not.

Henry's newspaper work steadily gained momentum, until, at the age of nineteen, he became editor of *The Smithtown Star*, and thereby "the youngest editor of a weekly newspaper in New York's second largest

10. Ibid., 30.
11. Ibid., 31.
12. Ibid., 32.

county, and probably the entire state."[13] Henry would also work as a stringer for papers such as the *New York Times*, *New York Herald Tribune*, and the *Chicago Tribune*.

Conversion

As new editor of a small New York paper, Henry was suspicious of what he perceived to be overly religious folks, even though he kept and occasionally read a Bible from his Episcopal Sunday school days. "Sometimes before retiring I read and reread parts of it, especially the fascinating accounts of Jesus' resurrection."[14] At the same time, there were several elements in Henry's life that placed the necessity and importance of new birth before him, including *The Islip Press*'s Mildred "Mother" Christy, who had commissioned a small circle of friends to pray for Carl. "To be on the prayer list of that triumvirate . . . was like being at the mercy of an air assault."[15] Henry would later dedicate one of his first books to "Long Island's 'Mother Christy,' who first pleaded with the author to receive Christ as Savior."[16]

The air assault finally had its intended effect when at the age of twenty Henry made a confession of faith in Christ. He had for a period of three consecutive Saturday's at first promised, and then later declined, to meet the houseguest of a local pastor. "Anyone who spent two weeks visiting a preacher, I decided, was incurably religious, and I had best beware."[17] Fatefully, though, that same houseguest was the guest speaker at a church event to which Henry chauffeured Mother Christy. And when Christy invited him to meet the speaker, Henry begrudgingly agreed. "For good or ill I had unexpectedly been thrust together with the chap with whom, in a village twenty-five miles away and weeks earlier, I had three Saturdays in a row broken an informal appointment."[18] The man whom Henry met, Gene Bedford, would shortly thereafter lead Henry to faith in Christ. "Sentence by sentence Gene prayed the Lord's prayer, and I followed. Then I acknowledged my sinful condition and prayed

---

13. Ibid., 41.
14. Ibid., 43.
15. Ibid., 36.
16. Henry, *The Pacific Garden Mission*, 5.
17. Henry, *Confession of a Theologian*, 43.
18. Ibid., 44.

God to cleanse my life of the accumulated evil of the years, to empty me of self and to make resident within me the Holy Spirit to guide and rule my life."[19]

Henry's conversion came with a profound burden for others who were lost. "If a month passed without my helping lead someone to Christ I began to wonder about the depth of my commitment."[20] To Henry's great disappointment, his father would not be among those he led to Christ.

Henry's conversion in 1933 came during an upheaval in world affairs. As Henry observed, that year marked the election of Franklin Delano Roosevelt as president, and the institution of his New Deal to restore American viability that had been drained by the ongoing Great Depression. It was a time in which Hitler had began his concentration camps in Europe, and in which a Humanist Manifesto was signed in the United States by a list of advocates that included thirty-four ministers. And yet, it was a time in which Henry later declared, "as for me personally, that year began a relationship with God through Christ, Savior and Lord, that can survive the crush of planets and the end of the world."[21]

The Call and Provision of God

Henry's call to ministry was marked by a couple of significant experiences of God's dynamic intervention. While Henry's newspaper career was beginning to gain tremendous momentum and he found himself promoted to more important and more prestigious editorships, he began to simultaneously discern a call to full-time ministry and the attenuating need for academic preparation in response to that calling. That is, at a time when most were struggling to find work, Henry enjoyed a blossoming and promising career that seemed to hold forth a bright and fulfilling future. Yet, Henry sensed this was not God's plan for his life. It was an unsettling prospect, to be sure, to contemplate giving up a secure job and trying to find a way to pay for college, at a time when, in Henry's words, "many persons could not afford even a sandwich or cup of soup."[22]

---

19. Ibid., 46. Later Henry would tell students at Beeson Divinity School, "Into the darkness of my young life, he put bright stars that still shine and sparkle. After that encounter, I walked the world with God as my friend"; George, "Daddy Evangelical," 61.

20. Henry, *Confessions*, 48.

21. Ibid., 49.

22. Ibid., 52.

Henry's nerves, though, were quieted when God assured him during a personal prayer time with an overwhelming sense that God would provide for his needs in college. Specifically, Henry felt God impressing upon him that he would earn his way through college by teaching typing, and by continuing to do newspaper work.[23]

At the recommendation of Frank E. Gaebelein, whom Henry had had occasion to interview from time to time in his role as a newspaper man, Henry applied to and was accepted at Wheaton College in 1935. Thus, by the age of twenty-two, Henry had worked in journalism for six years. His resignation from his post as editor garnered praise and commendations from the *Herald Tribune* and *New York Times*. There can be no doubt that this made even more difficult Henry's decision to leave. In the days following his resignation, Henry became debilitatingly ill. Desperate, he sought out a meeting known for Pentecostal healing, "in which a dynamic and voluble preacher professed to cast out everything from arthritis to demons." Turned off by theatrics, "disorder and confusion," Henry nonetheless trusted that God could heal him. "I was ready to put Him to the test in circumstances that, if he did not intervene, would surely frustrate his clearly revealed plan for my life." Henry, after finally going to the hospital, doubled over in pain, asked the doctor to delay an appendicitis operation because, though Henry believed in "hospitals, doctors and medical missionaries," he also believed "that, for his own glory, God sometimes heals without them."[24]

Henry then left the hospital to stay at Mother Christy's, who happened to be having her weekly Friday night gathering of "a band of soul-winners and prayer warriors."[25] The gathered company prayed over Henry until, after midnight, he fell asleep exhausted. By morning the pain was gone and the operation was not necessary. Henry later wrote of the event, "I knew . . . that the great God who is sometimes glorified by the courageous and victorious bearing of one's thorn in the flesh, is on other occasions, equally glorified in the direct healing of the body no less than the of the soul. I left for college in good time, reassured that God would supply every need."[26]

23. Ibid., 54.
24. Ibid., 58.
25. Ibid.
26. Ibid., 59.

Wheaton and Beyond

Within months of arriving at Wheaton, Henry became gainfully employed not only as a reporter and typing instructor, but soon was teaching classes on journalism as well. Academically he was thrust into Latin, philosophy, and Bible courses. He began to interact with professors who would become hugely influential and integral to his life, such as Gordon H. Clark, who would become a mentor to Henry. At Wheaton, Henry experienced denominational factionalism and infighting.[27] This may have been a factor in Henry's later emphasis on evangelical unity. Even Wheaton's motto seemed to shape Henry, as it would sum up much of his later theological thrust: "For Christ and His Kingdom."[28] Wheaton not only provided Henry with a solid foundation in theology, and was where he met not only Billy Graham and E. J. Carnell but also his future wife, Helga Bender.

Upon graduating *cum laude* from Wheaton and earning his BA, Henry entered simultaneously into a BD (now called an MDiv) program at Northern Baptist Theological Seminary in Chicago, and a newly formed MA program in Theology at Wheaton. He, of course, completed both degrees, finishing at Wheaton in 1941. His studies at Northern Baptist culminated in a doctorate a year later. His dissertation at Northern Baptist, titled, "Successful Church Publicity" embodied his later concern for the church's role in and relationship with culture, especially as it relates to Christian journalism.[29] This clearly helped pave the way for Henry's future, as he would go on to be the first of four consecutive editors of *Christianity Today* (CT) who were Northern Baptist graduates.

Henry was licensed to preach by the Babylon Baptist Church on October 5, 1939. He and Helga were engaged later that same year, and in 1940 he started at Northern as both a student and professor. Helga found employment, for a meager salary, as Northern's seminary librarian.

Henry's student days at Northern proved some of the most formative of his life. He writes, "In my solitary room I explored the New Testament in Greek, stretched my prayers around the world, and at times sank to my

---

27. Henry describes this in *Confessions*, detailing how Wheaton President J. Oliver Buswell Jr., and J. Gresham Machen were at odds with one another "over the purity of the church and over eschatology." The whole experience disavowed Henry of all inclinations about being ordained as a Presbyterian; ibid., 67–68.

28. Ibid., 65. For a thoughtful discussion of Henry's emphasis on the Kingdom of God as it relates to Christian theology, see Moore, *The Kingdom of Christ*, especially 21–22, 30, 37–38.

29. This work was published under the same title in 1943.

knees and wept, entreating God before an open Bible to forgive my sluggish spirit, redeem the failings of a religious life, and make me a worthy witness to his grace."[30] Henry laments that during his tenure as a student, "President [Charles W.] Koller was not yet offering his expository preaching course, which later became legendary in many evangelical circles and motivated the pulpit ministry of hundreds of Baptist pastors."[31] He adds that at the time, instead, "neither evangelical preaching nor liberal pulpiteering were plowing deep furrows."[32]

Among notable influences on his own life and theology, Henry especially cites Dr. William Emmett Powers, who not only taught philosophy of religion, but also pastored a Chicago church. "A powerful preacher, he could when at his best wrench one's very soul, it seemed, from one's body and speak directly to individual conscience."[33] Not only that, but Powers requirement that students "sharpen" their questions and address their presuppositions had lasting impact on Henry's own theological and apologetic method.

After Northern, he went on to pursue a second doctorate in philosophy at Boston University, which he completed in 1949. Henry's second doctorate "examined the impact of Edgar Brightman's personal idealism on the theological development of the preeminent Baptist theologian Augustus Hopkins Strong."[34] Thus, by the age of thirty-six, and armed "with no fewer than four advanced degrees in theology, Henry had laid a solid foundation for his later defense and exposition of scriptural teaching."[35]

The NAE

Harold J. Ockenga and others formed the National Association of Evangelicals (NAE) in 1942.[36] Henry early on handled the organization's yearly

30. Henry, *Confessions*, 89.

31. Ibid., 90.

32. Ibid.

33. Ibid., 91.

34. Thornbury, *Recovering Classic Evangelicalism*, 26. His second dissertation was published in 1951 by Van Kampen Press, under the title, *Personal Idealism in Strong's Theology*; cf. Henry, *Confessions*, 111.

35. Doyle, *Carl Henry*, 5–6.

36. Marsden, *Understanding Evangelicalism and Fundamentalism*, 69. The NAE provided an alternative to Carl McIntire's more separatist fundamental group, the *American Council of Christian Churches*; see also Carpenter, "From Fundamentalism

convention publicity and served as book editor for its publication, *United Evangelical Action*. Henry recalls, "I applauded NAE's determination to rise above a protest mentality and to shape a positive program."[37]

In addition, Henry served the NAE by heading a committee that recommended important books, and another focusing on evangelical education. As a direct product of these responsibilities, Henry delivered a keynote address at a two-day conference in Cincinnati in 1949 entitled, "Fifty Years of Protestant Theology," later expanded and published under the same title. This conference then founded the Evangelical Theological Society (ETS), as "an independent association with an 'affiliated' status in the NAE."[38] Henry served as society president from 1967 to 1970. He also became chair of the NAE's Commission on Social Action in 1952.

Henry the Professor

Henry's teaching career officially began at Wheaton, where he taught first journalism, and later, theology at various times between 1938 and 1947. He simultaneously taught as Assistant Professor of Theology at Northern Baptist from 1940 to1942, and later served as Chairman of the Philosophy department, from 1942 to 1947. The year 1947 proved a busy one for Henry. Of course, it was in 1947 the he published *The Uneasy Conscience of Modern Fundamentalism*, to which we will turn in detail later. Henry also became acting dean of Fuller Seminary that year in Pasadena, California. He served as professor of Theology and Christian Philosophy at Fuller until 1956. Finally, his last full-time stint as a professor came between 1969 and 1974, when Henry served as professor of Theology at Eastern Baptist Theological Seminary in Philadelphia.[39]

---

to the New Evangelical Coalition," 12-16. On Ockenga's contribution to evangelicalism, see Randy Frame, "Modern Evangelicalism Mourns the Loss of One of Its Founding Fathers." Also, as Sweeney, observes, in the years following, the NAE "wrote a constitution (1943) and a seven point doctrinal statement of faith (1943), founded a national Office of Public Affairs (1943), opened a lobby for media ministry (1944, the National Religious Broadcasters), founded a missions agency (1945) and a humanitarian arm (1945, World Relief), and started several other well-supported ventures"; *The American Evangelical Story*, 172.

37. Henry, *Confession of a Theologian*, 106.

38. Carpenter, *Revive Us Again*, 207.

39. Billy Graham Center Archives, "Biography" under *Papers of Carl F. H. Henry-Collection 628*, http://www2.wheaton.edu/bgc/archives/GUIDES/628.htm#3 (accessed January 25, 2014).

During Henry's time as a professor at Northern he would be offered, and decline, several posts in college administration, including the role of academic dean at what would later become Gordon-Conwell Theological Seminary, and the position of president at Western Conservative Baptist Seminary in Portland, Oregon.[40]

Henry at Fuller

Fuller seminary was founded in 1947 by a group of both rising and already recognized stars within the neo-Evangelical movement. Henry was in a sense both. He emerged from his studies at Northern and Boston as a thoughtful and critical thinker, and prolific writer. It is not surprising therefore that Henry was among a small group that included Charles F. Fuller, Harold J. Ockenga, Wilbur M. Smith, and Everett F. Harrison, that met in May of that year "to talk and pray about launching an evangelical seminary in California in September of 1947 or 1948."[41] Henry recalled that meeting, saying:

> we spent unhurried time in prayer. A common conviction gripped us of the need for what we envisioned: an evangelical seminary of uncompromising academic and spiritual priorities, and that granted professors built-in time for research and writing. Each of us knew that only a sovereign God could create such a seminary *ex nihilo* in less than four months. A spiritual imperative urged us on.[42]

Henry and Fuller seemed made for each other, as both sought to reform fundamentalism from within, and not, as it would appear later, to make a complete break with it.[43] Thus, as Marsden observes, "to understand Fuller Seminary, then, we must first know something about fundamentalism."[44] The same is true of Henry.

Especially important, and relevant to this study, is that evangelical Protestantism dominated the American religious landscape in the

---

40. Henry, *Confessions*, 107–9.
41. Ibid., 104.
42. Ibid., 114.
43. Marsden, *Reforming Fundamentalism*, 3. Marsden observes that "the early Fuller was in striking ways a fundamentalist institution with a thoroughly fundamentalist constituency," ibid.
44. Ibid., 4.

nineteenth century. At the close of the century, even the president of the United States was expected to abide by "evangelical piety."[45] By the 1930s however, "this extraordinary influence of evangelicalism in the public sphere of American culture collapsed."[46] Prior to this, evangelical doctrines were taught in most colleges and universities, and chapel attendance was mandatory.

At the heart of this dramatic shift, was the fundamentalist-modernist controversy that was dramatically and publically played out in Dayton, TN, in 1925. The Scopes Trial would leave fundamentalists appearing out of touch "as rubes and hicks," largely discrediting the entire movement in the public eye.[47] As Marsden observes of this change:

> not only did the cultural opinion makers desert evangelicalism, even many leaders of major Protestant denominations attempt to tone down the offenses to modern sensibilities of a Bible filled with miracles and a gospel that proclaimed human salvation from eternal damnation only through Christ's atoning work on the cross.[48]

It was from within this milieu that Henry and others called for a "new evangelicalism," one that "reaffirmed cognitive and apologetic concerns and social engagement."[49] Fuller stood at the very center of this new program. According to Ockenga, "undergirding the school . . . was the authority of the Bible and commitment to sound theology with an apologetic mission and responsible Christian awareness and involvement in social concerns."[50]

---

45. Ibid.

46. Ibid.

47. Marsden, *Reforming Fundamentalism*, 60. Jerome Lawrence and Robert E. Lee dramatized the Scopes trial in the historically inaccurate *Inherit the Wind*, starring Spencer Tracey and Fredric March, which only fueled the declining public image of fundamentalists.

48. Ibid., 4.

49. Henry, *Confessions of a Theologian*, 117. Henry also discusses the fundamentalist-modernist controversy at length in Henry, *Evangelical Responsibility in Contemporary Theology* (Grand Rapids: Eerdmans, 1957). In chapter one of this text he describes the modernist revision of Christianity and in chapter two focuses on fundamentalist reduction.

50. Ibid.

Henry and the Founding of Christianity Today

In 1938, when Henry was a senior at Wheaton, he was asked by the dean of students, Dr. Wallace Emerson, what he thought was Christianity's greatest need. His reply? "A counterpart to [the liberal Christian magazine] *Christian Century*."[51] That keen observation would become a reality nearly twenty years later, when, in 1955, Henry was presented an opportunity to edit just such a publication. *Christianity Today* (CT) had been the vision of Billy Graham and his father-in-law, Dr. L. Nelson Bell. They had charted out the vision and secured a promise of $150,000 for two years from J. Howard Pew.

Rumors of Henry's pending appointment raised concerns among some who thought his association with Fuller would mean an anti-denominational slant for the magazine. Amidst those, and other complaints, Henry insisted that he could only take the position if the magazine embodied "an irenic spirit with theological integrity."[52] The magazine's goal was clearly stated: "to articulate historic Christianity and its contemporary relevance primarily for the clergy and incidentally also for thoughtful lay leaders."[53] That is, the intended readership was not the average layman, but rather "every gospel minister in the English-speaking world."[54]

Christianity Today was born in the midst of social unrest in America, especially regarding race. Martin Luther King Jr. had led the bus boycotts in Montgomery, AL, in 1955, joining Rosa Parks and others, that would lead to the Supreme Court ruling the following year declaring bus segregation unconstitutional. The magazine handled the matter by placing it in the hands of Bell, who along with Henry and Marcellus Kik, comprised the magazine's editorial board. It was unwise for the magazine to get this task to Bell, a southerner, who had already displayed insensitivity regarding the issue. In a letter to Henry, Bell wrote, "our problem is in many parts of the south, one of ratio, not race. Also, in many areas in the deep South, Negro children are so filthy, infected with disease and immoral, that white parents will not send their children to school with them."[55]

---

51. Ibid., 144. For more on the role of CT in the emergence of American Evangelicalism, see Alsdurf, "The Founding of Christianity Today Magazine," 20–43.

52. Henry, *Confessions*, 147.

53. Ibid., 148.

54. Ibid., 155.

55. Ibid., 158.

Bell charged that King's call to social change skirted the authentic gospel, a position with which Henry disagreed. "Although we emphasized what liberal theology ignored, namely, the gospel's life-transforming power, we escalated it at times into a solvent sufficient for all social injustices."[56] That is, Henry felt the church should not expect that all needed and important forms of social concern should come from simply individually transformed lives. There are times when further action is required, even on the part of believers "whose sanctification is incomplete."[57] It was perhaps this very sort of forward thinking though that raised the suspicion among some, including Pew, who later charged, "Carl Henry is a socialist."[58]

Henry ultimately had a falling out with other leaders at CT. When Pew requested advance proofs of the content of the magazine, Henry felt this greatly restricted his freedom as editor, and threatened to resign if the practice continued.

Despite ongoing struggles of this nature, Henry made great personal sacrifices to continue at CT and simultaneously serve on the faculty at Fuller. In 1956 Henry took a year-long leave of absence from Fuller, fully expecting to one day return. By the second year of publication CT had 38,000 paid subscribers, making it "the most widely and most completely and most regularly read Protestant magazine."[59] Both the magazine and Henry were gaining notice. As Henry observed, "not only was *Christianity Today* the most frequently quoted religious journal, but the secular press also dubbed me—doubtless to Graham's embarrassment—"the thinking man's Billy Graham."[60] Thus, pressure mounted on Henry to choose between Fuller and CT.

---

56. Ibid., 158–59.

57. Ibid., 159. Henry also notes that the magazine as a whole did not entirely agree with Dr. King's practices, stating, "the magazine opposed the disrespect for law implicit in mob demonstration and resistance, when a single well-publicized protest could have thrown the issue into the courts where justice issues were to be resolved"; ibid., 158. It is unclear, however, how Henry and fellow editors distinguish between "demonstration" and "protest." Plus, this view seems to overlook the reality of the Jim Crow south, wherein courts often turned a blind eye to racial injustices.

58. Ibid., 162. Others who have championed evangelical social concern have faced similar charges, including one of Henry's contemporaries, Ron Sider. See Sider, *I Am Not a Social Activist*. This is not to suggest, however, that Henry and Sider are in agreement on the issue evangelical social concern.

59. Henry, *Confessions*, 179.

60. Ibid., 181.

Henry chose CT, and on December 30, 1958 cut his ties with Fuller. As CT gained in influence and positively affected the public perception of Evangelical Christianity, Henry continued to press the need for, among other things, scholarly reflection on a Christian worldview, including especially a focus on the doctrine of the church, and "a breakthrough in evangelical social action."[61] Indeed, these two foci would continue to be prominent in Henry's work up until his death in 2003.

From its inception CT had taken a firm position regarding both evangelism and social action. Specifically, CT stated its position in five tenets:

1. The Bible is critically relevant to the whole of modern life and culture—the socio-political arena included.

2. The institutional church has no mandate, jurisdiction or competence to endorse political legislation or military tactics or economic specifics in the name of Christ.

3. The institutional church is divinely obliged to proclaim God's entire revelation, including standards or commandments by which men and nations are to be finally judged, and by which they ought now to live and maintain social stability.

4. The political achievement of a better society is the task of all citizens, and individual Christians ought to be politically engaged to the limit of their competency and opportunity.

5. The Bible limits the proper activity of both government and church for divinely stipulated objectives—the former, the preservation of justice and order, and the latter, the moral-spiritual task of evangelizing the earth.[62]

The issue of these basic beliefs came up in ongoing confrontations between Henry and Pew over the editorial control of the magazine. Ultimately, these disagreements with Pew became an insurmountable obstacle, ending in Henry's "involuntary termination" in 1968.[63]

---

61. Ibid., 205. Patterson claims that "social caution" characterized the magazine more than did an emphasis on social action, but offers no evidence of this. Plus, one must keep in mind Henry's concern to also champion the cause of evangelism and an orthodox doctrine of Scripture, which tended to be absent in ecumenically minded churches; see Patterson, *Carl F.H. Henry*, 53.

62. Henry, *Confessions*, 270–71.

63. Ibid., 286. Thornbury says that regarding the problems that arose between

Henry though had done much to restore the public confidence in Evangelical Christianity that had been eroded by the fundamentalist-modernist controversy. He had helped give rise to an intellectually rigorous and culturally engaged Evangelicalism.[64] Under Henry, CT had "become the most effective evangelical thought journal on the contemporary scene" and had at the end of his tenure, 150,000 paid subscriptions. Furthermore, it proved the sustaining force of the emerging neo-Evangelical movement for which Henry's *Uneasy Conscience* had been a prime catalyst.[65] Yet, out of work at the age of fifty-four, Henry wondered what his future would hold.[66]

Henry and Evangelism and Social Concern

Much of the relevance of this study depends on the reality that Henry played key roles at nearly every evangelical conference in the latter half of the twentieth century that addressed the topics of evangelism and social concern. Understanding these conferences and Henry's role in them prove crucial to grasping his perspective.

Berlin 1966

The 1966 World Congress on Evangelism, held in Berlin from October 26 to November 4, was the brainchild of Billy Graham and Carl F. H. Henry. Following a White House meeting with President Johnson in

---

Henry and CT, "it was probably the case that Christianity Today did not deal forthrightly with Carl despite his honesty with them." Plus, "Henry tended to treat CT involvement like a one-year academic contract, and the board wanted a long-term commitment. In other words, he was not all that politically astute"; Thornbury, *Recovering Classic Evangelicalism*, 23.

64. One of Henry's most memorable moments at CT occurred when Karl Barth held a Q&A at George Washington University. Henry asked Barth, pointing to the press gallery, "if these journalists had their present duties in the time of Jesus . . . was the resurrection of such a nature that covering some aspect of it would have fallen into their area of responsibility?" Barth angrily retorted, "did you say Christianity Today, or Christianity *Yesterday*?" The audience, according to Henry, "roared with delight." But Henry, not being one to back down from a challenge, replied, "yesterday, today, and forever," which also delighted the audience. At the end of his lecture, Barth apologized for the way he had handled Henry's question; Henry, *Confessions*, 211.

65. Cf. Carpenter, *Revive Us Again*, 204.

66. Henry, *Confessions*, 286–87.

1964, Graham phoned Henry and asked that he accompany him to the airport.[67] Graham, fearing that a sponsorship of the event by his own organization would appear self-serving, asked Henry if CT could sponsor the event, and if Henry could serve as chairman. As Graham recalled, "the magazine had already gained worldwide prestige among both Protestants and Catholics."[68] Henry agreed, if Graham would be honorary chairman. Once this was agreed upon, much of the organizational work fell to Stan Mooneyham, who had worked closely with Graham, first serving as editor of *United Evangelical Action*, and later as Vice President of Graham's organization, the *Billy Graham Evangelistic Association* (BGEA).

This congress, according to Mooneyham, sought to "define biblical evangelism, expound its relevance to the modern world, identify and mark its opponents, stress the urgency of proclaiming the orthodox gospel throughout the world, discover new methods and share little known techniques of proclaiming it more effectively, and summon the church to recognize the priority of the evangelistic task."[69] Officially, the congress named several purposes for coming together:

1. To define and clarify biblical evangelism for our day.
2. To establish beyond any doubt its relevance to the modern world.
3. To underline its urgency in the present situation.
4. To explore new forms of witness now in use throughout the world and new ways of reaching contemporary man.
5. To deal frankly with problems of resistance to the Gospel.
6. To challenge the church to renew its own life through an intensified proclamation of the historic faith.
7. To show the world in a fresh and dramatic way that God is in truth Lord of all, and that he saves men through his Son.[70]

---

67. Ibid., 252; Martin, *A Prophet without Honor*, 326. Pollock wrongly has the meeting in 1962 and with President Kennedy; see Pollock, *Billy Graham*, 188. Graham himself does not mention the taxi-cab ride in his autobiography, so Henry being the only other person present, seems the most reliable source; see Graham, *Just as I Am*, 562. Also, according to Graham, even though CT would be the official sponsor, Graham's Evangelism Association would provide funding and do all the organizing; ibid.

68. Graham, *Just as I Am*, 562.

69. Martin, *A Prophet Without Honor*, 328.

70. Johnston, *The Battle for World Evangelism*, 171.

Henry points out that in 1966, the issue of the relationship between evangelism and social concern was becoming particularly contentious, especially among ecumenical churches. "The conflict in ecumenical circles that pitted social action priorities against evangelism was at that time already running at high tide."[71] When Graham arrived in Berlin early to conduct crusades prior to the congress, he was heavily criticized by ecumenically-minded churches. Ecumenical workers from the National Council of Churches (NCC) "were prone to dismiss evangelistic efforts as spurious and counterfeit."[72] In addition, an earlier conference held by the World Council of Churches (WCC) in Geneva that same year, also drew a sharp distinction between Evangelical approaches and those of the more theologically liberal churches. The NCC, for its part, actively promoted suspicion among its workers toward the Berlin meeting. Yet, as Henry observed, "to oppose the World Congress on the edge of quasi-official criticism was therefore to promote the bias of partisans hostile to personal evangelism and evangelical orthodoxy."[73]

It is important to understand then, that the World Congress on Evangelism in Berlin in 1966 itself stood in sharp contrast to the demise of evangelism among ecumenical churches. Two works are especially important for grasping the content, emphases, and passions of the congress. Henry laid out the concerns of the congress in his book *Evangelicals at the Brink of Crisis: Significance of the World Congress on Evangelism*. In addition, the congress produced a two-volume work containing the text of all plenary presentation and reports associated with the congress.[74]

In Henry's opening address, entitled "Facing a New Day in Evangelism," he began by challenging the delegates regarding the present day neglect of evangelism. "One major weakness of modern Christianity lies in its abandonment of the heavy burden of evangelism to a small company of professional supersalesmen." He then reminded the attendees, "our participation here is no occasion for self-congratulation; it is rather a call to self-crucifixion."[75] More importantly, Henry set forth here a maxim to which he would often return: "The God of the Bible is the God of justice and justification."[76]

71. Henry, *Confessions*, 253.
72. Ibid., 245.
73. Henry, *Confessions*, 255.
74. See Henry and Mooneyham, *One Race, One Gospel, One Task*.
75. Henry, "Facing a New Day in Evangelism," 11.
76. Ibid., 16; see also *GRA*, 6:402–17.

Henry, and many others as well, deemed the Berlin congress a triumph. One of the areas in which the congress drew criticism, though, was on the issue of social concern. Yet, here too Henry felt the congress had been right on track:

> The congress shaped the mood in which evangelicals sensed their larger need of each other and of mutual encouragement and enrichment. While it put theology and social concern within its purview alongside evangelism, its role was that of stimulating discussion and reflection rather than of issuing preconceived pronouncements.[77]

Henry adds regarding the task of evangelism and the impact of the World Congress, in a statement that could well sum up much of Henry's own career from this moment on:

> Berlin was therefore a milestone for the evangelical image . . . Berlin defined evangelism as uniquely proclamation, and it disowned 'all theology and criticism that refuses to bring itself under the divine authority of Holy Scripture, and all traditionalism which weakens that authority by adding to the Word of God.'[78]

Henry also says that those who were critical of Berlin for not giving more attention to social concern "do so from the standpoint of later ecclesiastical developments. They underestimate also its achievement of bringing together the disparate worldwide evangelistic forces to focus as a single body on the church's priority task."[79]

The closing statement issued by the congress elaborated, and in some ways, pointed to three dominant challenges facing the task of evangelism: racism, the exclusivity of Christian claims, and the singular task of the church. Regarding the latter, the delegates wrote:

> Our Lord Jesus Christ, possessor of all authority in heaven and on earth, has not only called us to himself; he has sent us out into the world to be his witnesses. In the power of the Spirit he commands us to proclaim to all people the good news of salvation through his atoning death and resurrection; to invite them to discipleship through repentance and faith; to baptize them into the fellowship of his church; and to teach them all his words.[80]

77. Henry, *Confessions*, 261.
78. Ibid.
79. Ibid., 262.
80. "One Race, One Gospel, One Task: Closing Statement of the World Congress

It is important to note here, that this "one task" was not an oversimplified understanding of the role of the church, but rather one in which the human race stood as one in need of Christ, revealed and made known through the one Gospel, the task of which had been set before the church by Christ himself.

Key '73

Like the World Congress in Berlin, Henry had been one of the main instigators behind the event known as Key '73, so named because the vision for this event was birthed at a meeting near the Key Bridge (named after Francis Scott Key) which connects Rosslyn, VA, to the Georgetown neighborhood of Washington, D.C. Yet, unlike Berlin, by this time Henry no longer held his influential position at CT, and without the magazine's support, the effort stood little chance of significant success.

The event came about through an editorial Henry wrote in 1967 in CT, titled, "Somehow, Let's Get Together."[81] Here Henry observed, "increasingly the need becomes evident for a greater framework of cooperation as evangelicals seek to witness to the world of the sovereignty of Christ."[82] While lauding the reality that evangelicals were a significant force in society "despite their mass-media invisibility," he warned that divisions were significant and damaging. "[Evangelicalism's] common ground is crisscrossed by many fences. Evangelicals differ not only on secondary doctrines but also on ecclesiology, the role of the church in society, politics, and cultural mores."[83]

The editorial proved one of the most noticed in the magazine's entire history, according to Henry. Clearly, others shared Henry's sentiments expressed in the letter, as more than one hundred denominations responded and made commitments.[84]

However, in addition to the lack of support from Henry's successor at CT, other factors contributed to the event's low impact. First, independent fundamentalist churches refused to be involved because of

on Evangelism," 1:6.
    81. Henry, "Somehow, Let's Get Together," 24–25.
    82. Ibid., 24.
    83. Ibid.
    84. Henry, *Confessions*, 344.

participation by ecumenically aligned churches.[85] Second, ecumenical churches threw fuel on the fundamentalist fire by trying to place social justice ahead of evangelism as the main emphasis. Finally, prominent Jewish spokesmen, who later recanted after irreparable damage had been done, initially condemned the event as anti-Semitic for encouraging the evangelization of Jews.[86] Despite this, Key '73 was not without positive results. As Henry observed:

> What Key 73 achieved most spectacularly was a massive alliance of evangelical Christians of all denominations on a community basis in evangelistic outreach, without direct dependence of this thrust on any one charismatic leader or single denomination or organization. In this respect the effort disclosed latent aspirations for evangelical awakening, and a ready disposition to transcend the ghetto concentration of Christians in their churches or in crusade meetings by programs of community outreach and penetration.[87]

Chicago Declaration

That same year, Ronald Sider invited Henry to attend a gathering of about fifty evangelical leaders to discuss the need for "unhesitating social involvement." Henry, at the outset, sensed an imbalance in the agenda being pushed, but feeling his presence might help offset things, agreed to attend. Negatively, Henry believed that the invitation list insured "an outcome serviceable to the merging social activist mood and critical of the evangelical establishment." Yet, "for all that, it seemed better to attend and to strive for a balanced position than to simply accommodate a one-sided outcome."[88] The meeting, which took place Thanksgiving weekend in 1973, concluded with the issuance of *The Chicago Declaration*. By this time, Henry was considered already an elder statesman of Evangelicalism. Sider, in his edited volume on the event, applauded Henry for the

---

85. For this and other objections by Reformed Fundamentalists, see Engelsma, "Key '73 – What Must We Say About It?," n.p.
86. Henry, *Confessions*, 345.
87. Henry, "Looking Back at Key 73," 7.
88. Henry, *Confessions*, 348.

courage to work with younger evangelical social activists, acknowledging that to do so was risky.[89]

Despite his initial suspicions, Henry did have some positive reflections on the importance of *The Chicago Declaration*, which he published in *CT* in May of 1974, and which Sider also published in his booklet, *The Chicago Declaration*.[90] Henry, in his assessment of the event, took advantage of the opportunity to point out the weaknesses of ecumenical social action, and thereby the genuine need for evangelical clarification and effort in this area. He criticized ecumenical social engagement especially for focusing exclusively on society while ignoring individuals, and for a failure to "elaborate the revealed biblical principles" which guide their social concern.[91]

"The paramount Chicago concern," Henry observed, "was not to advance one or another of the current ideologies but to focus on the divine demand for social and political justice, and to discover what the Kingdom of God requires of any contemporary option."[92] In other words, the participants avoided the liberal theological tendency toward an entirely earthly Kingdom of God by also emphasizing transcendent realities. Henry also observed that "Evangelicals are contemplating anew the Evangelical awakening," which not only kept England from something akin to the French Revolution, but also wrought dramatic social changes on multiple fronts. "In that movement of social reality," Henry said, referencing the earlier Awakenings, "evangelicals took an initiative in such matters as slavery, factory working conditions, child labor laws, illiteracy, prison conditions, unemployment, poverty education for the underprivileged, and much else." He then declared, "If ever America has stood in dire need of an awakening of both social and personal morality, the moment is now."[93] In his autobiography, Henry laments the unrealized potential of *The Chicago Declaration* and of Sider's *Evangelicals for Social Action (ESA)*. Plus, Henry felt that when Jerry Falwell's Moral Majority appeared, "it did so as something less than a specifically evangelical movement and

---

89. Sider, *The Chicago Declaration*, 9; Sider especially interpreted Key '73 as proffering the hope of greater evangelical cooperation and agreement on social concern, much as had taken place in the area of evangelism; ibid., 15.

90. Ibid.

91. Henry in ibid., 127–31.

92. Ibid., 130.

93. Ibid., 131.

skirted many concerns voiced by the Chicago Statement."[94] As will be evident later in the study, Henry particularly disagreed with the Moral Majority's direct endorsement of political candidates, when Henry instead preferred a less direct involvement that spoke more to policy issues. However, this is not to imply that Henry held a completely negative view of Falwell and the Moral Majority.

Lausanne I

When Billy Graham and others launched the *Lausanne International Congress on World Evangelism* in 1974, Carl Henry was invited to present one of the opening papers and to chair the subsection on "evangelism and personal and social ethics." He was also asked to serve on the redaction committee that would finalize the covenant to be produced, but declined because of ambiguity and uncertainty about the congress's goals.[95] This, of course, would be the first of several such international congresses, the most recent held in Cape Town in 2010.[96]

In his assessment of Lausanne I, Henry, citing Arthur Johnson's *Battle for World Evangelism* (Tyndale House, 1978), points out that Lausanne "carried forward the Berlin/1966 emphasis on personal evangelism but focused more fully on the church as a cross-cultural community, and stressed the gospel's this-worldly utilitarian values more than man's destiny in eternity." Moreover, "it meshed evangelism into the current ecumenical controversies over the visible church as its authorizing instrument and appropriated the concept of mission and 'holistic witness' that held together proclamation and service."[97]

Henry seems to approve of John Stott's position that social action "is integral to fulfilling the Great Commission," commenting that, "evangelism in the popular sense does not of itself fulfill the intention of the Great Commission."[98] He also observes, using a now anachronistic term, that 'Two-Thirds World' participants emphasize that the church should lead

94. Henry, *Confessions*, 348–49.

95. Ibid., 349–50.

96. For history and access to all Lausanne documents, see http://www.lausanne.org. For the documents from all Lausanne movement events and the many subsidiary commissions, see especially *Making Christ Known*; Tizon, *Transformation after Lausanne*; Hunt, "The History of the Lausanne Movement, 1974–2010."

97. Henry, *Confessions*, 349.

98. Ibid.

the way in seeking socio-economic change, and created some confusion as to whether this was "an integral facet of the gospel."[99] The debate pitted priority of evangelism advocates like Donald McGavran against "radical discipleship" advocates such as Samuel Escobar and René Padilla. Yet, many of these tensions were addressed, though not resolved, in Henry's subcommittee. In the end, the covenant affirmed that, "in the church's mission of sacrificial service, evangelism is primary." Oddly, John Stott, however, "interpreted the Covenant as championing an equal partnership of social action and evangelism."[100]

Reflecting something of the diversity that Henry observed, Al Tizon has classified participants in the evangelical conferences between 1966 and 1973 into one of three prominent groups:

> (1) the fundamentalists who maintained the primacy of evangelism largely at the expense of social concern as a continued reaction against the 'apostate ecumenical movement;' (2) the new or moderate evangelicals, who, while maintaining the primacy of evangelism, called for a return to historical evangelicalism that pro-actively engaged the social issues of the day; (3) The younger, radical evangelicals who called for an uncompromising socio-political commitment to biblical compassion and justice for the sake of the poor and oppressed in the world.[101]

Henry also points out that Lausanne "linked evangelism and social concern more tightly than did Berlin," but that "the theology of Lausanne needs clarification and buttressing in numerous respects."[102] Plus, because of certain ambiguities, perhaps such as those that led Stott to see in the covenant a more unified understanding than did others, "the gathering postponed rather than resolved the conflicts and ambiguities" over the precise relationship between evangelism and social concern.[103]

---

99. Ibid.

100. Ibid., 350.

101. Tizon, *Transformation after Lausanne*, 30–31. As Tizon rightly observes, these three strands should not be seen as necessarily progressive, as though one pushed out the other, but rather as running alongside each other in the contemporary context, "making evangelical missionary social ethics a very diverse and complex phenomenon; ibid., 31. One might observe, also, that these three groups closely parallel Hesselgrave's description of various approaches to the prioritism-holism issue.

102. Henry, *Confessions*, 350.

103. Ibid.

Finally, Henry feared the Covenant had an inadequate view of church as a spiritual body, emphasizing too much the visible institutional church.

World Vision

Henry's official role as lecturer-at-large with World Vision began in March 1974, following his six semesters at Eastern Baptist Seminary in Philadelphia. The offer of this position had come from Stan Mooneyham, who had previously led the Billy Graham Evangelistic Association (BGEA), but now served as president of World Vision.[104]

Part of what attracted Henry to World Vision lay in Mooneyham's belief that the tendency to educate promising young African and Asian scholars at American seminaries contributed to the "brain drain" in those places. Thus, "Mooneyham saw the need of transporting evangelical scholars abroad for short-term lectures and courses benefiting students in their own cultural contexts."[105] Plus, the position held forth ample opportunity for Henry to engage in writing and research. Henry served in this capacity until 1987, during which time he also saw the publication of his magnum opus, *God, Revelation, and Authority*.[106]

Conclusion

It is not difficult to see that the events of Carl Henry's life shaped his passions, both theologically and personally. Being the son of a poor alcoholic father gave Henry a keen awareness of the ill effect this issue had on a family. As a young man Henry had known first hand both poverty and injustice. As a theologian, he came to know that Scripture had something to say about both.[107]

Henry's conversion to Christ was one that set him aflame with a passion for evangelism. As he pursued God's calling upon his life, his studies only added to his incipient conviction that evangelism and social concern constitute not only non-negotiable aspects of the church's responsibility in

---

104. Ibid., 352.

105. Ibid., 352–53.

106. The first two volumes came out in 1976, volumes three and four in 1978, five in 1982, and six in early 1983; ibid., 361.

107. For example, see Deut 15:11; 24:14; 1 Sam 2:8; Job 24:14; Ps 72:13; 113:7; Prov 31:20; Isa 10:2; Ezek 16:49; 18:12; 22:29.

the world, but also aspects that must never be confused with one another. And in fact, his life in ministry bears out this reality, as these ideas were central to his work at the NAE, at CT, Fuller, World Vision, and the many conferences on evangelism and social concern that he either helped organize or in which he participated. To understand these passions more fully, and in order to move toward a deeper evaluation of Henry's thinking, we now turn to his theological and philosophical commitments.

— 3 —

Henry's Theological Method

"Evangelical Christianity refuses to put God under any category other than his own, yet it declines on that account to declare God inconceivable and unknowable."[1]

Part I: Alternative Approaches to Theological Method

CARL HENRY HAS BEEN variously accused of being a rationalist, a modernist, and a fideist in his approach to theology.[2] These divergent accusations indicate to some degree the complexity of Henry's writings on his epistemological and theological foundations. Yet, they also highlight a tendency to assign Henry to a particular category, apparently without having actually read his work, since he directly refutes many of these claims.[3]

---

1. *GRA*, 3:229.

2. Brand, "Is Carl Henry a Modernist?"; Carswell, "A Comparative Study of the Religious Epistemology of Carl F. H. Henry and Alvin Plantiga." Rationalism can be defined as a belief in "the rationality of the universe and in the power of reason to Grasp it"; see Brown, *Christianity and Western Thought*, 173; Allen, *Philosophy for Understanding Theology*, 181. Central to rationalism is the notion of innate ideas—that the mind has access to ideas apart from sensory experience. Three of the most prominent rationalists were Rene Descartes, Baruch Spinoza, and Gottfried W. Leibniz. Rationalists sought to counter skepticism by showing both the universe and human mind to be inherently rational. As we will see, this is patently not what Henry believed. Fideism, at the other end of the spectrum, emphasizes faith alone, apart from, above, or sometimes even contrary to reason; cf. Boa and Bowman, *Faith Has Its Reasons*, Kindle edition, chapter 16. Those who have in reality taken a fideist approach to Christianity include Martin Luther, Blaise Pascal, Søren Kierkegaard, and Karl Barth.

3. As Thornbury asks, "are these people reading the same Carl F. H. Henry that I am?" Thornbury, *Recovering Classic Evangelicalism*, 59; cf. Trueman, "Admiring the Sistine Chapel" 56.

Epistemological concerns and theological method rise and fall together. Or, as Thornbury has said more mildly, "epistemology matters in theological formulation."[4] In order to evaluate Henry's theological method and how it informs his approach to evangelism and social concern, it will be necessary to contrast his approach with the dominant option among evangelicals, namely a post-conservative method.[5] Much of the divide within Evangelicalism today can be described in terms of those who advocate the traditional conservative-propositional approach, and those favoring a post-conservative method.[6] Furthermore, these models are often distinguished, as we shall see, on the basis of their ability or inability to foster a holistic approach to Christian faith. For example, Steven B. Sherman says of the emergence of post-conservative theology, that proponents such as Roger Olson and others by advocating this method were moving "away from a defensive posture of rationalistic evidential apologetic, and toward a more holistic approach to theology and epistemology."[7] Similarly, Grenz and Franke claim that evangelical theology has generally taken a propositional and informational approach to the Bible. Against this trend, they wish to "rescue" Christian theology from rationalistic tendencies and promote a more culturally and socially relevant approach.[8]

---

4. Thornbury, *Recovering Classic Evangelicalism*, 35.

5. While an examination of all other models (neoorthodox and liberal for example) would also be a fruitful line of inquiry, the stated goal of this study is to better understand how Henry's model might inform the *evangelical* divide over this issue. Therefore, only models advocated by evangelicals lie within the scope of this study.

6. Reasons for focusing on these two approaches include (1), post-conservative theologians have been the most vocal critics of Henry, as we shall see; (2) their criticism centers especially on the issue of holism and the charge that a propositional approach leads to a concern for orthodoxy over orthopraxis. Furthermore, these two approaches, the conservative-propositional and post-conservative are arguably the dominant competing methods among Evangelicals; cf. Olson, *Reformed and Always Reforming*, Kindle edition, under "Introduction." Olson does distinguish between two types of conservative evangelical theologies, the first being a more Biblicist and propositionally oriented type, and the second being more heavily influenced by tradition (e.g., Methodism). But these do not necessarily represent two approaches to theological method, as both would prioritize Scripture, as Olson also points out. In the end, Olson places both of these in the category of "conservative" and proceeds to differentiate them from a post-conservative method.

7. Sherman, *Revitalizing Theological Epistemology*, 1–2.

8. Grenz and Franke, *Beyond Foundationalism*, 13–15.

In like manner, Allistair McGrath, reflecting an Augustinian idea, laments what he perceives as the loss in evangelical theology of the distinction between *scientia and sapientia,* or between knowledge and wisdom.[9] Thus, the two most common criticisms of the conservative propositional approach, are that it (1) tends toward an unbiblical rationalism focusing primarily if not entirely on information, and (2) it does not foster a holistic approach to Christian faith.[10] A basic examination of these models and their critics will be the subject of Part I of this chapter. Part II then will proceed to unpack Henry's methodology.

At the heart of this study is the relationship between evangelism and social concern, and an attempt to best understand how these things relate to one another in biblical faith. Along those very lines, a great deal of contemporary writing on the subject of theological method looks specifically to the issue of how word and deed, faith and practice, relate to one another. Or, as David Clark says, "Good theology is true to the Bible and powerfully transformative for real people in real cultures."[11] Thus, theological method, as Henry would surely concur, proves to be the crucial issue in discerning the proper relationship given to both evangelism and social concern in a biblically faithful and culturally relevant faith.

Epistemological Dualisms

Joseph Spradley, in *The Making of a Christian Mind*,[12] provides a helpful overview of how Christianity uniquely understands physical and spiritual anthropological qualities, and thus why Christianity by its very nature should avoid non-biblical dualisms.[13] Spradley shows that

9. See McGrath, "Evangelical Theological Method," 21–38.

10. Cf. Olson, *Reformed and Always Reforming*, chapter five, under "Postconservative Revelation: Narrative Before Propositions."

11. Clark, *To Know and Love God: Method for Theology*, Kindle ed., under "Evangelical Patterns in Theology." Similarly, Grenz says of theological method, "as theologians, the goal of our engagement in intellectual reflection on the faith commitment of the believing community is the construction of a model of reality that can foster a truly godly spirituality that translates into ethical living in the social-historical context in which we are to be the people of God"; ibid. See also Grenz, *Theology for the Community of God*, 17.

12. Spradley, "Christian View of the Physical World," 55–80.

13. Christopher Little is correct to assert that not all dualisms are unbiblical; but, conversely, neither are they all biblical; cf. Little, *Polemic Missiology*, chapter one. Also, for an excellent study of how dualistic worldviews have crept into and dominated

it is largely non-Christian ideas in philosophy and science that lead to false dichotomies between spiritual and physical realities. Spradley, for instance, points out that "a Christian worldview offers the possibility of a unifying perspective for seeing life whole and finding meaning in each part."[14] Key to this study is understanding how within a holistic framework the various components of biblical faith fit together. That is, just because they should not be unnaturally divided, does this thereby mean they should have equal place in Christian theology?

Biblical Foundations and Methodological Assumptions

Is it even legitimate to discuss "what the Bible says" on a given subject, prior to settling the issue of theological method?[15] Does not the claim to offer a "biblical basis" presuppose a particular methodology, namely one that takes for granted both the perspicuity and authority of Scripture? Even in methods that do not start with Scripture, unfounded presuppositions undergird the whole project. For example, George Lindbeck, in his *Nature of Doctrine*, argues for his cultural-linguistic approach based on the criteria of ecumenism, a criteria that he nowhere defends. Perhaps his lack of such a defense lies in this very conundrum: can one test or even put forth a theological method without first presupposing some theological conclusions? It seems obvious that one cannot, *and*, furthermore that this is not inherently problematic. That one has theological presuppositions should be taken for granted. "The important question," says Nancy Pearcey, "then, is what a person accepts as ultimate premises, for they shape everything that follows."[16]

Next, we examine two predominant approaches to method in theology, common in evangelical circles, prior to and as a necessary first step in presenting and evaluating the precise method articulated by Henry. This comparison is important precisely because much of the contemporary criticism of Henry comes from the post-conservative camp.

Western thought in ways that directly contradict a Christian worldview, see Pearcey, *Total Truth*.

14. Spradley, 57.

15. Cf. Thornbury, who observes of Grudem's *Systematic Theology* the lack of any mention of theological method, "the entire basis for doing evangelical theology was missing"; Thornbury, *Recovering Classic Evangelicalism*, 34.

16. Pearcey, *Total Truth*, 41.

Conservative-Propositional Approach

There are several key characteristics that define a general conservative-propositional (CP) approach to theology.[17] Central among these is that theologians from within this tradition have understood Scripture as especially conveying theological truths that are expressible in propositional form. In an earlier generation, this method characterized the work of Charles Hodge and B. B. Warfield. These theologians took for granted *Scottish Common Sense Realism* and sought to counter the liberal emphasis on subjective feeling by advocating an emphasis on intellectual apprehension. Their common sense approach also gave supreme importance to individual authority, and the ability of every person free from ecclesial authority to understand and appropriate the content and meaning of Scripture.[18] While there has been a general tendency to lump Henry together with the methods of Hodge and Warfield, Helseth has correctly pointed out that there is "significant discontinuity as well."[19]

This approach to theology has been criticized at several levels. For instance, Richard Lints has pointed out evangelical theology's lack of attention to its own extra-biblical influences and its neglect of church

---

17. For others who have used this designation, see especially Dulles, *Models of Revelation* and Lindbeck, *Nature of Doctrine*.

18. Scottish Common Sense Realism was originated by Thomas Reid. Reid had been a strict empiricist and emphasized common sense along with sensory experience as the source of all knowledge. As such, it highly valued Newtonian physics. Reid had sought, furthermore, to overcome Humian skepticism by declaring that all that exists is either mind or matter, and what the mind then perceives is not ideas as such, but real objects. Undergirding this was a foundationalist epistemology that proposed there are certain basic beliefs which need not be defended, but are rather grounded in common sense judgments; Livingstone, *Modern Christian Thought*, 303–4; cf. Marsden, *Fundamentalism and American Culture*, 110–12.

19. Helseth, "Carl F. H. Henry, Old Princeton, and the Right Use of Reason," 294. Although, I must strongly disagree with Helseth's conclusions, wherein he attributes to Henry a "naïve" realism that "flattens reality and promotes an epistemology that . . . .subverts what it means to know God in the fullest creaturely sense of the term"; ibid., 299. Helseth believes that Henry's emphasis on rational capacity and the receivability of revelation reduces the human soul as a thinking-feeling-willing whole, and is more in keeping with psychology than with biblical anthropology. I have to confess to not at all seeing this in Henry, whose concern for the rational nature of revelation means to deny the claim that revelation might be subjective, non-cognitive, and vague. As White has pointed out, Henry's epistemology is not as rationalistic as Helseth claims, nor is it as reductionist; White, "Word and Spirit in the Theological Method of Carl Henry," 65–66. Also, Grenz and Franke especially lump Henry and the Princetonians together; cf. Grenz and Franke, *Beyond Foundationalism*, 14.

history. Citing historian Nathan Hatch, Lints points out that evangelicalism has fully embraced the Enlightenment elevation of individual autonomy. Following Descartes, the individual thinking self (*cogito ergo sum*) became the ultimate arbiter of truth and meaning, and this notion has surprisingly become a distinct feature of American Evangelicalism. During the Second Great Awakening at the beginning of the nineteenth century, "many shifted the test of truth away from one's fidelity to the creeds of the church and instead measured it by one's personal experience of the Holy Spirit."[20] As Lints points out, "[Nathan] Hatch goes so far as to suggest that 'at one level then, the Enlightenment in America was not repudiated but popularized' by evangelicals of the early nineteenth century."[21] One of the effects of this was the turning away from historic Christianity and from "past communities of interpretation."[22]

Also, Stephen B. Sherman points out four areas where post-conservatives especially have criticized the methodology of Hodge and Warfield. First, critics question the prevalence of modernity and the reliance on Scottish Common Sense Philosophy in this approach. Second, critics commonly also question this method's confidence in scientific method and the supposed innate ability of the human mind to reason rightly.[23] Third, there was a tendency to elevate Calvinism itself to near infallible status and thereby lay claim to be the singular proper theological methodology. Fourth, post-conservatives express concern over theological method being tied too closely to the current regnant philosophy.[24]

Others have also criticized CP approaches to theology as borrowing too liberally from other disciplines without fully appreciating the impact of such actions. For instance, Alister E. McGrath has argued that evangelicals have not "paid adequate attention to theological method," and more specifically to the "intellectual environment that shapes their thinking."[25] Similarly, Kevin Vanhoozer has said that such a view fails to

20. Lints, *The Fabric of Theology*, 34.
21. Ibid., 38; Hatch and Noll, *The Bible in America*, 74.
22. Lints, *The Fabric of Theology*, 36.
23. Hatch and Noll, *The Bible in America: Essays in Cultural History*, 75. As Sherman points out, this confidence in the mind's ability to reason was at odds with Hodge's strict Calvinism, which emphasized total depravity; worse, Hodge himself seemed oblivious to this fact; Sherman, *Revitalizing Theological Epistemology: Holistic Evangelical Approaches to the Knowledge of God*, 103.
24. Sherman, *Revitalizing Theological Epistemology*, 92–105.
25. McGrath, "Evangelical Theological Method," 15. Also, Grenz and Franke, *Beyond Foundationalism*, 13.

take into account the full range of scriptural genres. For Vanhoozer, "the crucial point is that neither the covenant nor the canon can be reduced to a set of concepts."[26] Furthermore he argues that Scripture functions in a way beyond merely providing information. "The Bible is more than divine data." Finally, he adds that propositionalism is too derived from a very modern form of epistemology, namely foundationalism.[27]

Roger Olson, also an advocate for a post-conservative theological method, has criticized a conservative evangelical approach to Scripture for its alleged emphasis on information over transformation. Furthermore, he specifically cites Henry's *Toward a Recovery of Christian Beliefs* as advocating a view of Christianity that is primarily belief-informational centered.[28]

Olson, McGrath, and Vanhoozer can each be variously located within the spectrum post-conservative evangelical theology, which by definition seeks to pay greater heed to extra-biblical influences on theological epistemology.[29] At one level, their critique is valid: we do not enter the theological task in a vacuum. We are subject to countless influences that are endemic to our particular culture and perhaps alien to many other cultures, including those through which the Scriptures have come to us. To do theology is, therefore, not to simply skim away the cultural dross and reduce the content to its most basic and unadorned form. Theology is not about merely capturing the meaning of Scripture, but is rather about conveying that meaning in ways that are both biblically faithful and culturally relevant.

Assessment of the CP Approach

The question all this raises regarding the relationship between evangelism and social concern, is how might evangelical theological methods have skewed what Scripture says and teaches by not adequately considering all

26. Vanhoozer, "The Voice and the Actor," 64.

27. Vanhoozer, *The Drama of Doctrine*, 5.

28. Olson, *Reformed and Always Reforming*, chapter 2. However, against Olson's claim, as this study will show, Henry's emphasis on revelation did not focus merely on right belief. Rather, Henry and others like him advocated that the doctrine of revelation stood at the center of a vibrant Evangelical theology. Oddly, Olson seems to even admit this when he and Grenz say, regarding Henry's emphasis on revelation, "For Henry and others the focus on biblical authority is not an end in itself. Rather, its importance rests in the perception that 'the doctrine of the Bible controls all other doctrines of the Christian faith.'" Grenz and Olson, *Twentieth Century Theology*, 292.

29. Sherman, *Revitalizing Theological Epistemology*, 12–14.

of the relevant external influences that come into play? More importantly, do these critiques apply specifically to Henry? Can it be rightly said that Henry unbiblically narrowed the scope and content of Scripture with his propositional approach? For now, we will defer that question in order to first better understand the nature of post-conservative theology.

Post-Conservative Theology

History and Development

Post-conservative approaches to theological method by and large build on George Lindbeck's post-liberal method, outlined in his text *The Nature of Doctrine*. This approach is especially sensitive to the postmodern "linguistic turn"—meaning simply that the world is never viewed objectively, but rather especially through the linguistic concepts each individual brings.[30] Plus, post-conservative theology attempts to move past what proponents see as Enlightenment-based foundationalism.

Defining Characteristics

Roger Olson defines post-conservative theology as an outgrowth of the pietistic side of the evangelical movement. Citing especially three modern thinkers who have exhibited post-conservative leanings, namely Grenz, McGrath, and Vanhoozer, Olson details six ways in which post-conservative theology may be distinguished from a more traditional, conservative evangelical approach.[31]

First, post-conservatives conceive of revelation differently. Though, importantly, they too presuppose revelation, "they consider its main

---

30. Franke, *The Character of Theology*, 23–36. The so-called linguistic turn has its ancestry in Ludwig Wittgenstein's concept of "language games." As Franke explains, "according to Wittgenstein, each use of language occurs within a separate and seemingly self-contained system, complete with its own rules. Similar to playing a game, we require an awareness of the operative rules and significance of the terms within the context of the purpose for which we are using language." Furthermore, "meaning is an internal function of language," and not directly correspondent to external realities; ibid., 24; see also Wittgenstein, *Philosophical Investigations*.

31. Olson, *Reformed and Always Reforming*, under "The Postconservative Style of Evangelical Theology," chapter one. McGrath does not self-identify as post-conservative, though he frequently shows affinity for some of its key characteristics, as Olson has shown. Other prominent post-conservatives include John Franke and Clark Pinnock.

purpose to be transformation more than information." In this, "many post-conservative evangelicals are enamored with narrative theology, which emphasizes the power of story . . . in a way that propositions do not." Second, post-conservatives view theology as "a pilgrimage and a journey rather than a discovery and conquest." Third, post-conservatism can be seen as a rejection of Enlightenment ways of thinking, especially foundationalism. Fourth, post-conservatives are more concerned with the theological center and who is nearest to it, than with who is in and who is out. Fifth, post-conservatives emphasize evangelicalism's core as spiritual experience over doctrinal belief. Finally, post-conservative theologians tend to have less emphasis on tradition than conservative evangelicals.[32]

Defining Narrative Theology

As we have observed, an emphasis on narrative or story often characterizes post-conservative approaches to theology. Thus, at times, post-conservativism is lumped together under the broad banner of narrative theology. Narrative theology, though not necessarily a theological method, is more properly defined as an approach to hermeneutics that informs and shapes various (i.e., neoorthodox, post-liberal, and post-conservative) approaches to Scripture. Thus, it has its roots in one of Carl Henry's theological nemeses, namely Karl Barth. Hans Frei especially made use of Barth's understanding of Scripture as witness to move away

32. Ibid. Regarding the first point, Olson admits that theologians such as Henry and Paul Helm also contend that knowledge is for the purpose of transformation. Post-conservatives though question whether knowledge is "the only or best means of transforming persons"; ibid. On the second characteristic, Olson points out that the issue is not that post-conservatives reject outright the search for objective truths, but that they are unafraid of theological imagination and experimentation. On the third point, Olson especially cites McGrath's accusation, leveled at Hodge and Henry, of abiding an Enlightenment form of foundationalism. Olson summarizes the view of McGrath, who believed this approach to theology "prizes rational certainty and elevates propositions and coherent systems almost to idols." Regarding the fourth characteristic, Olson claims that "the center" is Jesus Christ and the Gospel, "but also includes the four or five common core commitments" that includes all of Bebbington's quadrilateral. On the issue of an emphasis on spiritual experience, Olson answers the charge of similarity to Schleiermacher by deferring to Grenz, who distinguishes between the two by saying that post-conservatives are not, like Schleiermacher, referencing a universal God-consciousness, but uniquely Christian conversion that includes commitment and devotion to Christ and acceptance of the authority of Scripture. On the final point, Olson cites both McGrath and Vanhoozer as claiming that conservative evangelicals give lip service to the principle of *sola scriptura*; ibid.

from a historical-critical method of interpretation, and to emphasize a Christo-centric reading of the Gospels.[33] Frei's work heavily influenced that of George Lindbeck, and nearly all subsequent theological methods that emphasize a narrative hermeneutical approach. While this trend as a theological movement has been difficult to define owing to its diversity, minimally it can be said that efforts within this category tend to emphasize community and linguistic analysis in contrast to historically situated, propositionally stated truth.[34] As Thornbury has observed, in *The Eclipse of biblical Narrative*, Frei argues that "Enlightenment epistemological categories supplanted the central feature of the biblical text: its narrative quality. That is, Frei contends that the Bible maintains a unity because of the story it tells, that of the person of Jesus Christ and his identity."[35] Thus, the truth of Scripture relates primarily to how the Scriptures are true for those within the community of faith. Thus, Frei rejects the idea that "the interpreter should be concerned with any supposed 'objective' truth standing outside the narrative of Scripture."[36]

Assessment of a Post-conservative Approach

The primary differences in a conservative-propositional and post-conservative approach to theology lies in the audience that each is addressing. Propositionally inclined methods, such as those of Warfield and Henry, direct their efforts against modernity's attack on the Bible and on the supernatural. Plus, at least in Henry's case, he aims to reclaim the Augustinian ground gained by the Reformation. Post-conservative theology

---

33. Jones, "Narrative," 395; cf. Grenz and Olson, who define narrative theology as an approach that "seeks to utilize the concept of story and the human person as storyteller as the central motif for theological reflection." Plus, among the key aspects of narrative theology is the belief "that all of our fundamental convictions, whether religious or non religious, are rooted in some narrative as the context in which they take meaning"; *Twentieth Century Theology*, 272; on the basis in neoorthodoxy, see 273.

34. None of this is to say, of course, that postliberalism and narrative theology, nor postconservatism and narrative theology, are the same thing, but that they constitute a related and overlapping cluster of approaches to theology.

35. Thornbury, *Recovering Classic Evangelicalism*, 89.

36. Ibid., 90. Also, as Clark observes, though narrative theology holds to the centrality of Scripture, the understanding of how Scripture functions proves especially important. Scripture in narrative theology functions to primarily shape the Christian community and the goal of theology is to "invite society into the thought world of the church"; Clark, *To Know and Love God*, 15.

addresses itself, conversely, to a postmodern world, suspicious of authority, scornful of absolutes, and skeptical of claims to timeless truth.

Regarding the claim to emphasize transformation over information, it is far from clear how transformation can take place within post-conservative theology apart from cognitive and clear information. That is, one is inclined to ask here, precisely how transformation is to be defined in a way applicable to all, if it is not first preceded by information available to all? Does not the very notion of "community transformation" come with the underlying assumption of some universal standard to which people are to conform? And does this not by necessity require a basis in information? Finally, in their claim to not be concerned with who is in and who is out, post-conservatives seem rather eager to declare conservative-propositional proponents as anything but "in." Thus, their claims to inclusivity appear more romantic than actual.

Henry's Assessment of Narrative Theology

Henry begins his assessment of narrative theology by immediately questioning whether such an approach is capable of upholding the "evangelical orthodox view of the Bible as an authoritative, divinely inspired book." Thus, it becomes apparent that for Henry, narrative theology and his own revelational epistemology are directly at odds with one another. Henry ascribes the rise of narrative, or canonical, approaches to Scripture as a reaction to the modernist reconstructions of the Bible often associated with an anti-supernatural bias. Advocates of a narrative approach, on the other hand, agree that the Bible should be taken as it stands, on its own terms. However, questions of historicity are largely irrelevant on this view.[37]

The emphasis in narrative theology on the linguistic nature of Scripture (contra the historical nature of Scripture), though, results in wildly diverse understandings of the significance of Scripture. This is evident not only in various claims regarding how Scripture should be understood ontologically, but also in the way that the term "story" is variously used.[38] It is, though, the turn away from historical verification that appears most troubling, especially when "the New Testament itself affirms

---

37. Henry, *Gods of This Age or—God of the Ages?*, 259–62; cf. Hunsinger, "What Can Evangelicals and Postliberals Learn from Each Other?," 166.

38. Henry, *Gods of This Age or—God of the Ages?*, 262.

that historical disconfirmation of the resurrection would undermine the Christian faith."[39] Furthermore, Henry identifies four issues with narrative theology that are especially troubling.

First, the emphasis on the literary phenomenon of Scripture and its unity as "narrative," "oversimplifies the unity of Scripture."[40] Because narrative theology treats Scripture as a unified story, in doing so it glosses over the obvious fact that much of it simply is not narrative. This, though, is not to say that proponents of a grammatico-historical interpretation method do not also understand Scripture as a unity. Rather, they do so without the same reductionist tendencies, and without elevating narrative portions in value above that of the non-narrative genres. Second, the low place given to historical confirmation of the biblical data in narrative theology ultimately drives a wedge between faith and reason. To separate Scripture from the events of redemptive history ultimately leaves the content of Scripture unstable.[41] Third, by focusing on the literary form of the text, the basis for the objective truthfulness of the text is lost. "Literary concentration on the risen Jesus by itself does not logically entail belief that he is alive and risen, nor does it preclude an identification of the risen Lord as mythical."[42]

Finally, this approach to Scripture fails to support the important and historical Christian doctrine of verbal inspiration and inerrancy, and thereby undermines Scripture's divine authority. In summary, Henry contends:

> Narrative theology in the broader sense offers us a hermeneutical theory that affirms the comprehensive authority of Scripture yet suspends the question of its ontological truth and historical factuality. It is a theory that affirms that the unity of Scripture has a canon conveyed by the church, yet not necessarily exclusive of pseudopigraphical authorships; a theory that insists on the plenary-verbal integrity of the story form, yet concedes that large portions of the Bible do not fit that form. Although the theory welcomes the whole received tradition as inviolable, it offers no objective criterion for distinguishing truth from error

---

39. Ibid., 263.
40. Ibid., 265.
41. Ibid., 266–69.
42. Ibid., 269–70.

and fact from fiction, as is apparent from rival schools identified with narrative exegesis.[43]

Thus, as Henry sees it, narrative theology, and therefore any system such as post-conservative theology that borrows from it or abides its basic presuppositions, explicitly lacks holistic promise because it leads to the loss of Scripture's objective authority and truthfulness.

Part II: Carl Henry's Theological Method

Carl Henry thought not only that balancing Christian social concern and evangelism was first and foremost a theological problem,[44] but he also believed epistemology to be *the* crucial issue in the theological task. "Unless theology clearly identifies and expounds its way of knowing God and its criteria for verifying such knowledge claims, its future as a serious academic concern is problematical."[45] Furthermore, Henry's epistemology was forged amid the challenges of modernism, neoorthodoxy, and narrative theology, each of which Henry found wanting. The goal of this chapter is to examine Henry's epistemological and theological assumptions in order to better understand how those assumptions informed his views of evangelism and social concern.

The Foundations of Revelational Epistemology

Henry's answer to the epistemological question dogging Christianity comes down solidly on the unrivaled necessity of divine revelation. "When revelation gets through," says Henry, "man has an ultimate and final word."[46] For Henry, Christian theism as revealed in Scripture remains

---

43. Ibid., 270–75. Hunsinger notes the differences in the approaches of Henry and Frei, when he says, "whereas Henry seems to think the narratives are finally about the doctrines, for Frei it is just the reverse"; Hunsinger, "What Can Evangelicals and Postliberals Learn from Each Other? The Carl Henry/Hans Frei Exchange Reconsidered," 172.

44. As Carswell has noted, "Because Henry's primary concerns are theological in nature, his views on epistemology are connected to the applications of that same epistemology to various theological issues"; Carswell, "A Comparative Study of the Religious Epistemology of Carl F. H. Henry and Alvin Plantiga," 31. For evidence that Henry sees the issue of evangelism and social concern as primarily a theological issue, see the subsequent chapters of this study.

45. *GRA*, 1:213.

46. Ibid., 1:93.

the necessary starting point not only for knowing anything about God, but for knowing anything at all.[47] This ultimately makes Henry a presuppositionalist—a label he gladly wore, so long as he was allowed to carefully define what that means.[48] More importantly though, Henry declares:

> The Christian's primary ontological axiom is the one living God, and his primary epistemological axiom is divine revelation. On these basic axioms depend all the core beliefs of biblical theism, including divine creation, sin and the Fall, the promise and provision of redemption, the Incarnation of God in Jesus of Nazareth, the regenerate church as a new society, and a comprehensive eschatology.[49]

Axioms and Presuppositions

Before unpacking these axioms, it is necessary first to explore the nature of presuppositions as Henry understands them, as this proves crucial to his overall approach to theology. Is Henry claiming some special privilege for Christianity by presupposing some of its basic truths? Not according to Henry. Even so, he is fully aware of the primary critique of the presuppositional method levied mostly by evidentialists, especially the charge of fideism.[50]

---

47. As Nash observes, this is rooted in the early church's Logos doctrine, to which we shall turn later in this study. For now, it will suffice to note that for early believers, it was widely held that "Jesus Christ, the eternal Logos of God, mediates all divine revelation and grounds the correspondence between the divine and human minds. The eternal Logos is a necessary condition for the communication of revealed truth; indeed, it is a necessary condition for human knowledge about anything"; Nash, *The Word of God and the Mind of* Man, 59.

48. For instance, Henry says, "If presuppositionalism implies that anyone who thinks has presuppositions, then I am unapologetically an evangelical presuppositionalist"; Henry, *Toward a Recovery of Christian Belief*, 42.

49. Ibid., 49.

50. Ibid., 38. For a defense of evidentialism as an apologetic method, see Habermas, "Evidential Apologetics," chapter two. Also, among presuppositionalists, there exists a variety of approaches, which Geisler, cited in Boa and Bowman, distinguishes according to four subtypes: revelational (e.g, Cornelius Van Til, Grag Bahnsen, John Frame), rational (Gordon Clark, Carl Henry), systematic consistency (E. J. Carnell), and practical (Francis Schaeffer); *Faith Has Its Reasons*, Appendix under "Norman Geisler." Also, against an evidential approach, Henry asks, "Is the Christian view of God and the world really well served by methodology, that at best, can affirm with 95 percent probability that Jesus died for sinners or 90 percent probability that he arose

This claim though, according to Henry, is based on a misconception of what presuppositionalists actually do and believe. Furthermore, the label of fideist is more aptly applied to thinkers like Søren Kierkegaard or Karl Barth, who expressly rejected public reason and rational verification. As Boa and Bowman observe, the key difference between Reformed epistemologists, with whom Henry can be closely associated, and fideists is that "Reformed apologists, though, contend that these truth claims are internally consistent and that they can show them to be rational from within a Christian system of thought, based on certain key Christian assumptions."[51] Not only this, but evidential approaches are also highly problematic. First, evidences cannot in any sense produce proofs of God, leaving one to the unfortunate need to "fallback to probabilities." In doing so, the evidentialist thereby "romances an un-scriptural deity more than it reinforces biblical theism."[52]

Beginning with an axiom or presupposition that is subject to testing and verification is common in every field of inquiry, says Henry. "Axioms are the ruling principles with which any system of thought begins." Furthermore, "the are never deduced or inferred from other principles, but are simply presupposed."[53] Even logic itself rests on an unprovable axiom, namely the law of non-contradiction. Furthermore:

> Even if empiricists may and do deny it, all systems are based on axioms; without initial axioms nothing can be demonstrated. Natural science is impossible unless one assumes that meaningful correspondence exists between the laws of thought and the order of the external world.

Plus:

> In Philosophy, the axiom that underlies naturalistic atheism is that physical process and events comprise the whole of reality. Empiricism rests on the axiom that all knowledge has its source in sensation alone. Kant's governing axiom is that knowledge is a joint product of innate forms and sense content. Logical

---

bodily from the grave?"; *Toward A Recover of Christian Belief*, 48. This though appears to be a misunderstanding in Henry's methods whereby he confuses theological method with apologetic method, when in fact the two are not the same.

51. Boa and Bowman, *Faith Has its Reasons*, chapter 16.
52. Henry, *Toward a Recover of Christian Belief*, 40.
53. Ibid., 64.

> positivism sets out from the axiom that only sentences verifiable by sense experience are meaningful and true.[54]

Therefore, as it applies to the Christian theologian, he is every bit entitled, even required, to also begin with basic presuppositions. "He has a right and even a duty to state his case on his own ground whether skeptical contemporaries believe it or not. If he does not do so, he throws his case away."[55] The only other option, as Henry sees it, is to presuppose some other system that is inherently foreign, and often contradictory, to a Christian worldview.

This by no means implies that Christianity is a speculative endeavor. And though there is some circularity to this, this owes to the unique nature of revelation itself. Even as Dulles has pointed out, one needs revelation in order to know what revelation is.[56] In fact, not only can circularity not be avoided, it actually should be seen as an asset in that it shows the "comprehensive unity of discourse."[57] This approach "is anchored in God's self-revelation. The proponents of the revelation axiom do not approach divine revelation as a merely speculative first principle, but rather affirm it in view of the self-revealing activity of God."[58] In summarizing a presuppositional approach to Christian theology, Henry says:

> The Christian knows that the axioms of his faith are grounded in transcendent realities and not in speculative fabrication. The biblical view is that human reason has no normative, creative role in respect to truth. God is truth and the fountain of all truth. In the Christian view, God's mind and will are the source of all truth, of mathematics, of logic, of law, and of cosmic order.[59]

God Exists: The Ontological Axiom

Henry's first axiom of biblical revelation is the ontological axiom, based on the presupposition that God exists. Human awareness of God must be deduced as a theoretical inference from an innate consciousness of God.

---

54. Ibid., 64–65.
55. Ibid., 67.
56. Ibid., 69; Dulles, *Models of Revelation*, 14.
57. Henry, *Toward a Recovery of Christian Belief*, 90–91.
58. GRA, 1:219.
59. Henry, *Toward a Recovery of Christian Belief*, 69–70.

"The human spirit stands always in direct relationship to the transcendent Creator, Sustainer, and End of all things." Furthermore, the apprehension of God flows not from evidential discovery—one does not "rise to God from the not-God"—but rather, comes by way of discernment in the "inner human spirit."[60] In fact, it is this very divine-human relationship that even in neoorthodoxy has been "definitive of human experience."[61] By this Henry means that human life itself from the beginning represents the reality of a primal knowledge of God. The knowledge of God's existence proceeds from both the reality of God's universal revelation, "which directly engages man as a carrier of the created image of God in both mind and conscience, and confronts him intelligibly in external nature and history."[62]

The Role of Reason

Most of the criticism leveled against Henry's epistemology, centers on his view of the role of reason, a view that has caused others to charge him with being a foundationalist and/or a modernist.[63] This criticism became especially acute after Henry gave a series of three lectures at Yale University in 1985, during which Henry criticized the narrative theology of Hans Frei. Frei responded in both a lecture of his own and in his *Types of Christian Theology*.[64]

---

60. *GRA*, 1:274.

61. Ibid. Bob Patterson presents many of the main notions of neoorthodoxy to which Henry strongly reacted. In defining neoorthodoxy, Patterson notes that WWI dampened liberal optimism and helped give rise to neoorthodoxy, which, (1) held not that the fall was an historical event, but rather a historical condition characterizing all humanity, (2) emphasized God's transcendence over liberalism's immanence of God, and (3) was Christo-centric concerning God's revelatory disclosure. Henry was especially critical of neoorthodox approaches to Scripture and Barth one of his most frequent targets; Patterson, *Carl F.H. Henry*, 46–47, 50.

62. *GRA*, 1:279.

63. Cf. Brand, "Is Carl Henry a Modernist?"; Waita, "Carl F. H. Henry and the Metaphysical Foundations of Epistemology:" Helseth, "Carl F. H. Henry, Old Princeton, and the Right Use of Reason: Continuity or Discontinuity?"; Hutchens, "Knowing and Being in the Context of the Fundamentalist Dilemma"; Patterson, *Carl Henry*, 165–166; see especially Purdy, "Carl Henry and Contemporary Apologetics."

64. Hunsinger, "What Can Evangelicals and Postliberals Learn from Each Other? The Carl Henry/Hans Frei Exchange Reconsidered." Center stage in the Henry/Frei debate lay the issue of Scripture and the possibility of knowledge of God. This question then is especially informed by one's understanding of the relationship between faith

What role then does reason play in understanding Christian truth? In expounding his approach to theology, Henry expounds his methodology according to seven basic principles relating to revelation. These will be unpacked in sequence in this and subsequent sections. However, as it relates to the role of reason, Henry makes several important points.

For Henry, human reason is not a creative source for truth but a means of recognizing it.[65] Knowledge is possible only because God wills it and makes it possible. Thus, as Thornbury has pointed out, this has Henry advocating a "Reformation-inspired voluntarism."[66] This distinction is important for Henry, in that it keeps reason in its proper place, prevents the exaltation of the human mind, and prioritizes the role of faith. "When human reasoning is exalted as the source of truth, then the content of truth is soon conformed to the prejudices of some influential thinker or school of scholars, or it may be conformed to the current consensus of opinion."[67]

The primary difference between Henry's approach and that of Evangelical empiricists lies in that the latter "encourages a theological appeal to particulars in search of a universal," whereas Henry's presuppositional approach postulates "a universal explanatory principle subject to testing." In other words, "to affirm the priority of faith need not mean, as evidentialists routinely charge, that all presuppositionalists adhere to faith alone *apart from, instead of or contrary to* reason."[68] Rather, in the tradition of Augustine, Henry starts with faith and Scripture, but then allows that these beliefs be submitted to the canons of reason and the law of non-contradiction. He derives this principle from the fact that the people of God have always been called upon to reason rightly regarding true and false prophets or teachings.[69] Thus, Henry ultimately holds to a modified

---

and reason, and indeed, Henry accused Frei of wrongly dividing the two; ibid., 168.

65. *GRA*, 1:225.

66. Thornbury, "Carl F. H. Henry: Heir of Reformation Epistemology," 68. Voluntarism stresses that the universe is as it is because God wills it and for no other reason. Furthermore, God could have just as easily willed a very different universe than the present one.

67. *GRA*, 1:226.

68. Henry, *Toward a Recovery of Christian Belief*, 40. As White points out, "if Henry is to be maligned as a deductivist on this score, then so too must Augustine, Luther, and Calvin be, along with every Christian thinker who takes revelation as an epistemological starting point"; White, "Word and Spirit in the Theological Method of Carl Henry," 32.

69. *GRA*, 1:232. As Nash points out, "for Augustine, the innate ideas which are a

correspondence theory of truth, that depends not first and foremost on human cognitive ability, but on the presupposition of divine revelation.[70]

As to the charge of rationalism, Henry replies by asking if irrationalism is to be preferred. Because this accusation features prominently in attacks on Henry's epistemology, his full reply is worth restating:

> If they are pleading the cause of irrationalism they are welcome to it. Christianity is a faith—but so are Buddhism, Shamanism, communism, and humanism. The main issue for the intellectual world is whether the biblical revelation is credible; that is, are there good reasons for believing it? I am against the paradox mongers and those who emphasize only personal volition and decision . . . . I insist on the reasonableness of the Christian faith and the "rationality" of the living, self-revealed God. I maintain that God creates and preserves the universe through the agency of the Logos, that man by creation bears the moral and rational (as opposed to the irrational) image of his Maker, that despite the fall, main is still responsible for knowing God. I believe that divine revelation is rational, that the inspired biblical canon is a consistent and coherent whole, that genuine faith seeks understanding, that the Holy Spirit uses truth as a means of persuasion, that logical consistency is a test of truth, and that saving trust in Christ necessarily involves acceptance of certain revealed propositions about him.[71]

God Speaks: The Epistemological Axiom

As David Clark has rightly observed, "an authority-based theology will recognize an authority principle at its epistemic center."[72] That epistemic center, for Henry, is divine revelation. As such, Christianity lays claim to the whole of human life and transcends historical situatedness. "A

---

necessary condition for human knowledge are explained in terms of a theory of divine illumination"; Nash, *The Word of God and the Mind of Man*, 79.

70. Brand, "Is Carl Henry a Modernist," 15; as Trueman observes, "for Henry, this is what makes revelation rational—not that it can, in some Cartesian sense, be predicated by the autonomous reflection of human beings, but that when God does reveal himself he does it in a way that is intelligible to individuals and communicable from one individual to another"; "Admiring the Sistine Chapel," 52.

71. Henry, "The Concerns and Considerations of Carl F. H. Henry," 21.

72. Clark, *To Know and Love God*, 30.

method whose primary axiom is transcendent revelation will encompass all the eras of cultural experience and call them to account."[73]

This epistemological axiom flows from the necessity of God's own revelation in order for humanity to know anything at all. This approach follows Augustine's model of faith seeking understanding (*fidens quaerens intellectum*). As Henry notes, the Reformers rejected the Thomistic model that placed too much confidence in reason alone, and instead returned to Augustine's insistence upon the priority to faith.[74] It is thus, not only the existence of God, but the reality that God graciously and sovereignly speaks to human beings in intelligible and rational communication that makes God knowable at all. As such, God's ontic and epistemic axioms are bound together. "The Christian knows . . . that it is only by divine grace that he believingly participates in the epistemic and ontic realities affirmed by the biblical heritage."[75] The main contours then of Henry's epistemological axiom are as follows.

First, "God in his revelation is the first principle of Christian theology, from which all the truths of revealed religion are derived."[76] As such "divine revelation is the evoking cause" of Christian faith as well as the "the ultimate criteria" by which one assesses Christian doctrine. This is because apart from God's revelatory acts, one could know nothing about God.[77] However, the focus on revelation does not minimize the histori-

73. *GRA*, 1:215.

74. Henry, *Toward a Recovery of Christian Belief*, 40; Henry, *Gods of This Age or-- God of the Ages?*, 225. Henry followed Abraham Kuyper in both attributing the loss of biblical authority to Aquinas's elevation of reason, and in preferring to return to an Augustinian approach; Marsden, *Reforming Fundamentalism*, 79. Also, Ramm, summarizes Augustine's approach to faith and reason, "the key to Augustine's apologetic is the motto: *faith leads the intellect.* For example, he wrote: 'If you are not able to know, believe that you may know. Faith precedes; the intellect follows'"; *Sermons*, CXVIII, 1. Augustine reasons at this point that it is impossible to see the truth in any system if the mind is in a state of unbelief. The person dominated by an acidic skepticism can learn nothing. A friendly disposition is the prerequisite for all learning. Furthermore, no hypothesis is ever verified without a provisional acceptance of its truthfulness else we would never have the motivation to test it. In the spiritual realm, the necessity is greatly increased. The intellect needs the aid, insight, and illumination of faith"; Ramm, *Varieties of Christian Apologetics*, 158.

75. Henry, *Toward a Recovery of Christian Belief*, 51.

76. *GRA*, 1:215.

77. Ibid., 1:216. As to nonbiblical claims to revelation, Henry makes several vital points. First, "almost all nonbiblical religions and philosophical visions of spiritual reality alike neglect transcendent cognitive revelation as a basic axiom"; ibid., 217. Even Buddhist's have protested neo-Protestant ecumenical claims to revelational content

cal realities attached to God's acts.[78] Second, "human reason is a divinely fashioned instrument for recognizing truth; it is not a creative source of truth."[79] Biblical faith in no way denigrates rational capacity and its role in apprehending God's truth.[80] Against the charge of rationalism, Henry claims that placing emphasis on the centrality of revelation in epistemology serves as a necessary means of chastening human quests for truth.[81] This importantly distinguishes Henry from the rationalistic approaches of the Enlightenment, wherein reason unaided by revelation was deemed sufficient.[82] For Henry, though, reason and revelation always work in tandem, as shown below, but never apart from or independent of one another. Furthermore, according to Henry, biblical faith everywhere presupposes the ability of fallen humanity to cognitively and logically reason as it concerns the apprehensive of divine truth.[83]

Henry's third principle of divine revelation as the basic epistemological axiom is that "the Bible is the Christian's principle of verification." Against the tendency to understand divine communication mystically and vaguely, Christianity stresses the understandability and universally communicable nature of Christian belief through coherent and intelligible propositions.[84] Even to sinners, revelation is intelligible, precisely because it was intended for them. This important aspect Henry summarizes as follows: "Inspired Scripture is the divinely authorized attestation of God's speech and acts, and as such is normative in all matters of religion and ethics." This is evident in that everywhere in Scripture the constant

---

in all religion, as this implies the notion of a personal God, a concept patently denied by many Buddhists. Second, the reality of the Christian revelation claim and God-consciousness accounts for the prevalence of pagan religions as corruptions of the true knowledge of God. Finally, "the presence of other revelation claims gives no reason to avoid divine revelation as the basic epistemological axiom of revealed religion. The presence of counterfeit currency does not prove the absence of the genuine, but rather presupposes it"; ibid., 218.

78. Ibid., 1:223.
79. Ibid., 2:225.
80. Ibid., 2:225.
81. Ibid., 1:226.
82. Ibid.
83. Ibid., 1:227; cf. Wells, "Evangelical Theology," 610.
84. *GRA*, 1:229. As White observes, theological truth in one sense is like all truth, in that it is cognitive and communicable. Yet, theological truth, being grounded in an infallible Scripture, stands above other truths, which by nature are subject to the need for constant correction; White, *What is Truth?*, 99.

safeguard for determining right beliefs is the reliability and centrality of the sacred Judeo-Christian writings as the primary controlling agent.[85]

Fourth, "logical consistency is a negative test of truth and coherence a subordinate test." According to Henry, without logical consistency and non-contradiction, no knowledge could be possible as one would have no means of distinguishing truth from fantasy.[86] Plus, given the biblical injunction to give a reason for one's hope, care should be taken to not do away with reason itself. Fifth, "the proper task of theology is to exposit and elucidate the content of Scripture in an orderly way." Here, Henry contends that the content of revelation especially lends itself to systematic representation, as a means of showing its logical consistency.[87] If the comprehensive unity, along with the logical consistency, of Scripture could not be shown, then no one should be obliged to believe them. Furthermore, the task of theology in doing this should be to first and foremost serve the church and advance biblical preaching. Finally, "the theology of revelation requires the apologetic confrontation of speculative theories of reality and life." By taking the approach outlined above, the Christian will present a challenge to every other postulated worldview by showing its internal contradictions and inability to offer a comprehensive explanation for reality. This is because "secular theories elaborated independently of the truth of revelation either exaggerate or limit the nature of reason and thought and language in a manner that the Christian knows distorts the actual state of things."[88]

Redemptive Religion

For Henry, Christianity must especially be understood in terms of its redemptive focus. As we shall see, this idea figures prominently in Henry's theology of both evangelism and social concern. Specifically, this means that Christianity originated from the historical life and work of Jesus Christ, whom the first-century church recognized as the promised Redeemer of the OT. Furthermore, this understanding of Jesus sprang from early Christian interpretations of Scripture (1 Cor. 15:3). "Christianity, therefore, is that scriptural revelation of the Creator-Redeemer

---

85. *GRA*, 1:232.
86. Ibid., 1:232.
87. Ibid., 1:238–39.
88. *GRA*, 2:244.

God incarnate in Jesus Christ."[89] It is this redemptive element that holds both evangelism and social concern together, and simultaneously necessitates the priority of evangelism. This is because, first of all, the need for redemption becomes explicit only through the precise verbal message that makes known both the plight of sinners and the hope offered in Christ. Jesus alone provides the substitutionary and propitiatory atonement from sin (Rom 3:25; 1 John 4:10). Yet, the Christian message offers not only hope for cleansing from sin once and for all, but also calls the forgiven to a life of holiness, setting before its adherents the necessity of good works that evidence a life surrendered to Christ and in conformity to his image.[90]

Henry's Reformed Perspective

G. Wright Doyle has articulated several characteristics that describe not only Calvinism in general, but that also the broadly Reformed theology of Carl Henry. Specifically, Doyle turns to William Johnson and John Leith's *Reformed Reader* for these essential characteristics.

First, Reformed theology is catholic in its affirmation of the historic doctrines of the church, especially concerning the first four ecumenical councils. Second, it is Protestant in that it stands in continuity with the Protestant Reformation and especially Luther's emphasis on the ultimate authority of Scripture, justification by grace through faith, the priesthood of all believers, the sanctity of the common life, and the necessity of faith expressed in intentional reception of the sacraments. Third, Reformed theology is scriptural in the subordination of all theological undertakings to the unique authority of Scripture. Fourth, it is experiential, wherein by emphasizing the experience of regenerating grace, the theological task does not contradict human experience or common sense. Fifth, it is practical and edifying since theology's purpose is not to produce speculative treatises, but to "glorify God, save human souls, and transform human life and society." Sixth, Reformed theology is God-centered in its emphasis on the awesome holiness of God, wherein God is especially transcendent, but also "personally and immediately active" in creation. Seventh,

---

89. Henry, "What is Christianity," 107.

90. Ibid., 110; cf. *The Uneasy Conscience*, 30, wherein Henry says, "the ideal Hebrew or Christian society throbbed with challenge to the predominant culture of its generation, condemning with redemptive might the tolerated social evils, for the redemptive message was to light the world and salt the earth."

there is a prominent emphasis on holiness, evident the Reformers emphasis on sanctification and that they "never set law and grace against each other." Finally, Reformed theology is comprehensive, emphasizing an all-encompassing vision for human life in obedience to God.[91]

Of these emphases, the one that most uniquely defines Calvinism must be its understanding of God's sovereignty, especially in relation to human freedom. Of course, this is not to say that Arminian theology does not hold to the sovereignty of God, but on this doctrine Arminians see things quite differently.[92] In fact, one of the main differences between Calvin and Arminius lay in the latter's belief that the former's view of God's sovereignty made God the author of sin and evil. Therefore, the differences were not on the sovereignty of God, *per se*. As Olson has noted, "All Christians have always believed that nothing at all can happen without God's permission, and almost all Christians have always believed God foreknows whatever will happen. But Calvinists typically go further and claim that whatever happens is planned and rendered certain by God. Calvin explicitly denied mere foreknowledge or permission by God— even of evil."[93]

It is this view of God's sovereignty within Calvinism that necessitates the doctrine of double predestination.[94] Yet, given this view, which is bound up in the doctrine of limited atonement (the "L" in TULIP), simultaneously advocating for evangelism seems contradictory.[95] For

---

91. Doyle, *Carl Henry*, 38–50.

92. Ibid., 47.

93. Olson, *Against Calvinism*, 40. As Olson points out, some Calvinists readily admit that "permissive" language is not strong enough and instead prefer to say God causes or brings about evil; ibid., 59.

94. Predestination and election are twin concepts in Reformed theology, wherein they are taken to mean the unconditional decree of God resulting in the effectual salvation of fallen sinners, apart from any merit on their part. Furthermore, their acts in responding to God's Grace are solely determined and foreordained by God; see "Election" in Olson, *The Westminster Handbook to Evangelical Theology*, 167–70. Also, as Reid pointed out, in the broader understanding of predestination, "from all eternity God has sovereignly determined whatsoever shall happen in history"; see Reid, "Predestination," 870–72. Also, as Olson has noted, any doctrine of predestination is necessarily double-predestination, whether overtly admitted or not; see Olson, *Against Calvinism*, 104–109.

95. As Olson observes, even some Calvinists have been acutely aware of this and have gone so far as to claim that a message of salvation should, therefore, *not* be indiscriminately offered to all on this very basis; Olson, *Against Calvinism*, 60. Lewis and Demarest offer seven responses to the question of why should believers preach

example, in responding to criticism of God's eternal decree of election as being arbitrary, Fred Klooster declares that, according to the Canons of Dort, though it is true that God sovereignly "discriminates" who shall be saved and who will be damned, and this without consideration of the merit of the individual, that this is somehow not arbitrary. Klooster, though, never defends exactly how or why this is not arbitrary, he simply declares that it is so. This though seems contradictory. Either the elect are chosen by their own merits, or they are chosen arbitrarily. It must be one or the other. Furthermore, one wonders, what does it mean to affirm, as Dort does, that preaching "offers forgiveness and eternal life for those who truly believe," while simultaneously declaring that "some are given faith and some are not given faith"?[96] In short, the Calvinistic emphasis on God's sovereignty that claims to necessitate double-predestination would appear to hinder evangelistic impetus, or at the very least, fail the test of logic and non-contradiction which Henry so ardently champions.

Henry clearly takes a Reformed approach to the theological task, and depends heavily on both Augustine and Calvin in his theology. Especially important to the present study, is that Henry understands this perspective to uniquely hold forth promise for both theology and cultural engagement. Henry believes that the positive impact of Christianity during the last two thousand years owes to its basis in biblical revelation and the saving grace of God in Christ. Where these emphases have been overrun by modern theories, Christianity's influence has been diminished. Therefore, it is imperative upon the church if it is to continue as a dominant force in society to return to its Reformation heritage.[97]

---

the Gospel if God has already sovereignly elected some to salvation. First, believers must preach the Gospel because Jesus commands it (Matt 28:18–20; Luke 24:46–48); second, in being obedient to God believers "honor God's two-fold purpose—universal and particular . . . in order that the chosen may recover their potential as his image-bearers; third, proclamation of the Gospel, though not " a sufficient condition" of salvation, is nonetheless "a necessary means in the divine plan"; fourth, we never know beforehand who is among the elect and who is not; fifth, in preaching the Gospel, we model the life of Christ; sixth, evangelism is to be a way of life for all believers, and especially for those gifted for evangelism; and finally, "why God desires all to hear the Gospel even though he has not purposed to save all is a question mortals do not fully comprehend," Lewis and Demarest, *Integrative Theology*, 3:61–62.

96. Klooster, "Predestination: A Calvinist Note," 82–94; see also in response, Dayton, "A Wesleyan Note on Election," in ibid.; 95–103.

97. Henry, *Gods of This Age or—God of the Ages?*, 230–31; for a helpful discussion on the theology as wisdom applied to the whole of life, as opposed to theology as mostly academic discipline (i.e. *sapientia* vs. *scientia*), see Clark, *To Know and Love God*, 176.

Henry defines an "Evangelical" as a Protestant "of broadly Reformed commitment, whether identified with Reformed denominations or not." According to Henry, the Reformed lineage of Christian orthodoxy offers a theologically rigorous means of understanding the role of the church and the life of the believer. As such, Christianity offers a distinct worldview, laying claim "upon the whole person, intellect, will, and emotion, and on the New Testament importance of the mind of Christ for obedient service to God."[98]

Reformed theology has historically emphasized that the church, as God's elect people, "is the primary sphere of Christ's lordship."[99] While there is within the context of a Christian worldview, an integrated nature to the role of the church in society, within this comprehensive scope, a certain priority is given to the redemptive role of the church in God's plan:

> It is for the people of God that the Christian world-life view provides first and foremost an integrating perspective, one that stretches throughout time and is vibrant with eternity. Yet the church is called to exhibit to the whole world the blessings of serving the true and living God.[100]

This concept especially defines Henry's unique position in the evangelism-social concern debate, as Henry understands within the Reformation lineage, the integration of faith to all of life, but the simultaneous priority of a redemptive focus. Of course, an ecclesiology that emphasizes a social mandate is by no means unique to Reformed theology.[101]

---

98. Henry, *God of This Age, or—God of the Ages?*, 231.

99. Ibid.

100. Ibid; in the Reformed tradition, the cultural/worldview emphasis is closely tied to its view of Scripture; as Henry Van Til observes, "Scripture was not only the authoritative guide for the way of salvation, but it furnished man with an authoritative interpretation of reality as a whole"; Van Til, *The Calvinistic Concept of Culture*, Kindle ed., under chapter four, "Calvinism Defined"; see also chapter three, "Religion and Culture."

101. See for example, Thompson, "Social Involvement, 689–732; see also Ro, "The Perspectives of Church History from New Testament Times to 1960," 11–40. Ro points to, among other things, "the close association between evangelism and social concern practiced in the Wesleyan tradition"; ibid., 28. Yet, concerning the Reformed perspective, the social emphasis was part of the Reformed heritage that Henry sought to recover. As Marsden observes, Henry's theology of social concern leaned heavily on the work of Abraham Kuyper. In this, "what Henry and the new evangelicals found in Kuyperian thought was a twentieth century conservative Christian articulation of a point that had been part of the reformist side of the American evangelical heritage, but which had diminished severely in Fundamentalism since the 1930s. The point was

Regarding the social mandate, Henry sets forth liberalism as a warning against too great a focus on society and not enough on individual regeneration. The failure of Protestant modernism and the social gospel it spawned flowed from a neglect of individual salvation. This though, should not be construed as implying that the church has no social mandate. But rather, informed by his ontological and epistemic axioms, Henry says,

> The church is to speak to the world first and foremost concerning the self-revealing God and his incarnation in Jesus Christ, concerning redemption from sin and the victory of divine truth and righteousness. Without that overarching canopy, all condemnation of evil lacks good news and merely multiplies pessimism over human existence. It is remarkable that so many writers who today appeal to the Old Testament prophets to advance their theology of social revolution and political liberation seem unheeding when those same prophets protest against false gods and emphasize the need of spiritual conversion.[102]

In other words, Henry does not minimize the need to denounce evil as part of a biblical social agenda. Rather, he proposes an integrated approach that prioritizes the redemptive over the social. This is his point in noting that social good without a redemptive focus falls short of actually being good news.

As it concerns the preservation of the Reformation heritage, Henry is keen to call for the centrality and necessity of emphasis upon God's sovereignty and providence, and the attenuating doctrine of predestination, along with the need to reiterate justification by grace alone, apart from

---

the broadly Calvinistic vision that the Christian mission involves not only evangelism but also a cultural task, both remaking the mind of an era and transforming society"; Marsden, *Reforming Fundamentalism*, 79; also, as Moore points out, Reformed covenant theology had a long history of emphasizing a soteriology that included God's renewing of the cosmos. Kuyper especially helped recover this aspect of the Reformers' thoughts. Yet, important differences exist between Henry and Kuyper, evident in Kuyper's direct involvment in politics, even becoming Prime Minister; but not only the Dutch Calvinist stream of the Reformed heritage, but also the Princetonians as well (e.g. Warfield), held to a "world-transforming" understanding of salvation. However, some Reformed thinkers (e.g. Berkhof) failed to embody this, and thought instead of salvation in the more narrow sense as primarily spiritual and otherworldly; Moore, *The Kingdom of Christ*, 96–97. For a lengthy discussion of Kuyper's approach to Christianity and culture, see also Marsden, *The Twighlight of the American Enlightenment*, 162–72.

102. Henry, *Gods of This Age*, 232.

works. Specifically, Henry observes that neglect of the doctrine of predestination results in a diminishing of belief in God's sovereignty over all of life. Plus, neglect of the historic Reformed priority given to justification by faith leads to confusion regarding the place of works in saving faith, despite Paul's insistence that it is by grace alone.[103] Nonetheless, the church must stringently avoid neglect of its social and cultural mandate. From the God Who is and the God Who speaks, Christianity derives its mandate:

> The axioms of the Christian world-life view retain their enduring power. It is God in his revelation that this earth needs to know. The knowledge of God and his will can teach us anew what life is all about and how tragic it is to give ourselves over to the demonic. To us falls the task of conveying ethical monotheism to the modern world along with its great correlatives, the dignity of the human person, equality before the law, the sinfulness and social responsibility of humankind, the prospect of divine redemption, the incarnation of God in Jesus the crucified and risen Savior, love as fulfillment of the law, and peace and justice as God's intention in history.[104]

The Imago Dei

The *imago dei*, from the Genesis account of the creation of humanity, operates as a central controlling feature in Henry's epistemology. Genesis 1:26–27 states that man was made in the image (*tselem*) and likeness (*demuth*) of God. That humans are made in God's image is repeated in Gen 9:6, wherein God condemns murder as a direct affront to this fact.[105]

---

103. Henry does not address here the charge that this view of predestination leads necessarily to double-predestination, or, that God sovereignly chooses some for damnation; ibid; see also Olson, *Against Calvinism*, under chapter five, "Unconditional Election *is* Double Predestination."

104. Henry, *Gods of This Age*, 244.

105. Westermann, *Genesis*, 65. For a discussion of the various approach to understanding the *imago Dei*, see Erickson, *Christian Theology*, 520–23. Erickson points out that most views fall into one of three categories: substantive, relational, or functional. A substantive view sees the *imago* as something inherent in human beings, in their very nature. The predominant take on the substantive view in church history has been that *imago Dei* refers to man's cognitive abilities, to his inner self and rational and moral capacities. A second view, the relational view, focuses on the *imago* in social terms; that is, in reference to human interaction with other humans and with God. Emil Brunner and Karl Barth were advocates of this view. Karl Barth rejected much of earlier Christian theology on the *imago Dei*, namely that it denoted human cognition,

While much will be said about the *imago* in the subsequent chapters as it relates directly to evangelism and social concern, here a few fundamental issues need to be presented.

First, Henry takes a substantial view of the imago Dei, meaning that he believes it is something that constitutes the essence of what it means to be human. Most importantly, reason is understood by Henry to be part of the *imago Dei* in that humanity's ability to comprehend revelation depends on the relationship between revelation and reason. All humanity in fact stands guilty in that all persons are inherently capable via the *imago* of comprehending God's revelatory acts, both in nature and in Scripture. Even the noetic effects of sin have not wrought a disastrous effect upon human reason. Henry also draws from his understanding of the *imago Dei* the universal notions of logic and rationality, or what he sometimes refers to as "public reason." As Thornbury has pointed out, the rational component of the *imago Dei* for Henry is primary, since this makes it possible for humans to receive divine revelation.[106] Not only this, though,

---

on the grounds that the text of Gen 1:26–27 says nothing of intellect or reason as the defining qualities of what it means to be made in God's image; Allison, *Historical Theology*, 336. Rather, Barth's interpretation depended on the text's reference to "male and female." As Allison says in explaining Barth's interpretation, this "plurality of gender" points to the "plurality of persons—Father, Son, and Holy Spirit" and the *imago* thus refers not to a substance or activity of humans, but a "confrontational relationality." This confrontational relationality was "first and foremost between the members of the Trinity, then between God and human beings, and finally between people and other people"; ibid., 337. Barth's relational view was a product of existentialism, and thus the question of essence was unimportant. As Erickson has noted, existentialism was not concerned with "what is it?" but rather "is it? ("Does it exist?")"; Erickson, *Christian Theology*, 527. In addition to this existential basis, there are other problems with the relational view. First, how does one account, given the emphasis on humans in relationship with God, for those who consciously rebel against God? How are such persons considered 'in relationship' with Him? Brunner, whose ideas on this topic had much in common with Barth, has said that the relationship is inherently present. But as Erickson notes, this conclusion seems forced; ibid., 530. Also, the animals in the creation account are also made male and female, and thus it seems that Barth must assume some validity to the substantive view to account for human relational uniqueness; cf. Bromiley, "Image of God," 805. Finally, some theologians have held to a functional view of the *imago* as highlighting not what humans are, but what they do. Proponents of a functional view prefer to focus on the latter half of Gen 1:26, ". . . and let them rule over the fish of the sea." Proponents of this view tend to focus on humans as God's viceroys, called to exercise dominion over the earth.

106. Thornbury, *Recovering Classic Evangelicalism*, 74. Henry also refutes the idea that the *imago* refers not to cognitive ability but to imagination, noting that advocates of this position claim that the rational understanding of the *imago* is more a Greek than Hebraic idea. Henry notes that this view tends away from propositional

but also the evangelical view of the *imago* is necessary for recovering the dignity of *homo sapiens*.

The Mediating Logos

According to Nash, few contemporary theologians have appreciated the historic doctrine of the Logos as well as Henry.[107] Nash also helpfully articulates the key issue at stake, in asking: "How can the mind of man know the mind of God? Since the Greeks used logos as a synonym for mind or reason, the question can now be worded: How can the human logos know the divine Logos?"[108] Henry develops the doctrine of the Logos, based on the Johannine prologue (1:1–18) as a fundamental aspect of his epistemology. Especially important is that Christ, as the incarnate Logos, mediates divine revelation, and thereby holds together the epistemic and ontological axioms. That is, "the Word brings and preserves rational order in the universe."[109] Thus, the Logos functions as only God could, as Creator, and Sustainer of creation. Much more will be said on this in the coming chapters, but for now the following will suffice.

For Henry, the Logos of God provides the essential means of human access to rational, divine revelation. "As the source of created existence, the Logos of God grounded the meaning and purpose of man and the world, and objective reality was held to be divinely structured by complex formal patterns."[110] In other words, for Henry the Logos directly enables and intends human creatures to access and understand a rational creation. Without this enabling and intentionality human knowing would be impossible. "Endowed with more than animal perception, gifted in fact with a mode of cognition not to be confused with sensation, man

---

revelation and is often employed in service of "leftist agendas"; see Henry, *Twilight of a Great Civilization*, 121.

107. Nash, *The Word of God and the Mind of Man*, 68.

108. Ibid., 59. Nash's excellent study traces the doctrine through its origin in Alexandrian Judaism, its NT foundations, and its development by the early church fathers; ibid., 59–69. In summary, Nash says, "reason has an intrinsic relationship to God, it has cosmic significance. Christians believe the rational world is the projection of a rational God who objectifies his eternal thoughts in the creation and who endows the human creature, the apex of his creation, with the image of God which includes a structure of reason similar to God's own reason"; ibid. 69.

109. Thornbury, *Recovering Classic Evangelicalism*, 74–76; White, "Word and Spirit in the Theological Method of Carl Henry," 38.

110. *GRA*, 3:168.

was therefore able to intuit intelligible universals; as a divinely intended knower, he was able to cognize, within limits, the nature and structure of the externally real world."[111] It is not then that humans are inherently rational and the human mind entirely self-capable. Rather, the Logos endows creatures made in God's image with a rationality reflective of God's own nature. As Bob Patterson observes regarding Henry's view of the Logos, "the Logos is the mind of God incarnate in Jesus Christ. The Logos is central to the Godhead."[112] But through the Logos, humanity can access transcendent reality that produces both a present and future hope. It does this by confronting humans with their sinful disposition through knowledge of the cross, the crucified Logos. Henry denies therefore that logic *per se* is a product of Western thought, but that reason is ontologically related to God, who is himself truth.[113] The Logos, recorded in English translations of the Bible as *the Word*, conveys, as Gordon Clark has noted, both a personal and propositional quality. "The eternal divine Word is at one and the same time ultimately personal and rational."[114]

Propositionalism

As noted earlier, one of the most debated issues in contemporary method centers on the issue of how propositions function in evangelical theology. In fact, Henry is well aware of the charge that a propositional approach to Scripture has been charged with imposing "rationalistic encumbrances" on discussions about the Bible.[115] Against this, Henry declares

---

111. *GRA*, 3:168.

112. Patterson, *Carl F.H. Henry*, 97.

113. For a comparative analysis of Henry's view of truth and reason, see James Emery White, *What Is Truth*, 107; As White points out, Henry has been criticized on this point for what some see as too much dependence on an Aristoteliain understanding of logical categories; ibid.

114. *GRA*, 3167.

115. Ibid., 3:455; cf. Olson, who, citing LeRon Shults, a now self-described atheist, advances the theory that a propositional approach to theology is (1) reactionary to neoorthodoxy's emphasis on personal revelation and revelatory acts, and (2) "an unconscious accommodation to the Enlightenment"; *Reformed and Always Reforming*, under "Postconservative Revelation: Narrative before Propositions." Henry's approach has also been criticized for being somewhat "Euclidian," that is, built primarily on abstract principles or presuppositions; Henry denies this though, claiming "a god preoccupied with abstractions is not my god"; Henry, "The Concerns and Considerations of Carl F. H. Henry," 20.

unapologetically that in order for God's revelation to be meaningful, it must be intelligible and coherent. "The biblical prophets and apostles, and Jesus of Nazareth as well, communicated in intelligible sentences with an eye to logical validity; without such rational and linguistic sensitivity it is impossible to engage in objectively meaningful human communication."[116] Furthermore, Henry defines propositional revelation in the following way:

> The Bible depicts God's very revelation as meaningful, objectively intelligible disclosure. We mean by propositional revelation that God supernaturally communicated his revelation to chosen spokesmen in the express form of cognitive truths, and that the inspired prophetic-apostolic proclamation reliably articulates these truths in sentences that are not internally contradictory.[117]

Thus, the content of the Bible either is by nature or can be stated in propositional form. But what of the charge that a propositional understanding of Scripture de-personalizes God's own communication? According to Henry, this claim confuses the two axioms of biblical faith. "Here the objection to propositional revelation stems from a confusion of ontology and epistemology."[118] Even though God himself transcends human beings and even conceptual truths revealed about Him, this reality itself is only known by way of revealed truth.

Furthermore, if one hypothesizes that revelation can be known in non-cognitive ways, then how can one distinguish that sort of revelation from say psychological presumptions or from demonic influence? "To render even the bare idea of revealed presence intelligibly defensible, one must correlate that view with a thoroughly cognitive content."[119] This does not mean that divine revelation exhausts the knowledge of God, though. "Unless the divine 'more' is revelationally vouchsafed, it is but

---

116. *GRA*, 3:456.

117. Ibid., 3:456-457. Or as Nash puts it in question form, "Is God's revelation a disclosure of truth? Does it have cognitive content?"; Nash, *The Word of God and the Mind of Man*, 50; cf. "The Concerns and Considerations of Carl F. H. Henry," wherein Henry defines propositional revelation saying, "by propositional revelation I mean not simply that the Bible is written in meaningful sentences—as most books are—but that God has revealed himself intelligibly and rationally in units of human speech involving sentences, words, and syntax that Scripture attests, and thus gives us an inspired literary document," 20.

118. *GRA*, 3:458.

119. Ibid., 3:458-59.

Henry's Theological Method

sheer speculation."[120] Furthermore, the propositional aspect of God's revelation is inherently necessary for salvation:

> Special scriptural revelation normatively sets forth the propositional content of general revelation, and does so as the framework of God's saving revelation. Scripture confronts fallen man objectively and externally with a divinely inspired literary deposit that states the intelligible components of God's ongoing general revelation in nature and history, and conveys as well the propositional content of God's redemptive revelation. Knowledge of revelational truths is indispensible for the salvation of sinners; saving faith in Christ involves appropriating divinely disclosed information.[121]

The scriptural foundations for asserting this view of propositional revelation, furthermore, are quite solid. In the OT, the prophets of Yahweh do not emphasize their interpretation of God's acts, but rather proclaim God's own words. "'Thus saith the Lord!' is their unqualified banner."[122] Plus, it was the accurate conveyance of God's verbal message that distinguished true prophets of Israel from false. This verbal prophetic nature of God's word also characterized the expectation of the Messiah. "The Gospels center the discussion of who Jesus is in the scriptural context of prophecy and fulfillment."[123] His whole life and ministry, Jesus explicitly appealed to the OT verbal witness in Scripture to both define himself, and as the source of his teaching. Furthermore, any experience of God can only be understood in light of Scripture. Even Barth could not escape the necessity of declaring that Scripture conveyed "authentic information about God."[124] Yet, and here is where almost all of Henry's critics wrongly assess him, Henry unambiguously declares that he is not reducing all of Scripture to a single literary genre:

> By its emphasis that divine revelation is propositional, Christian theology in no way denies that the Bible conveys its message in many literary forms such as letters, poetry and parable, prophecy and history. What it stresses rather, is that the truth conveyed by God through these various forms has conceptual adequacy, and that in all cases the literary teaching is part of

120. Ibid., 3:459.
121. Ibid., 3:460.
122. Ibid., 3:460–61.
123. Ibid., 3:461.
124. Ibid., 3:466; cf. Barth, *Church Dogmatics* II.1, 210.

a divinely inspired message that conveys the truth of divine revelation. Propositional disclosure is not limited to nor does it require only one particular literary genre. And of course the expression of truth in other forms than the customary prose does not preclude expressing that truth in declarative propositions.[125]

Regarding the biblical idea of the Divine Logos and its relation to propositional theology, Henry makes an important and astute observation when he observes the then current tendency to affirm, "that the Word of God became flesh," but to thereby "demean and disown the propositional teaching of the Bible as the Word of God."[126] That is, "If propositions as such are not to be considered as carriers of truth, neither can the Johannine proposition that asserts the enfleshment of the Logos (John 1:14)."[127] His point is that if one is to affirm the Word made flesh then one must affirm propositional theology, since this doctrine comes inherently by way of biblical proposition. So, despite a general tendency away from the Bible as proposition, Henry shows that propositional content lies at the center of the Christian message. Though Christianity certainly is historical, it is through Scripture that its historical content is defined. As George Eldon Ladd says, historical events "are revelatory only when they are accompanied by a revelatory word."[128] Thus, there is a certain necessity given to the priority of God's Word. Furthermore, this emphasis in Henry stands as a direct challenge to some contemporary expositors and preachers, such as Brian McLaren, who downplay the informational side of evangelism in favor of the relational aspect of Christian community. McLaren's tendency toward postmodernism overlooks what Henry has demonstrated, namely that Scripture itself requires assent to objective truth, a notion that McLaren finds objectionable.[129] McLaren

125. Ibid., 3:463; cf. Trueman, "Admiring the Sistine Chapel," 57.
126. Ibid., 3:164.
127. Ibid., 3:165.
128. Ibid., 3:458; Ladd, *Theology of the New Testament*, 31. Problems with Henry's view of propositionalism and his attenuating concept of truth and reason are described by White, and include especially the fact that one can formulate a formally correct logical syllogism that is patently false. Plus, Henry's system is often challenged for perhaps over emphasizing reason to the detriment of other possible avenues of knowledge, and the very idea of presuppositionalism, though of some value, becomes, if all other avenues such as historical evidences are ruled out, impossible to execute as one would have to refute all other systems; White, *What Is Truth?*, 105–9; 188–90.
129. See Crouch, "Emergent Evangelicalism"; cf. also Gundry, who once quipped that perhaps the Fourth Gospel's opening verse might be translated, given the actual

therefore serves as a practical example of how the same notions to which he adheres, and which are also present in postconservative approaches, diminish the objective content of the Christian faith.

Problematic Approaches to the Knowledge of God

Carl Henry's concern for epistemology and rationally defined revelation centers on his belief that "the West has lost its moral and epistemic compass bearings."[130] At the center of this demise, according to Henry, is the loss of Scripture as the "absolute norm." He says, "the Bible could tell us, 'where we are,' 'from where we have come,' and 'where we are going.' Thanks to its scriptural commitments, the West towered head and shoulders above its pagan past."[131] This, though, can no longer be taken for granted.

In volume one of *GRA*, Henry surveys several potential means of knowing and finds them wanting. For example, mysticism—the idea that "direct insight into the invisible world is available through personal illumination as a means of access to the Divine"—fails on several accounts. According to proponents of this view, "the Divine . . . is ineffable, not knowable in terms of criteria applicable to daily life; God transcends distinctions of truth and falsehood and is beyond good and evil."[132] First, in mysticism, if God is supra-rational or beyond truth, how is one to know truth or error at all? Second, if the mystic themselves becomes lost in transcendental ecstasy, how can they then claim to give a reasonable account of their own experience? The answer is that they cannot. "The mystic must . . . respect the canons of reason and the convention of logic if he is to communicate anything whatever about ineffable reality."[133] The mystic further has no assurance that her experience is not a product of an over active imagination. Besides, what possibly can mystical experiences that supposedly transcend space-time reality really affirm about the nature of God? Henry is correct to point out, as he does, that they can affirm nothing at all.

---

meaning λογος "In the beginning was the Proposition." Gundry, *Jesus the Word*, xv.
    130. Henry, *Toward a Recovery of Christian Belief*, 15.
    131. Ibid., 15–16.
    132. *GRA*, 1:71.
    133. Ibid.

In this attack on mysticism, Henry has his sights set firmly on Schleiermacher's Protestant liberalism, and the claim inherent there that Scripture merely records the religious experiences of a particular people. While not entirely disagreeing that God contains a mysterious element, Henry points out that revelation is given precisely on that account. "While there is a mystery side to God, revelation is mystery dispelled and conveys information about God and his purpose."[134]

Henry is careful, however, to distinguish mysticism from "rational intuition" such as that held by Augustine and Calvin based on the *imago dei*. The idea Augustine and Calvin advocated centered on the idea that beings created in God's image are endowed with a certain rational intuition and that this is not the same thing as mysticism.[135]

Henry also denounces empiricism as a failure concerning religious knowledge. "Taken by itself, the empirical method provides no basis for affirming or denying supernatural realities, since by definition it is a method for dealing only with perceptible realities."[136] Henry thus

---

134. Ibid., 73.

135. Ibid., 74, 76.

136. Ibid., 85. Empiricism arose in England during the seventeenth and eighteenth centuries as a response to rationalism. Its main proponents were John Locke, George Berkeley, and David Hume. Like rationalism, empiricism has been associated with the rise in Phyrronian skepticism in the sixteenth century. Empiricists "were skeptical of general, theoretical explanations." This can be traced back to Francis Bacon (1561–1626) and the beginnings of inductive reasoning; Brown, *Christiainity and Western Thought*, 216. John Locke (1632–1704), though, is considered the originator of British empiricism, as he set out to "trace all ideas back to their origin in experience"; Before Locke though, there was Thomas Hobbes (1588–1679). Hobbes was a contemporary of Descartes who sought rationalistic justification for philosophy in a very different manner than Descartes. By making sense perception his starting point, Hobbes is considered to have helped lay the foundations for British Empiricism. In many ways, Hobbes moved both theology and philosophy in the direction of secularism and naturalism. He would influence both rationalists, like Spinoza, and empiricists like Locke; see Allen, *Philosophy for Understanding Theology*, 181. Henry though especially had his sights set on the empirical apologetic methodology of John Warwick Montgomery, who, along with Pinnock, "rest the care for Christian theism on historical evidences, beginning with Jesus' bodily resurrection"; *GRA*, 1:220; cf. ibid., 231; 234; et al.; see also Henry's observation that "although there is no philosophical consensus on how we must define experience, the limits of scientific empiricism (or laboratory observation) are now so widely recognized that strict empiricists concede that the method can provide no verdict on theological entities and moral imperatives. Empirical observation deals with the phenomenal, with our sense perceptions of reality. Standard inductive techniques do not allow us to go beyond perceived data"; *Toward a Recovery of Christian Belief*, 73.

shows how philosophers have attempted to overcome the weaknesses of mysticism, including the empiricist program of rooting knowledge in "inferences from observation."[137] But Kant showed that this ultimately leads to skepticism. This brings Henry then back to Augustine and Calvin, who "formulated the whole possibility of human knowledge in the context of transcendent divine revelation." [138]

In brief, Henry argues that Christianity exists as revealed religion and as such can only be properly explicated when revelation is the starting point. As Henry observes of other more philosophical approaches:

> The mystical approach inexcusably shrouds the self-revealed God in ineffability. The empirical approach cannot arrive at truth because it is committed to an unending search.... [And] the rationalistic approach subordinates the truth of revelation to its own alternatives and has speculated itself into exhaustion.[139]

Therefore, "if we are again to speak confidently of metaphysical realities, the critical decisive issue is on what basis—human speculation or divine revelation?"[140] To avoid human speculation, mysticism, empiricism, and rationalism are simply not viable options.[141] Henry clearly delineates his epistemology centered on the necessity and priority of revelation when he says:

> Divine revelation is the source of all truth, the truth of Christianity included; reason is the instrument for recognizing it; Scripture is its verifying principle; logical consistency is a negative test for truth and coherence a subordinate test. The task of Christian theology is to exhibit the content of biblical revelation as an orderly whole.[142]

---

137. *GRA*, 1:75.

138. Ibid., 1:76.

139. Ibid., 1:95.

140. Ibid.

141. See also Henry's critique of Pentecostalism, which he deems problematic especially on its loss of community or creedal orientation and its "occurring in a theologically imprecise context"; Henry, *Toward a Recovery of Christian Belief*, 26–27. For a contemporary view of Pentecostal epistemology, and one with which Henry would surely have issues, see Smith, *Thinking in Tongues*. Land also emphasizes, following Wesley and Edwards, "affections" as central to a Pentecostal epistemology; Land, *Pentecostal Spirituality*, 129.

142. *GRA*, 1:215.

Henry defended this view on the grounds that "divine revelation is the first principle of Christian theology, from which all the truths of revealed religion are derived."[143] However, Henry points out that this view is not plucked somewhat randomly out of thin air, but derives necessarily from the historical nature of Christian faith—from God acting dynamically in human history to reveal himself and his purposes. Thus, a key aspect of Henry's epistemology is that revelation and the activity of God in human history form a unified whole.

But, does this not seem to suggest that historical events such as the resurrection provide an equally viable starting point for doing theology? For Henry, the answer is a resounding *no*. Divine revelation constitutes the necessary starting point for Christian theology, and as such has no equal. "That Christianity is a historical religion is no less compatible with the primacy of revelation as the Christian epistemic axiom than is the centrality of the resurrection. Revealed religion was historically grounded before the resurrection."[144] Furthermore, Christian revelation stands as a unique source of knowledge, particularly fitted to the formation of Christian doctrine. This is because the Bible shows explicitly the human dilemma and its solution in Christ.

Conclusion

Post-conservative theologians have been some of the fiercest critics of Henry's approach to theology. Yet, Henry himself has shown, that despite the claims of its proponents, post-conservative theology is in fact not as holistically capable as is sometimes claimed. This is true especially because its view of Scripture reduces its content to unverifiable and ambiguous truth having a questionable objective quality both outside and inside the faith community. Plus, not only does Henry not fit the charge of rationalist, neither does he stand in direct continuity with the methodology of Hodge and Warfield. The latter's use of Common Sense Realism and the empiricism it was founded upon lacks the biblical and scriptural grounding found in Henry's revelational epistemology. This is evident in Henry's dependence on an Augustinian, and not an Enlightenment, approach to theology.[145]

143. Ibid.
144. *GRA*, 1:220.
145. Cf. Carswell's observation that "while it may be true that in the end Henry's

There does in fact, seem to be a great deal of confusion, especially among post-conservative theologians, over the difference between the terms "rational" and "rationalism." The former, as Henry defends it, affirms the ability of the human mind to cognitively and intelligibly understand the world and to weigh the content of revelation, precisely because God exists and because he communicates to those created in his image in rational ways. Otherwise, we could know nothing about him or about anything at all. "Rationalism," on the other hand, is the elevation of rationality above and apart from any connection to divine revelation wherein reason functions entirely under its own power and supposedly comes to unaided clarity about what is real and true. This is patently not what Henry believed.

Henry's advocacy of revelational epistemology does indeed appear the only natural way for evangelical theology to proceed and thereby be faithful to its content and subject matter, or more precisely, to be faithful to the God to which theology refers and points. This method has an ancient lineage in the theological method of Augustine, and rightly places both faith and reason in their proper place. In this, Henry has articulated the basic necessary axioms from which any truly evangelical theology must proceed: God exists, and by his grace, he has spoken in self-revealing and intelligible ways. Through the *imago Dei* humanity comprehends enough of God's general revelation to stand condemned, but through the mediatorial work of the Logos, is able to comprehend God's love and grace in and through special revelation. Furthermore, the content of God's speech must be intelligible and coherent, or else its meaning becomes lost in subject speculation.

Henry's Reformed Baptist perspective undoubtedly led to his emphasis on the sovereignty of God, the priority of Scripture, and application of Scripture to all of life. But even these clearly find expression in other (e.g., Wesleyan) theological approaches. While a study of Henry's theology of election must wait until the next chapter, logically it would seem that an emphasis on the necessity of evangelism and simultaneous belief in supralapsarianism, owing to an emphasis on the decretive

---

propositionalism is not a completely adequate account of divine revelation, the reason behind this position is not an intellectual slavery to the tenets of modernism or classical foundationalism." Instead, Henry's reaction to the neoorthodox tendency to "de-emphasize the cognitive aspect of divine revelation" must be understood in order to rightly read Henry; "A Comparative Study of the Religious Epistemology of Carl F. H. Henry and Alvin Plantiga," 113.

will of God, are at odds with one another. At the very least, it seems that a consistent Reformed theology would hinder evangelistic efforts, and that any emphasis on God's predestining individuals to salvation and damnation while simultaneously emphasizing the need for evangelism is contradictory.

Henry's theology of the *imago Dei*, however, deserves careful attention. Here humanity has access to reason in general and to God's revelation, both general and specific. Furthermore, this doctrine underscores the inherent dignity of all human persons, and as we shall see, features prominently in Henry's theology of evangelism and social concern. Furthermore, it is through the mediating Logos that humans are able to know both general and ultimate truth.

Despite numerous critiques to the contrary, Henry is absolutely correct to emphasize the propositional nature of God's revelation. Apart from this, one cannot know assuredly whether one's thoughts about God are true or merely human constructs. Scripture as the verifying principle insures factual, truthful, and requisite knowledge of God needed for the salvation of sinners. Those who would deny this have woefully misunderstood Henry on this point, as he by no means reduces all genres of biblical literature to propositions. He merely affirms along with Scripture itself in the long prophetic and apostolic tradition of Judeo-Christian faith, "thus sayeth the Lord!"

Neither can it be rightly deemed that Henry is modernist. Henry's is a distinctly revelation-centered epistemology that derives from the necessity of God's revelatory words and deeds in order for anything at all to be known about God. The task of theology then, is to expound the content of this revelation in ways faithful to its source in both Scripture and in God.

Most importantly, Henry's method by no means fosters a divide between faith and practice, or between evangelism and social concern. Calvinism itself tends to be a worldview oriented theological approach, and thereby oriented to the whole of life. Plus, the prioritizing of Scripture holds forth the best opportunity for both individual regeneration and social renewal. Apart from this, humanity has no means to determine "true north." The Christian Good News is not for mere social uplift, but personal salvation. As Henry himself declares, one's options for where to begin in the theological task, are either human speculation or divine revelation. There simply can be no other way. He has unashamedly chosen the latter.

— 4 —

Henry and Evangelism

A church without evangelism invites extinction.[1]

Introduction

PERHAPS ONE OF THE most overlooked aspects of Henry's *GRA*, is that it is, from beginning to end, evangelistic in nature. Henry's purpose throughout is to call humanity back to the knowledge of God, via the Word of God, and he does this not only by directly challenging non-Christian and pseudo-Christian ideas about divine disclosure, but also by championing the firm belief that God has spoken and issued a sure Word able to save sinful human beings.[2] In fact, the lack of attention to God's Word in contemporary culture constitutes an urgent crisis. The day of God's redemptive mercy has been and is upon us, and the word of God must therefore be proclaimed before the time of judgment arrives. As Henry says, "grateful we may be for the sake of those still unsheltered from the coming storm, that the God of the end-time has not yet spoken his final Word."[3]

Henry described the problem of evangelism in the late 1950s in America, pointing out that ecumenical (liberal) churches mostly, though not entirely, dismissed the idea of evangelism altogether, whereas fundamentalists, though concerned for evangelism, "tended to narrow the 'whole counsel of God,' and felt little obligation to exhibit Christianity as

---

1. Henry, "The Road To Eternity," 32.

2. *GRA*, 2:7; as to Henry's passion for evangelism, Timothy George observes "Carl Henry was ever the evangelist—though few think of the great theologian in this way"; George, "Inventing Evangelicalism," 48.

3. *GRA*, 2:16.

a comprehensive world and life view."⁴ Henry also notes that fundamentalism's failure to engage in the production of exegetical and theological literature could be traced to its burden for missions and evangelism "bequeathed by the modernist defection."⁵ Yet, fundamentalism's reductionist tendencies which emphasized evangelism but tended to truncate Scripture by avoiding its social implications were not the sole cause for concern. Others sought to completely diminish the need for evangelism, or to so redefine it that it bore no resemblance to the biblical picture. Especially troubling for Henry was the growing tendency to focus on altering social structures while ignoring the need for redemption. Henry understood this development as an unbiblical redefining of the church's purpose.⁶ Thus, the appearance of Henry's *GRA* reflected his life-long passion to correct both of these deficiencies by advocating a theological method capable of unifying Christian thought and practice.⁷

In addition to the minimalistic outline Henry articulates, a few other historical issues prove important to understanding the current debate over evangelism and social concern. As Arthur P. Johnson has pointed out, "the 'substance' of the nineteenth century evangelistic impetus was composed of the Reformation doctrine of Scripture as emphasized and applied in pietism."⁸ Liberal theology, though, wrought havoc on the doctrine of divine special revelation by both the loss of belief in an inspired

---

4. Henry, *Evangelical Responsibility in Contemporary Theology*, 33. Also, on the ecumenical tendency to deny evangelism, Henry writes, "It was significant that the Berlin Congress of 1966 registered growing impatience over any and all ecclesiastical forms that impede evangelism"; Henry, *Evangelicals at the Brink of Crisis: Significance of the World Congress on Evangelism*, 82; cf. Carpenter's observation that in the early part of the twentieth century, "fundamentalism's commitment to urban evangelism and foreign missions suggests that the movement was primarily concerned with preaching the evangelical gospel"; "Fundamentalist Institutions and the Rise of Evangelical Protestantism," 74; also, Thomas C. Berg provides an historical overview of the loss and recovery of evangelism in mid-twentieth century American Christianity. He notes especially that evangelism and social concern became the two poles around which opposing sides of the fundamentalist-modernist controversy coalesced; "'Proclaiming Together'? Convergence and Divergence in Mainline and Evangelical Evangelism, 1945–1967," 49–51. Henry's emphasis on worldview thinking owed much to James Orr's *Christian View of God and the World*; see Henry, "Fortunes of a Christian Worldview," 3.

5. Henry, *Evangelical Responsibility*, 34–35.

6. Henry, *Evangelicals at the Brink of Crisis*, 34.

7. Cf. Olson, *The Westminster Handbook*, 41.

8. Johnson, *World Evangelism and the Word of God*, 23.

Bible, associated closely with the denial of the supernatural, through false notions about the Kingdom, especially in the thought of Ritschl, and finally, through the rejection of historical dogma via Harnack. Thus, the error of liberalism may be seen as reverting from a top-down approach to Christian mission, or one that begins with God's own revelation, to a bottom-up approach that begins with human prognostication and that moves consequently away from historic orthodox understandings.[9] But not only have these ideas dominated liberal theology, they have also seeped into evangelical thinking, especially through seminaries and Bible colleges where the basic presuppositions of higher criticism have at times been uncritically utilized.[10] What makes Henry especially valuable then, is the fact that he, more than any other twentieth century theologian, has labored extensively to recapture a revelation-centered approach and reestablish a fundamental basis for evangelism.

Defining Evangelism

Though much of what follows should be seen as Henry's unfolding definition of evangelism, it may be helpful to start with something more concise. In *Evangelicals at the Brink of Crisis,* the follow-up text to the Berlin Congress on World Evangelism in 1966, Henry cited, with varying degrees of approval, two definitions of the evangelistic task of the church. The first was the definition produced by the Congress itself. The second, which he described as "highly serviceable," was produced in 1918 in England by the Archbishop's Committee on Evangelism. After providing each definition, Henry then cited six reasons why the former should be preferred. The 1966 definition is as follows:

> Evangelism is the proclamation of the Gospel of the crucified and risen Christ, the only Redeemer of men, according to the Scriptures, with the purpose of persuading condemned and lost sinners to put their trust in God by receiving and accepting Christ as Savior through the power of the Holy Spirit, and to serve Christ as Lord in every calling of life and in the fellowship of his church, looking toward the day of his coming in glory.

It is interesting to note that this definition does not explicitly mention repentance, even thought it is implied. Also, it is important to observe

---

9. Ibid., 72–81.
10. Cf. Osborne, "Historical Criticism and the Evangelical," 84–86.

that in this phrase, the words "with the purpose of" signal a key aspect of Henry's theology, namely that he understands evangelism as a verbal activity ("proclamation"), and that serving Christ in the church and in the world ("every calling of life") results from the proclamational task. The 1918 definition, however, though more succinct, suffers for lack of precision:

> To evangelize is so to present Christ Jesus in the power of the Holy Spirit, that men shall come to put their trust in God through Him, to accept Him as their Saviour and serve Him as their King in the fellowship of his church.[11]

The Need for Evangelism

Against the backdrop of an increasingly secular culture, Henry declares that the needed theological renewal in America must begin with a renewed attention to God's Word, not only in personal devotion, but also in prophetic pronouncement. "The preached Word must speak to society in general, to great modern cities whose clichés about urban renewal fade into discouragement."[12] Thus, as will become evident, Henry's constant emphasis on the priority of evangelism is closely tied to his doctrine of revelation.

---

11. For both definitions see Henry, *Evangelicals at the Brink of Crisis*, 37. Henry's reason for preferring the 1966 definition were (1) it stressed more clearly the mediatorial role of Jesus, (2) it better emphasized the hopelessness of humanity apart from Christ, (3) it is more explicit regarding Christ's substitutionary death, (4) the eschatological hope remains more in view, (5) the need of Jesus' disciples to penetrate the world and not withdraw from it is emphasized, (6) its explicit connection to the Gospel—"regarding both content and proclamation"; ibid., 37–38. Though this study is primarily concerned with theological foundations, this should not lead one to assume therefore that Henry had nothing to say about methods of evangelism. Rather, he says that (1) "every method of not evangelizing is wrong," and (2) "the best method is, always has been, and always will be person-to-person evangelism"; Henry, *The Christian Mindset in a Secular Society*, 50–51.

12. Henry, *The Christian Mindset in a Secular Society*, 36; cf. Leung, who observes of Henry, that "his passion for evangelism and mission was no less than the zeal for social justice"; "With What is Evangelicalism to Penetrate the World," 227; also, as Henry himself says, "the key intellectual issue for the 80s, as I see it, will still be the persistent problem of authority. It will concern especially the problem of hermeneutics, and centrally the question of revelation and culture. Those who argue that revelation is enculturated will be unable to exempt their own pontifications. Christianity's true immortals will insist that God addresses the truth of revelation objectively to all humans of whatever diverse cultures"; "American Evangelicals in a Time of Turning," 1062.

Theological Foundations for Evangelism

Though not a systematic theology, Henry's *GRA* contains his most developed theological foundations for understanding God's self-giving revelation in Scripture and in Christ.[13] As Henry unfolds the essence and implications of this Divine disclosure, the implications for evangelism frequently emerge. Therefore, what follows constitutes an exposition of not only *GRA* as the fundamental moorings of Henry's theology of evangelism, but also includes Henry's numerous other works where he touches on these same issues.[14] But the focus in this chapter will be especially on those aspects of Divine revelation that provide the necessity for Henry's prioritizing of evangelism.

The Awesome Disclosure of God

Henry's first thesis in *GRA* states that "revelation is a Divine initiated activity, God's free communication by which he alone turns his personal privacy into a deliberate disclosure of his reality."[15] Henry argues that this revelation alone has the power to shake us loose from our self-centered temporality, and issue to us a dire warning about future things. In other words, God's revelatory self-disclosure is supremely evangelistic. "Like some piercing air-raid siren it sends us scurrying from life's preoccupations and warns us that no escape remains if we neglect the only sure sanctuary."[16] As indicated by the heading of this section, Henry empha-

---

13. Cf. Mohler Jr., who observes, "though Henry is first and foremost a theologian, he has not produced a systematic theology, choosing instead to concentrate upon the doctrines of revelation, God, and religious authority; the major points of compromise in twentieth-century theology"; "Carl F. H. Henry," Kindle ed., under chapter 15.

14. To be as true as possible to Henry's own thoughts, I have taken the topics of this study directly from Henry's chapter and section divisions in *GRA*. This, though, is by no means to say that only his thoughts in *GRA* are taken into consideration. Rather, the whole of Henry's body of works are considered as they relate to these dominant issues.

15. *GRA*, 2:17. Contra the claims of Avery Dulles, Henry affirms unapologetically that indeed the idea of revelation is central to Scripture. As Henry says, "Revelation is in fact a core doctrine of the Bible. Without it the entire scriptural message would lose its authority"; Henry, "The Priority of Divine Revelation: A Review Article," 77; Patterson, *Carl F.H. Henry*, 84.

16. *GRA*, 2:17. Henry frequently posits the necessity of biblical revelation as the necessary foundation for a Christian worldview, as argued in the previous chapter. This is in fact the dominant theme of *GRA*, and many of Henry's other writings as well; cf. Henry, "Christianity and Resurgent Paganism," 87–92; Henry, "Fortunes of the

sizes here the "awesome disclosure of God," that is, God's gracious, self-revelatory act of making known that which was hidden, namely God's own nature and purposes.

The issue of the necessity of God's self-revelation in order for humanity to know God or anything about Him at all, represents one of the few areas in which Henry stands in agreement with Karl Barth. With mild approval he cites Barth's description of theological existence as "wonder" and Brunner's notion of God's revelation as "incursion from another dimension."[17] However, for Henry, "wonder" is insufficient given that "the truth of revelation can be evaded even where wonder is present."[18] Henry's key point here is that first, according to Scripture, revelation is an unveiling of something hidden, as made clear by the Hebrew word *galah* and the Greek verb *apokaluptō*.[19] In this, Henry does not deny general revelation, as "both the Old and New Testaments emphasize that God is universally and ongoingly revealed in his creation (Ps 19; Rom 1:17ff)."[20] In contrast, though, "[God's] special redemptive revelation . . . is given once-for-all time." In addition, God's revelation has not been made universally, but through God's chosen agents, Hebrew prophets and NT apostles, "who witness to the incomparable news that God in redemptive grace comes by way of fulfilled prophecy in Christ Jesus."[21] Specifically here Henry points out that *apokaluptō* occurs in Peter's declaration of Christ's deity (Matt 16:17), and occurs eighteen other times in the NT. Such revelation constitutes precisely what Paul appeals to in his own Gospel message (Gal 1:12).[22] As it

Christian World View," 163–76.

17. GRA, 2:17. See also Barth, *Evangelical Theology*; Brunner, *Revelation and Reason*. For a helpful summary of Barth's view of revelation, see Hardy, "Karl Barth," chapter one. Also, see directly Barth's *Church Dogmatics* I.1–I.2.

18. GRA, 2:27.

19. Ibid., 2:21. As Henry observes, *galah* appears some twenty-three times in the OT in reference to God's self communication (cf. Num 24:4; 1 Sam 3:21; 2 Sam 7:27; Dan 2:47). Also, *apokaluptō* is notable in the NT for its abundance of usage compared to non-biblical occurrences. See also "ἀποκαλύπτω/ ἀποκάλυψις" in *NIDNTT*, and the point that in the NT usage the focus is almost always on the content rather than the means of revelation.

20. GRA, 2:22.

21. Ibid.

22. Ibid. Also, as Henry says of the apostles, "their driving passion was obedience to Christ's Great Commission: to proclaim the good news and to make personal disciples; their passion was not to engage the church as a corporate body in political action aimed at restructuring social and political forms"; Henry, *Evangelicals at the Brink of Crisis*, 36.

relates to evangelism, then, this is crucial. As Henry says, "the content of church proclamation is therefore not just about anything and everything. The church's message to the world is not about the energy crisis, pollution, white or black power, détente, the Israeli-Arab conflict, *ad infinitum*. It is the very specific Word of God."[23] He adds, with equal force, "nor is the Christian minister anything and everything—a fundraiser, marriage counselor, pulpit orator, public relations specialist, *ad infinitum*. He is primarily the proclaimer of God's revealed Word." In short, "the unmistakable priority of God's people, the church in the world, is to proclaim God's revealed Word." Henry goes on to argue that apart from this distinctive, the church has no unique role in society and no possibility of enduring. Even worse, it becomes "an affront to God."[24]

Importantly, Henry points out the inherent cultural significance of proclaiming God's Word. It is not, says Henry, the fault of Christianity itself nor the fault of either "evangelistic or social failures of past generations of believers," that contemporary society has attached itself to power, money, and sex instead of God's Word. Rather, "the fault lies in timid preaching of God's revelation by professional pulpiteers, in presumptuous tampering with God's revelation by contemporary critics, and in subtle evasions of God's revelation" at the denominational, seminary classroom, and personal levels. "The Word of the Lord is not being sounded in the land as it ought."[25] Of course, Henry is not oblivious to the fact that Scripture itself attests that many will reject God's Word.[26]

---

23. *GRA*, 2:22. For a helpful survey of challenges in Henry's day to the value and centrality of the Bible to Christian theology, see Preus, "The Nature of the Bible," especially part II, under "The Modern Revolt Against the Bible," 121–28.

24. *GRA*, 2:22; all quotations in this paragraph are from this page. We might recall that this emphasis on the unique role of the church as it concerns evangelism echoes Christopher Little's claim as well from chapter one. A similar note is echoed by Michael Cassidy, in his essay "The Nature of Evangelism," in Padilla, *The New Face of Evangelicalism*, 67–86. While emphasizing the proclamation must accompany dialogue, that is, effort given to help those to whom the message is proclaimed to understand what is being said, Cassidy, in concert with the Lausanne Covenant and with Henry, affirms the primacy of evangelism. Cassidy also articulates a point to which Henry here also refers, namely that the task of evangelism in the NT is especially directed toward those who have not heard at all; ibid., 80.

25. *GRA*, 2: 23.

26. See Deut 28:68; Ps 41:9; 55:12; Zech 11:12; Isa 53:1; Jer 5:21; Matt 26:15, 21-24; John 1:11; John 13:21.

A Place in God's Kingdom

Henry's second thesis is that "divine revelation is given for human benefit, offering us privileged communion with our Creator in the Kingdom of God."[27] On this, Henry carefully points out divine graciousness in the reality that God's offer of revelation is yet available. For though "the human species is on the receiving end of a divine initiative" in revelation, and since humanity is the capstone of God's creation, neither of these are necessarily so. That is, God could have chosen other creatures (i.e., angels or beings on another planet) as the sole recipients of his divine disclosure. The uniqueness of human creatures then lies especially in their ability to be in relationship with the covenanting-redeeming God.[28]

Henry especially emphasizes here the non-necessary aspect of this redemptive plan, as God might sovereignly choose at any moment to bring about an end to the time of gracious revelation. In other words, the opportunity and time for decision is of utmost importance and urgency. "In his revelation God has published news incomparably important to every generation, past and present, of momentous value to each of us who live in this present opportunity for decision." Or, as Henry the consummate journalist puts it, "God's revelation is the headline above all headlines, directed to us from the world beyond all worlds, from God himself."[29]

The personal nature of God's revelation constitutes for Henry one of its chief features. "God's purpose in revelation is that we may know him personally as he is, may avail ourselves of his gracious forgiveness and offer of new life, may escape catastrophic judgment for our sins, and venture personal fellowship with him."[30] In other words, God's self-revelatory Word and acts, indeed take into view the broad sweep of humanity, but more importantly hone down to emphasize the divine disclosure aimed at individual lives. This emphasis will prove a crucial point to this study and one

---

27. Ibid., 2:30; see also Henry, "Reflections on the Kingdom of God." On the key role played by Henry and George E. Ladd in advocating for inaugurated eschatology as it relates to the Kingdom of God, see Moore, *The Kingdom of Christ*, especially chapter one; Snyder, *The Community of the King*, under chapter one, "Kingdom Consciousness"; cf. Henry's statement that Jesus' "purpose in the conquest of sin is not a mere cleansing of rebellious creatures from guilt, but their full liberation from the power of Satan and sin, and their transfer from the realm of moral darkness to the messianic kingdom which has already been manifested in Christ"; "The Purpose of God," 26.

28. *GRA*, 2:30.

29. Ibid., 2:31.

30. Ibid.

to which we will return often. To make this point, Henry argues that the broad strokes of the "unto yous" of the creation account (as Henry cites, "Every herb ... and every tree ... to you shall be food," Gen 1:29), ultimately culminate in the more personalized *unto you/unto us* statements of the NT. "Unto you is born this day ... " (Luke 2:11, KJV). "For the promise is unto you, and to our children ... " (Acts 2:39, KJV).[31] At the very heart of this personal offer, lies not only forgiveness of sin, but entrance into God's kingdom.[32] The Kingdom of God constitutes that which underlies the whole OT, wherein Yahweh is king,[33] and to whom human kings are but representatives (1 Sam 8:7; 10:19; 12:19). The longing of God's people especially centered on God's coming rule, and that longing itself served as evidence of God's redemptive work. "That the people of God yearn for God's kingdom rule to prevail ever more fully and absolutely is a mark of Yahweh's redemptive work in the life of sinful mankind."[34]

The point Henry makes here is that the essence of NT proclamation was that God's rule, and thereby God's Kingdom, was tangibly present, and not merely a future hope. "The kingdom-theme as it relates to the person of Jesus Christ must be correlated with the Old Testament prophecies and the dawning of the age of fulfillment." This is what Jesus himself preached, "the glad tidings of the kingdom" (Luke 8:1), and in his beatitudes emphasized the blessedness offered to those who presently and willingly participate in God's dawning kingdom (Matt 5:3, 10).[35] In fact, in Jesus the kingdom is especially present, for he "mirrors the new

---

31. Ibid., 2:33. See also other texts cited by Henry, including Luke 22:19–20; 1 Cor 11:24; 2 Cor 5:21; Gal 1:4; Gal 3:13; 1 Peter 2:21; 1 John 3:16; Eph 5:2; Heb 2:9; John 6:51; Rom 5:6; 5:8; 8:34; 1 Cor 15:3; 1 Thess 5:10: Heb 6:20; 9:24; 7:25; 1 John 3:1; et al.; cf. Henry, "Facing a New Day in Evangelism," 15.

32. Cf. Patterson, *Carl F.H. Henry*, 85–86. For an excellent discussion of Henry's contribution to evangelical discussions about the Kingdom of God, see Moore, *The Kingdom of Christ: The New Evangelical Perspective*. As Doyle points out, "Henry always insists that God's revelation speaks to every domain"; Doyle, *Carl Henry*, 53.

33. Ps 47:2, 7, 9; Jer 10:7; Dan 4:34.

34. *GRA*, 2:34. Thornbury summarizes Henry's theology of the Kingdom, noting that "in *GRA*, the kingdom is God's and God's alone, only as he bears the sovereignty, authority, wisdom, and freedom required to rule as the Creator. The universe is fashioned as intrinsically and vitally redemptive. Jesus is the Lamb, "slain from the foundation of the world" (Rev 13:8; KJV). Even now, Jesus, who died and was raised for us, "pleads our cause" (Rom 8:34) before God in heaven. He died so that we might live with him (1 Thess 5:10). God has offered us a place in his kingdom. He liberates us so that we will have faith in him"; Thornbury, *Recovering Classic Evangelicalism*, 64.

35. *GRA*, 2:34–35.

man who inherits God's kingdom." The way to avoid the error of overly temporalizing the kingdom centers on keeping the person and work of Jesus preeminent.[36] Yet, one must not only keep Jesus central, but also keep Him central within the full scope of attributes and authority attributed to Him in Scripture. There is, furthermore, in the context of the proclamation of the kingdom an ethical demand placed upon those who heed God's call. After the birth of the church, "the Christian goal now became 'to live lives worthy of the God who calls you into his kingdom and glory' (1 Thess 2:12, NEB), and under persecution to show oneself 'worthy of the Kingdom of God' (2 Thess 1:5, NEB)."[37] This means then that the biblical concept of the Kingdom of God requires of believers an embodiment of the ideals of the kingdom, including God's judgment against injustices in the social and political realms. Especially important here is that the Kingdom of God appears in and through the church, in the lives of the redeemed, even though the church is not to be equated with the Kingdom. As Russell Moore has noted, this aspect of Henry's theology marks him, along with George Eldon Ladd, as in important figure in the emergence of the current Evangelical consensus regarding inaugurated eschatology. Specifically, Henry laments the apprehension over Kingdom preaching among fundamentalists, and attributes this to a reactionary response to liberal theology.[38]

Henry will have more to say on the practice of Kingdom ideals in the next chapter, but his emphasis here on Kingdom preaching is an important emphasis, especially in light of some, like Little, who still show reluctance about the Kingdom. While Little does helpfully offer a corrective to some poor exegesis done in the name of the biblical Kingdom of God and the mission of the church, he also demonstrates what appears to be the same sort of Kingdom apprehension to which Henry warns against regarding fundamentalism.[39] The lesson Henry offers is the idea

36. Ibid., 2:35. To the extent that Julian N. Hart says Jesus is the "supreme witness" to the Kingdom of God, he seems on target and approximating that which Henry says; Hart seems less correct though to also say that Jesus *is* the kingdom; see Hart, *Toward a Theology of Evangelism*, 26, 39.

37. Ibid. The theme of God's kingdom as the necessary rubric for understanding the church's mission has featured prominently in several important works, including Ladd, *The Gospel of the Kingdom*; Stassen and Gushee, *Kingdom Ethics*; Wright, *Surprised by Hope*.

38. Henry, *The Uneasy Conscience*, 41–54; Moore, *The Kingdom of Christ*, 22.

39. For Little's corrective to some of the excesses of the holistic mission/mission as transformation movement, see his *Polemic Missiology*, under chapter 1, "The Contours

that previous abuses of a genuine biblical concept, no matter how grave, should by no means lead to the wholesale and uncritical rejection of the idea itself. Rather, theological excess should drive one back to Scripture as the primary source for theological reflection. Yet, more important is Henry's point that prophetic pronouncements in the OT stand behind the NT expectations and understanding of the Kingdom in such a way that proclamation becomes fundamental to both right expectation and faithful application.

Not by Good Tidings Alone

Reflecting concern for one of the church's most endangered doctrines, Henry next addresses the issue of God's judgment.[40] Not only is the Christian evangel an offer of Good News in Jesus Christ, but also features prominently a stern warning against coming judgment. Here Henry returns to, and more fully addresses, those who would reject God's gracious offer of salvation. Specifically, Henry's concern focuses on two extremes relating to revelation and salvation. First, willful unbelief not only brings end-times judgment, but brings about a form of judgment in the present. In the same way that the church anticipates the future glory and the qualities of the Kingdom of God, so too does unbelief anticipate future judgment. In support of this, Henry cites Cyril of Alexandria, who observed that the unbeliever "is condemned already because his refusal of the offered way of salvation is a kind of advance vote against himself as deserving punishment."[41] Or as Henry puts it, "the unbelievers confidence in his own ingenuity and works condemns him. His refusal to

---

of Christian Mission"; yet, Little oddly sets the biblical concept of the Kingdom in contrast, and perhaps in opposition to, doxological mission; see Little, "What Makes Mission Christian?," 69–70.

40. As Doyle has observed, theological liberalism especially shifted the focus of Christian theology away from any notion of divine wrath: "Theologians such as Schleiermacher and Ritschl responded to [the onslaught of modernity, higher criticism, and Darwinism] by shifting the focus of revelation from God's Word as written in the Bible to the human soul and its consciousness of dependence upon the Ultimate." Plus, "since hell seemed a concept from pre-Enlightenment days, God's love received primary attention; his justice and wrath were replaced by universal forgiveness"; Doyle, *Carl Henry*, 22.

41. *GRA*, 2:39. Henry here is citing a secondary source on Cyril, namely M. F. Wiles' *The Spiritual Gospel: The Interpretation of the Fourth Gospel in the Early Church* (London and New York: Cambridge University Press, 1960).

appropriate divinely proffered salvation reveals his true character and motives."[42] In other words, "in expounding the implications of faith and unbelief, the New Testament focuses not simply on the eschatological end-time, but also on the present in which God's eschatological action is already anticipatively underway."[43] The point here is that revelation does not necessarily lead to salvation; the requirement of personal decision and faith is abundantly evident in Scripture.[44]

The second error Henry addresses though is Barth's equating revelation with salvation. In his critique of Barth on this point, Henry defers to G. C. Berkouwer, who was in Henry's words, "biblically justified in rejecting Barth's notion that all human beings already share universally in the salvation wrought by Jesus Christ and therefore need only to be informed of the fact." As Henry notes, though Jesus' "substitutionary redemptive provision is indeed complete, it prevails only for those who appropriate it."[45] Barth, though, has, in his efforts to emphasize the surety and finality of God's grace and work, obscures this fact by equating revelation with salvation. In contrast, Henry points out that Scripture frequently emphasizes not only God's grace and mercy, but also the reality of pending judgment for those who reject Christ.[46] In addition to Barth, Henry also notes that Paul Tillich and Thomas F. Torrance "likewise perpetuate the fallacy that revelation is salvific." Torrance, for example, claimed that knowing theological truth was concordant with "being drawn into" God's redemptive activity, and therefore to possess knowledge of God was to participate in salvation.[47]

---

42. *GRA*, 2:39.

43. Ibid. See especially John 5:24–25, wherein Jesus says "Anyone who gives heed to what I say and puts his trust in him who sent me has hold of eternal life, and does not come up for judgment, but has already passed from death to life. In truth, in very truth I tell you, a time is coming, indeed, it is already here, when the dead shall hear the voice of the Son of God, and all who hear shall come to life" (John 5:24–25, NEB); ibid.

44. In support, Henry cites John 1:12; 3:16; 20:31; 1 Cor 1:18; see *GRA*, 2:40. Of course, Henry as a Calvinist sees the role of personal decision within the context of the elect; cf. *GRA*, 3:17, wherein Henry observes, "the eternal election of believers is experientially effected in the personal reception and appropriation of the now openly revealed mystery."

45. *GRA*, 2:40.

46. *GRA*, 2:41–42.

47. Ibid., 2:43. On Paul Tillich see Burch, "Tillich on Salvation," 246–51.

Not so says Henry, turning to his former professor and mentor, Gordon H. Clark in support, who pointed out that according to James (2:19), even demons have knowledge of God, a knowledge that would be impossible apart from revelation. Thus, Barth is wrong to say, as he does that knowledge and obedience must necessarily go together. According to Barth, if one possesses true knowledge of God, then this should be taken as an inherent indication of obedience, for one cannot be found without the other.[48] This view though conflates revelation and salvation, and results in a radical redefining of both.[49] Henry's point is that any understanding of God's redemptive revelation that does not include the reality of judgment and the necessity of a decision to enter into believing faith falls short of what God says in Scripture about his revelatory Word.[50]

Henry's frequent interaction with Karl Barth should be cause for reflection among Evangelicals who continue to debate the value of Barth in formulating an evangelical theology. Henry's thoughts should be taken as a warning against uncritically adopting the methodology of Barth and thereby ignoring his problematic views of revelation as it relates to Scripture and tendency toward universalism.[51] Conversely, Henry might also be criticized here for giving too little attention to the eschatological judgment of God, especially as emphasized in Revelation. However, one must also take into account that Henry's is not a systematic treatment of the subject.[52]

The Hidden and Revealed God

Under the banner of his third thesis—"divine revelation does not completely erase God's transcendent mystery, inasmuch as God the Revealer

---

48. GRA, 2:44; CD, I/1.

49. GRA, 2:44.

50. Ibid., 2:45; see also Henry's lament regarding the neglect of the need for justification, in Henry, "Justification: A Doctrine in Crisis," 57–65.

51. See especially McCormick and Anderson, *Karl Barth and American Evangelicalism*. On universalism in Barth, see McCormick's essay, "So That He May Be Merciful to All: Karl Barth and the Problem of Universalism," and McDonald's essay, "Evangelical Perspective from the Reformed Heritage," in ibid., 227–70. Also on the interest among conservative oriented Protestants, see Morrison, who observes that Barth has often been turned to as a *tertium quid* between liberalism and Protestant orthodoxy; Morrison, "Barth, Barthians, and Evangelicals," 188.

52. For such an emphasis, see Köstenberger and O'Brien, *Salvation to the Ends of the Earth*, 243–50.

transcends his own revelation"—Henry makes two salient points that relate directly to the evangelistic task.[53] First, he points out that no man can understand God without God's revelation (cf. Job 36:26; Ps 139:6), but second, and thankfully, God *has* revealed himself. Human beings, either regenerate or not, have no special capacity to discern the nature of God. On this account, God's nature is hidden from view.[54] However, and second, this does not mean that humanity is without hope. For though the revelation of God by no means exhausts the knowledge of God, that knowledge of himself that God has sovereignly chosen to reveal is sufficient for salvation, especially in and through Jesus, who is himself "the way, the truth, and the life" (John 14:6).[55]

Varieties of Divine Revelation

In what manner has the nature and will of God been revealed? This question occupies Henry's discussion of the varieties of revelation, wherein he examines the differences and nature of the forms taken by God's revelation, according to God's sovereign will. This discussion thus falls under Henry's fifth thesis—"not only the occurrence of divine revelation but its very nature, content and variety are exclusively God's determination."[56]

Henry's first point in this regard is that "human expectation or prognostication" can never suffice as a starting point for determining the forms of God's revelation as this amounts to a limit upon God's freedom.[57] In fact, no concordism whatever can suffice. Scientific, historical, and linguistic issues, for example, though important, must always be secondary to determining the manner of God's revelation. This indeed is the failed legacy of both idealism and naturalism.[58]

---

53. The bulk of this section deals with the question of whether God's revelation exhaustively discloses his nature and in the context of Henry's resounding "no" addresses other supposed forms of revelation.

54. GRA, 2:50.

55. Ibid., 2:57; cf. Patterson, *Carl F.H. Henry*, 86–87. Thornbury calls Henry's third thesis "the most ignored declaration in the entire body of Carl Henry's work"; Thornbury, *Recovering Classic Evangelicalism*, 65.

56. GRA, 2:77.

57. Ibid.

58. Ibid., 2:78. For Henry's critique of personal idealism in the theology of A. H. Strong, see Henry, *Personal Idealism and Strong's Theology*. See also Wacker, *Augustus H. Strong and the Dilemma of Historical Consciousness*. Idealism is the belief that

The issue of evangelism intrinsically raises a vital question regarding lost humanity and the varieties of God's disclosure. Specifically, how are general and divine revelation to be defined and in what way do they relate to one another? On this, Henry is quick to declare that "a general revelation of the Creator in his creation is integral to Christian doctrine founded upon Scripture and beyond that upon the factualities of the universe."[59] The Scriptures abundantly attest to this, especially Psalm 19, and in the NT, John 1:4, 9; Acts 14:17; 17:26–28; and Romans 1:18–20, 28–32; 2:14–16. Or, "in other words, no one anywhere at any time can escape the inner, secret, guilty knowledge of the true God and of his demand for spiritual submission and moral obedience."[60] But especially important regarding general revelation, and the aspect perhaps most often misunderstood or misapplied, according to Henry, is that general revelation does not avail itself for what has been called natural theology. General revelation does not produce true or accurate knowledge of God, but rather only the knowledge of one's guilt before God. "It is not into 'proofs' of the living God's existence, but into an occasion of revolt and estrangement that man the sinner turns the general disclosure of God. The Bible connects the universal or general revelation of God not with 'natural theology' but with man's guilt (Rom 1:20)."[61] This thereby leaves unregenerate humanity in a condition only remedied by special

---

reality consists primarily in ideas or minds. This notion owes its development to Kant's emphasis that the mind actively shapes one's ability to know, and his denial of reason and revelation as means for knowing God. Also, Hegel's dialectic view of history as developing toward an absolute ideal emphasized the imperfect nature of the knowing subject; cf. Ewing, "Idealism," n.p.

59. Ibid., 2:83.

60. Ibid., 2:85. Barth especially denied general revelation on the grounds that liberal theology abused the concept. However, as Clark Pinnock has pointed out, this is no basis for rejecting what Scripture clearly affirms; see Pinnock, "Revelation," n.p.

61. *GRA*, 2:86; 96; 253. Henry's concern with theistic proofs in the Thomistic sense lies in his belief that such a methodology gives too much to modern empirical method. His point is that if one adopts the methodology of empiricism, then it becomes rather difficult to argue against it; cf. Thornbury, *Recovering Classic Evangelicalism*, 73. Also, see Dulles' critique of Henry's denial of natural theology in Dulles, "God, Revelation and Authority 2 (Book Review)." Berkouwer also traces the Hegelian influence that gave rise to a broader understanding of general revelation that eventuated in understanding Christ "as a special illustration of the general revelation of God in the world"; Berkouwer, *General Revelation*, 12. It was also on this point of natural theology that a new rift emerged in dialectical theology between Barth and Brunner; see Brunner, *Natur Und Gnade: Zum Gespräch Mit Karl Barth*; for an English translation see Brunner and Barth, *Natural Theology*; cf. Berkouwer, 15.

revelation.⁶² Apart from that, humanity remains mired in its rebellion. Together, though, general and special revelation work in tandem affecting God's salvific purposes.⁶³

As it concerns natural theology, Henry appears to have fallen victim to Hume's critique that natural theology can never prove the existence of God, and is thereby a pointless endeavor.⁶⁴ In this Henry fails to adequately distinguish between theological method and apologetic method, as the two are not the same thing. Whereas the theologian sets out to explain the content of Christianity, primarily, though not exclusively, for the believing community, the apologist attempts to defeat barriers to the acceptance of Christianity among the unconverted and skeptical. Though its true that in theology Scripture can rightly be presupposed as a valid starting point, in apologetics the truth content of Scripture cannot be but the end goal. And, to the extent that natural theology can move the proverbial ball in that direction, it may be seen as an appropriate endeavor for the Christian apologists. After all, who can seriously cast doubt on the success that William Lane Craig, for example, has had in showing, in part via natural theology, the reasonableness of believing in the existence of God. That said, Henry is correct to assert that the search for religious truth apart from God's special revelation accounts for the presence of pagan religions and philosophies, and leads to the necessity of lost humanity being lighted by the Truth.⁶⁵ But the unregenerate mind's search for

---

62. Henry also warns against the fallacy of equating Jesus with the Bible, or vice versa, as some fundamentalists seemed prone to do, by failing to give full acknowledgement to the varieties of God's revelation. In this, Henry also has his sights set on Barth's three-fold form of the Word of God, though Henry's interaction with this idea seems underdeveloped; *GRA*, 2, 88. Barth develops his three-fold form of the Word of God in *Church Dogmatics* I/1 and I/2, wherein he understands the word of God as the Word preached, written, and revealed. In I/1 he focuses on the first two forms, wherein he expounds upon the commission, theme, judgment and virtue, which lay at center of proclamation. As to the written Word, and a point on which Barth is often misunderstood, he argues that the Word of God becomes in the present, by faith and the Holy Spirit, what it is in the past, that is, the written word of God. He then develops the idea of the Word revealed in I/2, wherein Christ is the supreme revelation of God to whom Scripture points.

63. Ibid., 2:90.

64. See Hume, *Dialogues Concerning Natural Religion*; on Hume's argument regarding the failure of natural theology to produce adequate proof, see Sennett and Groothius, *In Defense of Natural Theology*, 12.

65. Cf. Little, *The Revelation of God Among the Unevangelized* especially chapter 2, "The Role of General Revelation Among the Unevangelized," 7–46.

religious truth cannot be equated with the efforts of Christian apologists who employ natural theology. The two are simply not the same thing.

The Image of God and Evangelism

The biblical concept of the *imago Dei*[66] proves central for Henry in both his theological foundations for evangelism, as well as social concern. As it relates to evangelism though, Henry makes a number of salient points. While admitting that "the Bible does not define for us the precise content of the original *imago*," this in no way necessitates ambiguity. Rather, biblical revelation defines human persons especially in terms of their relation to God, especially as it relates to rational and moral aptitudes. Furthermore, "these are presuppositions not simply of human civilization and culture, but of meaningful and responsible fellowship with God as well."[67] In other words, apart from human beings having rational and moral aptitude, such as provided by the *imago*, their ability to know and love God seems impossible.[68] Henry's view stands in clear distinction from the neoorthodox views of Barth and Brunner. Contra Brunner, Henry argues that the *imago* consists in more than its formal aspect, but also involves a material component as well.[69] As Doyle observes, "the

---

66. Genesis 1:26–27 states that man was made in the image (*tselem*) and likeness (*demuth*) of God. That humans are made in God's image is repeated in Gen. 9:6, wherein God condemns murder as a direct affront to the fact that humans are made in God's image. The image of God, or *imago Dei*, is sometimes considered the quintessential statement in the Bible regarding human nature; see for example, Anderson, *On Being Human*, 69. Here Anderson eloquently describes Gen. 1:26–27 as "the superscription which biblical revelation places over the archway leading to the arena of the human."

67. Ibid., 2:125; cf. Vorster, who observes of Gen. 1:26–28, "the text does not attempt to give an exact content of the image"; Vorster, *Created in the Image of God*, 12.

68. Ibid., 2:125.

69. It was Brunner especially who distinguished between the formal and material aspects of the *imago Dei*. For Brunner, the formal aspect can be equivocated with what modern theologians term the "substantive" aspect of the *imago Dei*. This is the *humanum*, or what constitutes personhood. The material aspect describes what is commonly referred to as the "relational" aspect of the imago. In short, according to Brunner, humans *qua* humans stand, after the fall, as bearers of the divine image only in that they by faith are in relationship with God, and not because there is something in their being that contains the *imago*. Though that may have been true prior to the fall, it no longer is; Brunner, *The Divine Imperative*, 44–51; cf. Ramsey, *Basic Christian Ethics*, 263; Moltmann, *God in Creation*, 230. For discussions in contemporary theology on these substantive vs. relational views of the *imago*, see especially Erickson,

'material' aspect of this knowledge consists in some basic awareness of the existence and character of God, and of our moral accountability before him, as Romans 1:18–25 demonstrates."[70]

Henry's reason for emphasizing both aspects centers on his belief that biblical faith, especially because of the nature of the *imago Dei*, incorporates both knowledge and responsibility in a unified whole: "Man's ethical responses are not disjoined from intellection, however; his comprehension of truth is not sealed off from conscience, nor are his knowledge of the truth and his moral insights divorced from an awareness of answerability to God."[71]

Having pointed out these various interrelated components, Henry goes on to say that "the rational or cognitive aspect has logical priority."[72] Henry grounds this notion in the Johannine prologue, which "declares that man by creation is lighted by the Logos (John 1:4, 9), that is, logically lighted."[73] Paul also in Romans 12:1 presupposes the logical capacity of human beings, when he speaks of the believer's "logical service (literal)" in terms of a living sacrifice. Thus, without this capacity, says Henry, one "could never intelligibly discriminate God from the not-God, right from wrong, truth from untruth."[74] In other words, both of these aspects, the formal and the material, come to bear on the issue of evangelism. As Henry has already noted, general revelation in nature condemns sinful humanity of its guilt. But, special revelation in Scripture, and the faculties humans

---

Christian Theology, 520–31; Grenz, *Theology for the Community of God*, 218–29.

70. Doyle, *Carl Henry*, 56.

71. GRA., 2:125; the moral component Henry bases on the declaration of Gen. 1:31 and the superlative "very good" in reference to the creation of humanity and the implications of this for moral responsibility; ibid., 126; cf., Henry's declaration that "despite man's universal spiritual revolt, the Living God daily confronts the more than two billion persons of our generation as a fundamental fact of their human existence"; Henry, *Evangelicals at the Brink of Crisis*, 113. Or, as Thornbury observes, "When Barth argued that the imago Dei was obliterated by the fall, Henry repeatedly retorted that Barth summarily closed off the conduit through which God speaks to human beings, whether regenerate or not"; Thornbury, *Recovering Classic Evangelicalism*, 55. Thornbury also wisely notes that it is somewhat perplexing, given recent interest in Barth, and furthermore, given Henry's potent critique of Barth's neoorthodoxy, "how Barth's acceptance of Kant's radical phenomenal-noumenal distinction can produce a worldview that simultaneously engages and yet challenges the prevailing secular culture"; ibid.

72. GRA, 2:125.

73. Ibid., 2:126.

74. Ibid.

possess by means of the *imago Dei* provide a sure solution by providing for the reception of God's revelation and "the truth of redemption."[75]

Thus it is the *imago* especially that sets humanity in a position of accountability before God, owing to an innate awareness, "a perception . . . of God in the cosmos." But also in his relation to the rest of humanity, human beings are inherently aware of a certain moral responsibility. "General divine revelation embraces God's disclosure in all of created reality; to this man stands in moment-by-moment relationship alongside direct imago-relationship with the Creator and is thus hedged in on every hand—outside and inside—by God's unyielding claim."[76]

This concept proves a crucial component in understanding the relationship between evangelism and social concern, as the *imago* provides for both the reception of revelation and moral accountability before God. Henry's thoughts here are reflective of Augustine, though Henry does not fully develop the *imago* in the trinitarian sense that Augustine does.[77] Yet Henry did see rightly the connection in Augustine between the *imago Dei* and the Logos doctrine, to which we shall turn shortly, and that these are foundational for human access to God's truth. In the formulation of an evangelical theology of evangelism and social concern, this understanding of the image of God, especially as it relates to the reception of revelation, proves important and provides tremendous weight to the priority argument. Not only are human beings valuable by virtue

75. Ibid., 2:130; cf. 2:133.

76. *GRA*, 2:134; cf. Vorster, *Created in the Image of God*, 12. Vorster points out that this relational aspect of the *imago* both sets forth humanity's relationship to and with God, but also distinguished human beings from God. Human beings stand in unique relation to God as his image bearers, but are not God.

77. Augustine believed humanity created in the image of God is a reference not merely to the one God, but more precisely to the one God in three Persons. One way in which Augustine developed this thought on the trinitarian nature of humanity was by considering the relationship between various aspects of the human mind. The mind, consisting of memory, understanding, and will, reflected the *imago Dei*, in Trinitarian form. Just as the Father, Son, and Holy Spirit, were One, with one mind, so too was the human mind one, though with three distinct aspects. These aspects, though, were each inherently related to one another. Memory forms the central part of the mind because will and understanding are both equally dependent on the preexistence of memory. "Memory" is thus analogous to God. "Understanding" is likened to the Son, who as the living Word brings enlightenment, and "will" finds a correlate in the Spirit, for our will is determined ultimately by love. The Trinitarian likeness in humanity is renewed by God's love being poured into our hearts by the Holy Spirit, and so love forms the core of the spiritual life; see Augustine, *De Trinitate*, books XII–XIV.

of being created in God's image, they are also responsible, and they are responsible because God has both spoken and given them the means to hear and understand.

The Names of God

In Scripture the names of God serve to reveal God's personal nature. This is the essence of Henry's sixth thesis, namely that God's revelation is intensely personal.[78] They declare God's essence and desires, and set Him apart from the pantheon of mysterious and speculative deities of world culture. In connection to Henry's discussion of the *imago Dei*, this constitutes a distinct feature of Hebrew religion, as any graven image could only serve to "denigrate the self-revelation of God who makes himself known by his own personal manifestation in his audibly spoken Word."[79] Thus, the recurrent theme in Hebrew Scripture forbidding the making of graven images stands in contrast to God's self-revealed name and revelatory Word.[80]

The issue of the divine Name in Scripture is no mere trivial point of theology. As Henry points out, it is an essential aspect of understanding God's self-revelation, and thereby to engaging in the theological task. Furthermore, this reality of God's names is necessary for God to be known at all. Wherever God's self-revealed name is not known, God is not known, either.[81] As it relates to the task of evangelism, a few points emerge as pertinent. First, "the divine Name . . . serves as a medium of

---

78. "Its personal originator is God, and persons are its recipients; it involves personal thought and speech as when God addresses Abraham and Moses; sometimes in addition to God's direct address it involves also personal agents as bearers of revelation. Here one thinks especially of the Angel of Yahweh, during the Old Testament era (Gen 16:7; 18:4–4, 22–23; 21:17; 32:24–30; Exod 3:2; 14:19; Isa 63:9), of the inspired prophets and apostles, and supremely of Jesus Christ"; *GRA*, 2:151.

79. Ibid., 2:151–52.

80. *GRA.*, 2:152; cf. Hamilton, who observes that God's prohibition of graven images is meant in Genesis in contras to his revelatory act on Sinai; "Since at that holy mountain God does not manifest himself in an image, images are therefore excluded as means by which God reveals himself"; Hamilton, *Exodus*, 330–31.

81. Ibid., 2:172. In this statement Henry presents a challenge to the idea that God is known apart from his name, as some have claimed. Henry, for instance, cites Catholic scholar Paul Heinisch's proposal that God, owing to his transcendence, be nameless; see Heinisch, *Theology of the Old Testament*, 48; see also Grudem, *Systematic Theology*, 159–60.

revelation of the first magnitude, and denotes the self-revealed God as he desires to be known by his creatures."[82] In other words, there is inherently an evangelistic component to God's revealed names, which express God's desire to be known. God's names reveal God's character, and the names of God can only be known because of God's own self-revelatory acts.

Second, "the variety of names through which God identifies himself give an enlarging revelation of God's nature."[83] Though there is an anthropomorphic nature to God's names, they by no means should be understood as merely human constructions. Rather, God in speaking appropriates human language for his purposes and intents. Most importantly though, God's names reveal "distinct epochs in the progressive manifestation of God's redemptive purposes."[84] Finally, the designation "Yahweh" represents a specific progression of God's self-disclosure, centering on his covenant faithfulness and presence. This is evident in that Yahweh stood in close etymological connection in Hebrew thought to *hayah*, "to be," as in "I shall be to you a God" (Gen 17:7; Exod 3:14).[85] Thus, inherent in the name Yahweh is the notion that the redemption of God is a present tense reality. "The 'glory of Yahweh' comes to dwell in the very midst of Israel."[86]

---

82. *GRA*, 2:173.

83. Ibid., 2:175.

84. Ibid., 2:181.

85. Ibid., 2:221–222; cf. Exod 6:7, Lev 11:45; 26:12; et al. Also, as Knowles has observed, Yahweh is the name used in Scripture for the God of Israel, and Him alone; Knowles, *The Unfolding Mystery of the Divine Name*, 34. And, as Blackburn points out regarding Exodus 3:14ff., the meaning of "I AM" indeed centers on God's presence as guarantee of the success of the Exodus. It is the presence of God, specifically the God of Abraham, Isaac, and Jacob, the God of Moses' ancestors, who is now especially with Moses and the people of Israel. Yet, even this declaration of abiding Presence does not exhaust the meaning of "I AM" but opens it to further unfolding in chapters 5–15 of Exodus; Blackburn, *The God Who Makes Himself Known*, 37–39.

86. *GRA*, 2:223; see also Brueggemann's discussion of Yahweh who both commands and covenants; Brueggemann, *Theology of the Old Testament*, 198–201. Also Hamilton's discussion of Exodus 3:14, "God said to Moses, 'I WILL BE WHO I WILL BE,'" is illuminating. Hamilton observers that the main idea in this passage is God's presence. "That is to say, God will always be there for his people, in a distant Egypt too, even if that divine presence is questioned or imperceptible"; Hamilton, *Exodus*, 66.

Jesus: The Revelation of the New Testament Name

God in the midst of his people finds fullest expression in the NT, in the Person and work of Jesus. Citing Raymond Abba, Henry points out that the prominent feature of the NT as it concerns the Divine name is the interchangeability of Jesus and God. As Abba says, "prophesying or speaking in the name of God becomes prophesying or speaking in the name of Jesus."[87] In addition, John's Gospel especially associates Jesus with the "I am" of the OT (esp. John 8:28; 13:19). At several points, the glory only ascribed to God in the OT is ascribed to Jesus, as in John 12:23, 28; and 17:5. Thus, "according to John's Gospel Jesus Christ's mission in the world was to make the Name of God known (17:6), and this mission he fulfilled (17:26)."[88] Furthermore, "God with us," which is declared emphatically through the prophetic declaration of the OT (e.g., Isa 7:14) and at the outset of the NT (Matt 1:23), rings aloud with the truth of Yahweh: "*Present is what I am*.[89] The Gospels offer us, in a word, Yahweh unchangeably

---

87. Cited in Henry, *GRA*, 2:226.

88. Ibid., 2:227; as Köstenberger observes, "According to John's Gospel . . . God is characterized by Jesus, and once one has understood the gospel's characterization of Jesus, one has understood its characterization of God. Nevertheless, Jesus and God—the Father—are separate and so must be considered individually"; Köstenberger, *The Theology of John's Gospel and Letters*, 361. Also, as Dodd says, Jesus' revelation of the Name of God is "associated with Christ's enunciation of the ἐγώ εἰμι . . . which is bound up with ἐγω καὶ ὁ πατηρ ἕν ἐσμεν"; Dodd, *The Interpretation of the Fourth Gospel*, 417.

89. Cf. France's helpful summary of the immediate and messianic understandings of the Isaiah text, where France says, "Matthew's typological interest leads him rather to find patterns which will recur repeatedly throughout God's dealings with his people. In this case, he has good warrant for taking the prophecy concerning Immanuel as having a relevance beyond its undoubted immediate aim, for the name Immanuel will occur again in Isa 8:8 as that of the one to whom the land of Judah belongs, and its meaning will be developed in 8:10, 'for God is with us.' Moreover, the prophecy in 7:14 of the birth to the 'house of David' (Isa 7:13) of a child with so extraordinary an honorific title prepares us for the even more remarkable description in 9:6-7 of a child who is to be born 'for us,' and whose multiple and still more extravagant title marks him out not only as the Messiah of the line of David but also as 'Mighty God, Everlasting Father.' The theme will be taken up again in 11:1-5 with the prophecy of the spiritually-endowed 'shoot from the stump of Jesse.' These last two passages would have been recognized then, as they still are today, as messianic prophecies, and it seems likely that Isaiah's thought has moved progressively from the virgin's child, "God with us," to whom the land of Judah belongs, to these fuller expressions of the Davidic hope. If then Isa 7:14 is taken as the opening of what will be the developing theme of a wonder-child throughout Isaiah 7–11, it can with good reason be suggested that it points beyond the immediate political crisis of the eighth century B.C., not only in Matthew's typological scheme but also in Isaiah's intention"; France, *Matthew*,

faithful to his covenant engagement, the present I am, the incarnate God."[90] This carries with it, also, an important evangelistic reality: "The three-year public ministry transforms claims for the Word become flesh into a global message, God with us incarnate and crucified and risen. The resurrection and exaltation effect the personal presence of the crucified Jesus in a more permanent way—Christ in us."[91]

Jesus. "The name Jesus (from Jehoshua-Joshua) means 'he whose salvation is Yahweh' (or in brief, "God's Salvation)." Citing Longenecker, Henry observes that Peter's sermon in Acts (4:12; RSV) captures well the significance of this, by emphasizing the definite article that appears in the Greek text: "there is *the Salvation* in no one else."[92] Thus, the very name *Jesus* underscores that God has offered salvation only through Christ.

Messiah. Henry further articulates the importance of the divine name by turning to the term Messiah. When the NT community referred to Jesus as Messiah they had in mind the same usage as in the LXX, which also used *Christos* for OT references to the promised Son of David.[93]

Son of Man. Though other "Son" designations certainly appear (e.g., Son of David, Son of God), throughout his life and ministry, Jesus' preferred title or name was Son of Man. This phrase "occurs sixty-nine times in the Synoptics, twelve times in John, once each in Acts and Hebrews, and twice in Revelation." Eighty-one times the designation is located in

---

Accordance, ed., n.p.; cf also Keener's commentary on Matt 1:20–21; Keener, *Matthew*, 63.

90. *GRA*, 2:228.

91. Ibid.

92. Ibid., 2:230; cf. Keener, *Acts* 2:1150–52. Especially important to our present discussion is Keener's observation that despite contemporary objections to the soteriological exclusivism of Christianity, Luke makes it quite clear that Jesus alone is able to save sinful humanity; ibid; also, Calvin's observation is likewise potent, wherein he paraphrases Luke, saying that Luke's point is that "since salvation is in God's power only, he will not have us partakers of it by any other way than that we seek it from Christ alone"; Calvin, *The Acts of the Apostles*, 118.

93. *GRA*, 2:231–232; The word/title Χριστός appears over 500 times in the NT; in the NASB95, six times it is translated as Messiah (Matt 1:1, 16–17; 2:4; John 1:41; 4:25). Also, as Henry observes, in popular Jewish thinking, "messiah" referred not to the concept of God's divine intervention, but rather the notion of agent featured most prominently, and often in connection with political insurrection. Perhaps because of this, Jesus waits until after his resurrection before explicitly linking his role as Messiah to the OT background (Luke 24:26, 46). Whereas the Gospels apply the term to Jesus, it becomes in the Epistles almost equivalent to a proper name, thus *Jesus Christ*; ibid. For a contemporary study the term "Messiah", see Porter, *The Messiah in the Old and New Testaments*.

the Gospels and each time coming from Jesus himself.[94] As Henry observes, following the usage in Daniel 7, Jesus' use of the term "combined in himself as God's agent the emphasis on supernatural intervention and divine unction."[95] Plus, there seems to be an aspect of the usage that includes the notion of community. This is evident in that the interpretation of Dan 7:13 occurs in 7:18, and refers to not one individual but to the *saints*. That is, in some ways, this designation seems to anticipate the disciples and thereby the church, or the community of those centered around the Promised One.[96]

Lord. Whereas Jesus' preferred the self-designation *Son of Man*, his followers preferred Lord. That this term was not unknown outside Christianity in the ancient world, possibly accounts for its widespread use by Gentile Christians. But this generic usage cannot be the only background, and the use of this in the LXX for the name of God must also be considered significant, as it uses *kurios* (Lord) for both Adonai and Yahweh. In the NT, the term occurs both as simply an informal address, meaning "master," or "sir," and in the technical sense as referring to one equal to Yahweh.[97]

Son of God. The designation Son of God for Jesus occurs roughly eighty times in the NT. "In the Synoptic Gospels the term is almost invariably used to emphasize the unity of purpose and function of the Father

---

94. Ibid., 2:233.

95. Ibid., 2:234.

96. As Henry points out, in the OT the title "Son of Man" is used in three distinct ways: for mankind as whole (e.g., Isa 56:2; Jer 49:19; Ps 8:4; 80:17; etc.); as a formal address by Ezekiel (in over one hundred passages, e.g., 2:1); for the saints of God (Dan 7:18); regarding the latter, Henry's point is that Son of Man of Dan 7:13–14, described as one "coming" and to whom it is "given" is later (7:18) interpreted as "the saints"; *GRA*, 2:233–35; also as Bird says, "Daniel 7 sets forth a well-worn biblical pattern of suffering and vindication situated in corporate terms, where the Son of Man's exaltation and enthronement can be understood as the vindication of the saints"; *Evangelical Theology*, 262.

97. Specifically, Henry, citing Taylor (*The Names of Jesus*, 1953) mentions that the term is used by Matthew only once in the technical sense of the resurrected Lord of life (Matt 28:6), whereas Luke uses it in this sense twelve times (cf. 11:39), Acts more than one hundred times, and Paul over two hundred times; *GRA*, 2:236. Also especially significant are that the use of *kurios* (or some form of) by the Palestinian church, as is evident in Peter's sermon at Pentecost (Acts 2:36), shows that this name was common among both the Greco-Roman churches, as evident by Phil 2:6–11, as well as by Jewish converts; *GRA*, 2, 237.

and the Son."⁹⁸ It especially highlights Jesus' "obedience in the mission of divine revelation and redemption." In every occurrence in John, Acts, and the rest of the NT the emphasis is on the "unique functional relation of Jesus to the Father."⁹⁹

The names of God emphasize several important points relative to the subject of evangelism and social concern. First, as we have seen, the Divine Names from Yahweh to Jesus, underscore both God's self-revelatory nature, and redemptive self-initiative. God desires to be known, to restore fallen humanity to relational knowledge of himself, and his acts in redemptive history are meant for that purpose. But not only this, according to God's self-revelation, it is through "The Salvation," as Jesus the Christ, that constitutes the only means by which humanity may come to God.¹⁰⁰ This stands in sharp contrast to Karl Rahner's "anonymous Christians," as well as inclusivistic approaches to other faiths, such as that of Clark Pinnock.¹⁰¹ Therefore, if God's own self-designation emphasizes God's redemptive purposes, then any theological formulation of evangelism and social concern that takes seriously the doctrine of God must take this into account. Also, the revelatory nature of God's Names underscore the exclusivistic claims of God as the sole means of salvation, and furthermore emphasize the redemptive thrust of revelation.

---

98. Ibid., 2:240.

99. Ibid, 2:240. In support, Henry cites Mark 13:32; John 20:31 as evidence that the disciples used this term because Jesus himself used it; that is, they did not merely invent it nor were they using it in the more generic sense used by Christians of themselves, as sons of God. Plus, Jesus uses the self-designation Son four times in the Synoptics. Also, Matt 11:27 and Luke 10:22 are supposed Q passages in which Jesus refers to himself as Son. In addition, Jesus use of "my Father's house" (Luke 2:49) attests to Jesus self conscious unique relation to God the Father. The idea Henry is getting at is that even though each of these examples don't always use the phrase "Son of God," the idea is the same when Jesus speaks of himself as Son in relation to the Father; *GRA*, 2, 241–42.

100. This idea also stands in stark contrast, for example, to the pluralism of John Hicks; although, admittedly, given Hicks ambivalence toward Scripture, he's not likely to be persuaded by the argument; see Hicks, "Pluralism," under chapter one.

101. For Rahner's articulation of the idea of anonymous Christians, see Rahner, *Theological Investigations*, 283; Pinnock is somewhat more ambiguous about the fate of adherents to non-Christian religions, though still advocating for the possibility of grace at work within those religions, especially in a preparatory way for the Gospel; see Pinnock, "Inclusivism," chapter two; see also Moore's critique of Pinnock's inclusivism in Moore, "Leftward to Scofield," 436.

Disclosure of God's Eternal Secret

Henry's eighth thesis in *GRA* focuses on the reality that Christ is the climax of God's special revelation, and that "in Jesus Christ, the source and content of revelation converge and coincide."[102] Contra Greco-Roman usage of the term "mystery"—as in the mystery religions—to represent knowledge only accessible to select religious initiates, and equally contrary to contemporary usage focusing on "an insoluble enigma," the Bible gives the term "mystery" a unique meaning. Specifically, "it designates what is no longer concealed because God has now revealed it, and has done so for all at a given point in time."[103] Thus, mystery belongs to God and it has been God's prerogative to make known what had previously been unknowable.

Though uncommon in the OT, and found only in Aramaic portions of Daniel (2:18–19, 27–30, 47; 4:9), the NT uses the Greek term *mustērion* over thirty times.[104] Furthermore, the NT usage cannot be attributed to borrowing the concept from the mystery religions, for NT consistently uses the term in relation to what God has sovereignly made known and "published to all mankind." As S. S. Smalley has observed, there is a close affinity then between *mustērion* and *apokalypsis*, which refers to a "temporarily hidden eventuality."[105] More importantly, though, it is revelation that unveils the mystery. In explanation, Henry cites Bornkamm: "Hence the mystery does not disclose itself. At the appointed time it is in free grace declared by God himself to those who are selected and blessed by Him."[106] Or as Henry puts it, "the mystery itself as unveiled secret is revelationally disclosed (1 Cor 15:51)."[107] Henry then describes the nature of this revelational disclosure, following Smalley, in the following terms. First, it refers to the content of the Good News (Eph 6:19), centered on Christ (Col 2:2), decreed from eternity (1 Cor 2:7), but

---

102. *GRA.*, 3:9.

103. Ibid., 3:9.

104. For example, Matt 13:11; Mark 4:11; Luke 8:10; Rom 11:25; 16:25; 1 Cor 2:7; 4:1; 13:2; 14:2; 15:51; Eph 1:9; 3:3–4, 9; 5:32; 6:19; Col 1:26–27; 2:2; 4:3; 2 Thess 2:7; 1 Tim 3:9, 16; Rev 1:20; 10:7; 17:5, 7; cf. "μυστήριον" in *NIDNTT*, wherein it is shown that the term in the NT is especially Christocentric.

105. Ibid., 3:11; Smalley, "Mystery," Accordance ed., n.p.

106. Ibid., 3:11; see Bornkamm, "Mustērion," *TDNT*, 4:802–28.

107. Ibid., 3:11; cf. Fee, *The First Epistle to the Corinthians*, 800. Fee points out that Paul's emphasis in this passage is on the necessity of all "to be transformed so as to bear the likeness of the man of heaven"; ibid., 801.

hidden from understanding apart from supernatural Divine disclosure (1 Cor 2:8; Rom 8:25), historically manifest (Eph 1:9; 3:3–4) in the "fullness of time" (Gal 4:4; KJV).

Especially important for Henry is that this revelation cannot be known, according to Scripture (cf. Eph 3:3–5), apart from God's divine special revelation through the apostles and prophets. "The truths of God are not a prerogative of human knowing but belong to the 'deep things' of the Deity who reveals them optionally."[108] As Paul makes clear in 1 Corinthians, the content of God's mystery is both divinely determined and divinely revealed (see 1 Cor 2:7–9). This forms the basis of church's proclamational mandate. "Preaching carries to those who are strangers to God the already given content of divine revelation."[109] That content has been revealed especially in Christ. "The secret counsel or mystery of God's will in the created cosmos and in human history is therefore openly published in the manifestation of Jesus of Nazareth."[110] Furthermore, this message resounds with both future and present tense demands.[111]

In keeping with Reformed theology, Henry carefully affirms within this context the Calvinistic notion of predestination and election. "The eternal election of believers is experientially affected in the personal reception and appropriation of the now openly revealed mystery."[112] At the heart of this Divine mystery, is the reality of "Christ in you" (Col 1:27), a reality in which Jews and Gentiles are made one in Christ. Of this inconceivable reality, Paul attributes to himself the role of herald, or proclaimer.[113] Henry summarizes Paul's primary redemptive emphases:

---

108. *GRA*, 3:13.

109. Ibid., 3:14.

110. Ibid; as Thornbury observes of Henry on this point, the testimony of Scripture is such that the mystery of God is overcome only by God's acts of self-revelation. Thus, "the divine mystery should not terminate in apophatism"; Thornbury, *Recovering Classic Evangelicalism*, 67.

111. Ibid; cf. Rom 12:1, 11; 1 Cor 12:15; Eph 6:7; Phil 2:10; Col 2:6; 3:23.

112. Ibid., 3:17.

113. As Bruce observes of Col 1:27; "Christ is himself 'the mystery of God' (Col 2:2); in him the *deus absconditus* has become the *deus revelatus*. But Paul's special stewardship of this mystery involves its disclosure to Gentiles. 'Christ is in *you*,' he assures his Colossian readers, 'Christ is in you (even in you Gentiles) as your hope of glory.' The phrase 'in you' might mean 'in your midst' (as a community) or 'within you' (as individuals). Neither sense should be excluded, but the thought of Christ as indwelling individual believers is completely in line with Pauline thought"; Bruce, *The Epistles to the Colossians, to Philemon, and to the Ephesians*, Accordance ed., n.p.

The redemption of sinners has its ground in the incarnate and crucified Jesus as the promised Messiah, the saving knowledge of God is extended to Gentiles in eager worldwide invitation, and the Risen Christ indwells each and every believer. While these truths and privileges were unknown equally to Jew and Gentile, they are now the glorious good news openly proclaimed to all (Col 1:28).[114]

In other words, only through proclamation is the divinely revealed secret of God's redemptive plan known. As it relates to evangelism and social concern, Henry's statements raise an important issue. Does not the fact that the proclamation of Scripture is required in declaring the once hidden mysteries of God, now revealed in and through Christ and proclaimed in the past through the prophets and apostles, necessarily lead to the priority of evangelism? This seems to be obviously true. If it is, then to describe evangelism and social concern as partners, or as "two blades of a pair of scissors, or the two wings of a bird," applies to them an equality that simply does not cohere well with the testimony of Scripture.[115] Christianity exists as revealed religion and it is through the preaching task of the church that the precise content of that revelation is made known. As such, no other task of the church can be described as fully equal.

The Content of the Gospel

As part of thesis eight in *GRA* titled, "God's Personal Incarnation," Henry addresses the content of the Gospel. He begins by observing that Scripture is quite clear on what is contained in the Christian good news: "the gospel is the good news of God's merciful rescue of an otherwise doomed

---

114. Ibid.

115. Stott, *Making Christ Known*, 182; cf. Escobar, *The New Global Mission*, 153. This equality in nature was one of three ways of relating evangelism and social concern put forth by the Grand Rapids Consultation (CRESR) of 1982, the other two being "a bridge to evangelism," and "a partner to evangelism." Stott's commentary notes that there was wide disagreement on this issue prior to the consultation, as evidenced in the papers that were written and distributed before hand. Thus, these views likely represent a lack of consensus among those gathered; see Stott, *Making Christ Known*, 169–73. This is not to argue for an unqualified priority in every concrete situation, but to observe, even as Sider has, that "evangelism has a certain logical priority"; Sider, *Good News and Good Works*, 170.

humanity through the mediatorial life and work of Jesus Christ."[116] Elsewhere, Henry says:

> the gospel is good news about what God is like and what he has done. It is supremely about Christ, who made the restoration of sinners to fellowship with the living God possible. The gospel is about what Jesus did, not just what he taught. It is the good news that, though we deserve divine repudiation and punishment, God offers the guiltiest of us sinners forgiveness for Christ's sake. That is the unchanging gospel, and a Christianity that dilutes this content is not worth its weight in words.[117]

Henry, as already pointed out in chapter one, also argues that the word *euaggelion* or "gospel" was used outside the Bible in a general sense for joyful news, such as when the Greeks used it to refer to a political or military victory, or when the Romans employed it to announce the birth of a royal child. However, it took on a much different meaning in the ministry of the OT prophet Isaiah. Isaiah used the cognate *euaggaelizesthai* ("to announce good news"), specifically to refer to a theology of salvation. As such, "the prophetic good news revolves around Yahweh's rule of righteousness, salvation, and peace. And the prophet's divine call is to proclaim this good news to a desperately needy people."[118] The issue of proclamation as it relates to evangelism cannot be overstated, as this is precisely one of the points where the prioritism-holism debate divides. For Henry, evangelism is proclamation, even though this proclamation has social implications. "A major consequence of this of this proclamation (Isa 61) is the blessing and liberation of the hungry, the poor, the suffering, and the oppressed."[119] Henry's emphasis on social concern as a consequence of evangelism is fundamental to his approach.[120]

The NT presents the good news always in the context of God's gracious initiative. As Henry notes, "Paul uses the noun gospel (*euaggelion*),

---

116. *GRA.*, 3:63.

117. Henry, *New Strides of Faith*, 95.

118. *GRA*, 3:62.

119. Ibid. Obviously, given that *euaggelion* is Greek and the OT was written primarily in Hebrew, Henry means to refer to the LXX in this case, the Scriptures used by Jesus and his contemporaries. Others, though, such as Orlando Costas, see social concern, or what he calls "transformation," as part of evangelism; cf. Costas, *Liberating News*, 30. While undoubtedly theologians from the global south such as Costas do indeed help those from the west to see past certain cultural blinders, it might also be added that they too stand to benefit from dialogue with others for the same reasons.

120. See also Stott, *Making Christ Known*, 181.

and everywhere the subject matter is unmistakably clear." The primary, though not exhaustive, emphasis of the NT use of the term refers especially to "God's offer of forgiveness of sins and new life on the ground of the substitutionary death and victorious resurrection of the divinely incarnate Redeemer. This one mediator, moreover, now exalted, rules already as the supernatural source of the church's continuing life and as the invincible Lord."[121]

What especially makes this news "good" is not that God judges humanity, nor that Jesus is God's agent of judgment, though both of these are certainly true and part of the "historic Judeo-Christian theology." That part of the message which is especially "good" is that Yahweh "takes up in himself the cause of the oppressed and the aggrieved, God by his grace tempers judgment with mercy toward the penitent and believing." Again, Henry's emphasis here lies in God's initiative over against human effort or achievement.[122]

In inaugurating his Kingdom, Jesus has stayed the coming judgment of God. Now is the time to repent and believe (Mark 1:14–15). In "applying to himself the Isaian prophecy of liberation" (Luke 4:18–19; Isa 61:1–2), Jesus omits the declaration of coming judgment, thereby emphasizing that now is the time of mercy.[123] In Jesus, the Kingdom has come. "The Word incarnate actualizes the eschatological good news in his personal being."[124] The response of Jesus' followers then is to "proclaim and exhibit" the Messianic Kingdom. However, Henry also warns against presuming against the evidence of Scripture that God's judgment lies solely in the future. "Jesus Christ, the divinely appointed agent in the final judgment, is even now active in the rise and fall of nations, including modern China, England, Germany, Israel, Korea, Russia and the United

---

121. GRA, 3:64. In support of this, Henry cites 1 Cor 15:1–5; Rom 1:3–4; and Gal 1:6–9; 4:4, while also noting that none of these passages exhausts the content of the Gospel, and each may emphasize different aspects.

122. GRA, 3:65. In Henry's reference to "the cause of the oppressed" he seems to have in mind both the oppression from sin and from the causes of human suffering that afflict the poor and needy. Indeed, in biblical theology, these two are inseparable in that the former gives birth to the latter.

123. Ibid., 3:65–66.

124. Ibid., 3:66; As Henry also says, "Jesus proclaims the good news of the Kingdom of God, his miraculous signs exhibit the healing of individuals and of peoples as part of God's sovereign rule and redemptive plan (Matt 4:23; 9:35; Luke 8:1; 16:16). In view of the very imminence of the kingdom, he exhorts multitudes to repentance and faith"; ibid.

States." Thus, the end-times judgment serves merely as the final step of what has already begun (John 12:31; 16:11).[125]

Henry's reference to Luke 4:18–19, above, enters a discussion that lies at the center of the evangelism-social concern debate.[126] Before looking at that debate in more detail, it will be helpful here to clarify Henry's emphasis. When Henry refers to the "Isaian prophecy of liberation," he clearly means this in a redemptive sense, and not in the way the word is used in liberation theology, which emphasizes God's so-called "preferential option for the poor." As we have seen, Henry understands the essence of the Gospel to be salvation first and transformation second as a consequence of the received Good News.

Darrel Bock interprets Luke 4:18–19 similarly when he says that the passage offers no blanket endorsement of poverty nor does it provide any political manifesto. Rather, "the poor" in mind are those whom are spiritually poor and aware of their need of God. This can and does often entail economic poverty, but this need not be so. Joel B. Green also points out regarding this passage that the Luke 4:18–19 reference to "release" especially refers to those in need of release from sin, even though economic deprivation and the effects of sin are never far from view.[127] In other words, there is an implied close association between material poverty and the recognition of one's need of God. Yet, one must be careful to not overlook the aspect of spiritual poverty, as some have done as it relates to this passage.[128] Plus, as Sharon Ringe observes, the Year of Jubilee, which stands behind the Isaiah 61 text, came to mean in Israel's religion not actual economic liberation, as intended in Leviticus 19, but rather the prophetic call of renewed allegiance to God's reign.[129] Thus, Jesus' citation of the passage focuses on the proclamation of God's now dawning reign and the opportunity of release from sin.[130] So when David Bosch claims regarding Luke-Acts that salvation is, in part, "release from every kind of bondage," his failure to distinguish the salvific, redemptive

---

125. Ibid., 3:67.

126. For example, see Litfin, who questions whether this passage ought to be a basis for evangelical social concern; *Word versus Deed*, chapter thirteen, under "Luke 4:16–21"; Sider, *Good News and Good Works*, 49; Costas, *Christ Outside the Gate*, 45; Little, *Polemic Missiology*, chapter one.

127. Bock, *Luke*, 89; Green, "Good News to Whom?," 73.

128. See, for example, the liberation theology perspective of de Santa Ana, *Good News to the Poor*, 13–17.

129. Ringe, *Luke*, 68.

130. Cf. Just, *Luke 1:1—9:50*, 190.

intent of Luke 4 as primary is problematic. One can agree with Bosch that salvation has both vertical (God-ward) and horizontal (social) implications, but simultaneously one must also insist that the vertical dimension of salvation takes precedent, or it would not be salvation at all.[131]

In light of these realities that constitute the core of the Gospel, Henry then expounds what he believes to be the "crucial turning points of the scriptural good news."[132] By "turning points" it seems that Henry has in mind the contours of the Gospel beyond what might be considered the core. But the way in which Henry presents these aspects, though, would appear to indicate that he by no means considers these facets optional, but rather extensions of those core elements. These "turning points" then bring a fuller understanding to what is meant by the "good news." Among these turning points are the demand for justice,[133] the centrality of Jesus to human history as Messiah, Servant, and Judge, that fact that the Gospel is availed for every race and ethnicity, the requirement of conformity to the image of Christ (1 John 3:2), the overturning of sin's oppressive effects, the ethical demands of Kingdom participation (John 3:21),[134] the church's central role in God's redemptive plan, the believer's responsibility to work through civil authority for the establishment of God's just demands, and the offer of hope in the midst of pending Divine wrath.[135]

Though the phrase "turning points" is admittedly vague, and one wishes Henry had been more articulate in stating his meaning here, the fact that he delineates the core verbal aspects of the Gospel message from its implications in the life of the believer is helpful. Looking closely though, one notices that Henry has essentially distinguished, as did

---

131. Bosch, *Mission as Transformation*, 107.

132. GRA, 3:67.

133. See Isa 1:23; 27–28; 3:12–14; 5:19–20; 29:9–11.

134. Ibid., Henry echoes this same idea of necessary social concern within the priority of proclamation when he declares, the church "is called above all to proclaim the truth and the righteousness of God, to proclaim on the public scene what God says and wills." He adds, when the church does engage in "a moment" of social protest, then also "let the church bells ring to remind the community that forgiveness of sins and the offer of a new life is sounded by the churches." Furthermore, if the call to social justice is all the church has to offer, "where in that is Good News for sinful men?" Henry, "The Tensions between Evangelism and the Christian Demand for Social Justice"; see also Henry, *A Plea for Evangelical Demonstration*, 58–60; here Henry observes that the early church understood that though it had a horizontal fellowship component, its primary identity was derived from the unique relationship it had with the risen and exalted Lord.

135. GRA, 3:67–74.

C. H. Dodd, the Gospel message (*kerygma*) from the Gospel demands (*didachē*).[136] As Dodd says of the early church, "while the church was concerned to hand on the teaching of the Lord, it was not by this that it made converts. It was by *kerygma*, says Paul, not by *didaché*, that it pleased God to save men."[137] By similarly distinguishing, as does Henry, the message from its demands, he again finds valid support for the priority of evangelism, because regeneration must precede the ethical demands of the Gospel. Therefore, Costas is simply wrong to say that there can be no differentiating between the Gospel's message and its effects. Furthermore, to do so should not be classified as "dichotomizing" if in fact the two are distinguished in Scripture, as Dodd has shown.[138] Plus, others who seem to blur the line between the Gospel and its effects are guilty of confusing evangelism with repentance. To correctly say that repentance requires the performance of Gospel deeds is ultimately a matter of soteriology, and not proclamation, *per se*.[139] The point here is to simply say that evangelism may be seen as one component part of a biblical soteriology, and so too can social concern. But this does not mean they carry the same weight, as it were, within an evangelical theology. That which leads to salvation must logically be of greater import than that which is its direct result, even though lesser in importance does not mean unimportant, or non-essential.

Jesus and the Word

Next, Henry turns his attention to the question of what precisely it means when the NT equates Jesus with the Word. To answer this, Henry avers that against contemporary tendencies to look for the answer in Greco-Roman philosophical musings, one must understand Jesus as Word against the OT background of prophetic utterance. "Deep parallels with Judaism underlie Jesus' life and work, and his teaching is set in the thought-world of the Old Testament writers rather than in any other."[140] Not only that,

---

136. Dodd, *Apostolic Preaching and Its Development*, 13–38; cited in Stott, *Christian Mission*, 2008b, 67–68.

137. Dodd, *The Apostolic Preaching and Its Development*, 8.

138. Costas, *Christ Outside the Gate*, 38.

139. For example, C. René Padilla in his discussion of evangelism and repentance ethics seems to minimize the distinction between *kerygma* and metanōia. Though they are certainly related, they are not the same; see Padilla, *Mission Between the Times*, 19.

140. *GRA*, 3:77.

though, Jesus surely also moved beyond the OT understanding of Messiah, bringing about his "distinct interpretation."[141]

Regarding the NT understanding of Jesus as the Word of God incarnate, Henry says this emphasis is especially important, and as such, points out several scriptural realities that underlie this teaching. First, it is by the Word of God that believers are "spiritually and morally" reborn (1 Peter 1:23; James 1:18, 21). Second, Jesus explicitly connected the Spirit's life-giving work to his own words (John 6:63). Third, Jesus' words are supremely authoritative, even calling the dead to account (John 6:63). Fourth, "the words and works of Jesus Christ are creatively and cohesively interrelated," as the One who speaks creation into existence and sustains it "by his word of power," (Heb 1:3; cf. John 1:3). Finally, he is the eternal word of God who will judge all humanity (Rev 10:13).[142]

Henry's point here is to emphasize that Jesus is not merely a form or mode of divine communication, but is uniquely God "communicating to man directly in and through his incarnation and the word of revelation." To bring the point home, Henry cites Bonhoeffer: "If Jesus is the Christ, the Word of God, then I am not primarily called to emulate him; I am encountered in his work as one who could not possibly do this work myself."[143] Therefore as it concerns church proclamation, the goal is not primarily to advance a great moral agenda, but to bring every individual to a moment of crisis:

> The proclamation of the Word of God—that is, of the revealed truth of the Gospel centering on the incarnate, crucified and risen Logos—therefore propels every hearer into a crisis of decision, since it calls for an immediate verdict on redemption by Jesus Christ that leads either to or away from eternal life in the present and to the future eschatological salvation or damnation.[144]

Also, particularly relevant to the issue of evangelism, is the fact that, as Henry observes, Jesus' status as incarnate Word, gives tremendous authority, finality, and thereby urgency to his own preaching. One sees

---

141. Ibid. As Henry notes, Jesus in many respects moved beyond OT expectations and exceeded them, precludes the notion that his followers conjured up his Messianic status based solely upon their expectations. N. T. Wright makes much the same argument in Wright, *The Resurrection of the Son of God*.

142. GRA, 3:76.

143. GRA, 3:76; see Bonhoeffer, *Christ the Center*.

144. Ibid., 3:79.

this especially in Jesus' avoidance of the term "thus saith the Lord," as was common among other prophetic utterances. Instead Jesus spoke saying "but I say unto you." In addition, Jesus' uniquely used the Aramaic term "amen." The predominant Jewish usage of the term centered on a congregational response after a prayer or reading, and uttered by someone other than the speaker. But Jesus used the term in reference to his own words, thereby underscoring his unique authority. Thus, on the basis of this authority, Jesus calls for full commitment (Matt 7:28–29; 22:37).[145]

In his discussion on Jesus and the Word, Henry articulates yet another theological foundation that adds weight to his priority model. To describe Jesus as the Word, is to underscore the especially verbal nature of his mission, as alone Jesus makes possible the knowledge of God necessary for salvation, and that knowledge is conveyed primarily in verbal form.[146] In short, it is the words of Jesus alone, not his actions disconnected from his words, that are capable of calling sinners to repentance. Henry will continue to develop this idea as he expounds on the Logos doctrine.

The Biblically Attested Logos

After affirming that Jesus is the Word incarnate, and as such the appearance of divine revelation in the flesh, the truth of God in human form, Henry turns his attention to what this then means for the Bible as God's Word. In this, Henry is especially keen to refute the views of Barth, Brunner and Bultmann that tend away from understanding the Bible *per se* as God's Word, and also thereby diminish the importance and necessity of propositional statements derived from Scripture. Against this, Henry points out that these theologians take their starting point from the Johannine *proposition* that Jesus is the Logos of God in the flesh (John 1:14), and then oddly go on to deny the validity of propositional statements, apparently oblivious to the contradiction.[147] By emphasizing that the

---

145. Ibid., 3:80–82. In much of the remainder of this chapter, Henry addresses with a typically mastery of the relevant literature, the oddity of scholarly consensus that simultaneously upholds Jesus' use of the introductory formula, but denies the words of Jesus that often follow. "We seem—according to this verdict—to have the *ipsissima verba* of Jesus only in his prefatory introduction, while what he truly taught is almost wholly lost to us in his original wording"; GRA, 3:83.

146. Cf. Gundry, *Jesus the Word*, 54–55.

147. GRA, 3:164–65.

Word became flesh, Scripture thereby places prime importance on God's revelation as communicative action.

The Logos and the OT. Underlying the NT concept of *logos*, is the Hebrew OT term *dabar*. More specifically:

> The term *dabar*, or "word," focuses on the conceptual background or meaning through which an event becomes intelligible; it seems originally to have had associations with the "holiest of all" and the "back of the temple," hence the etymology suggests the background of a matter or meaning. Additionally, *dabar* focuses on a dynamic manifestation or life-giving power that creatively achieves its ends in history. The Old Testament uses the term dianoetically, that is, in respect to a nous, mind, whereby the inner reality is grasped, and dynamically, that is in respect to the effective energy of that reality.[148]

In addition, a few OT passages explicitly link the divine word with divine truth, in a way that emphasizes the divine origin of God's Word (see Ps 119:160; 2 Sam 23:2; Num 24:4, 16). Thus, "the Old Testament portrays the Word of God as an intelligible Word audibly conveyed to chosen spokesmen as a means of blessing to mankind, visible insofar as the divine message is written, and anticipating in God's fullness of time the enfleshed Word or visibly manifested Logos."[149]

The Logos in the NT. The NT presents Christ as the fulfillment and enlargement of OT divine revelation (John 1:17). While the NT at times uses logos in a more generic sense of "word," one must not overlook the distinctive function of the concept that reflects the OT concept of *dabar*. "The New Testament uses the term additionally of the enfleshed Word and also to summarize the theme and content of the major New Testament events, centrally the message of the incarnate Christ."[150]

Especially important, is that "Jesus' work consisted largely of a spoken message, and this message the evangelists depict in terms of both *logos* and *rhema* (cf. Luke 9:44–45; Matt 26:75; Mark 14:72)." But Jesus'

---

148. Ibid., 3:173–174; cf. the phrase "dabar YHWH," or "the word of the Lord," "offers clear evidence of an established theological conviction" that Israel's God should be especially understood as a God who speaks; *NIDOTTE*.

149. *GRA*, 3:175.

150. Ibid., 3:177; for a history of interpretation and for claims to Hellenistic or Platonic backgrounds, plus NT usage, see D. H. Johnson, who concludes that John takes the meaning of logos from the OT background, especially the Hebrew *dabar*, and as referring especially to God's word that brings forth creation, as well as judgment, renewal, and redemption. Also, the term, as such, emphasizes the evangelistic thrust of the Fourth Gospel; "Logos," Accordance ed., n.p.

words never stood apart from his actions. "Jesus Christ is at once in his very own person the Word and Act of God, dramatically exhibiting the unity of God's revelation."[151]

> Jesus is indeed identified as the proclaimer of the Word (Mark 2:2; 4:33; Luke 5:1; Acts 10:36), but he is usually identified far more profoundly because his mission is so much more comprehensive than simply preaching the divine Word. The prophets and apostles relay what they have heard, or seen and heard. But Jesus' words and works together embody the creative Word of God. In him the Word of God is both audible and visible.[152]

In fact, this coming together of word and event constitutes a distinct feature of Hebrew-Christian thought. What is especially important in the unison of these things is their relation to the creative force of God's word.[153] Thus, as it relates to proclamation in early Christianity:

> In all the apostolic writings the Word is the message about Jesus. Primitive Christianity was fully aware that proclamation of what had occurred in the person of Jesus of Nazareth is, indeed, preaching of the Word of God, and that human reception of that Word involves faith in Jesus Christ. Ministers of the good news stressed not simply what Jesus said about who he is and what he did and does. The Word, as Paul wrote the Colossians, is the mystery formerly hidden but now disclosed, Christ Jesus himself, the hope of coming glory (1:25-28). The Word that God has spoken is Christ enfleshing the Father's will for the redemption of lost

---

151. *GRA*, 3:178. Cf. Mk. 1:25; 2:10; 4:39; Luke 7:14–16. On the difference/similarity between *rhema* and *logos*, see also Clark, *The Johannine Logos*, 38–46. Clark points out that logos often refers to what can only be understood as true propositions (John 4:37), and also frequently must be understood as referring to teaching or doctrine (John 4:41–4:50). It is also used in reference to OT passages, as in John 12:38 and 15:25, et al. Clark goes on to say that the Logos of the Johannine prologue must be understood especially as the Wisdom of God, and therefore the relation between the Logos and *logos* as propositions lies in the fact that God communicates in rational means the very mind of Christ, and "in them, we grasp the holy Wisdom of God," ibid., 40. But, contrary to the tendency among dialectical theologians to draw a sharp contrast between rhema and Logos, in order to emphasize the divinity of Christ, but to also deny the infallibility of Scripture, Clark argues that this cannot be sustained by a study of the use of each within John's Gospel.

152. Ibid., 3:178.

153. Ibid., 3:179; here Henry cites Psalm 33:6, and Calvin's commentary on this passage in his *Institutes*.

men. Jesus is not only proclaimed but is the Word of God. The Word of God is Jesus' very thought and deed, his very person.[154]

In this, John's Gospel presents Jesus as the Logos of God, as also the pre-existent One sent by God into the world (see John 1:30; 3:31; 6:38; 8:23; et al.). The main point made by the Johannine reference to Christ as Logos of God is that "the Logos affirmations of the New Testament are not mythical or conjectural, but are rooted in the reality of supernatural historic revelation."[155] Thus, "revelation" is the key word, and this must be understood primarily as verbal activity. Whereas the works and words of Jesus are both in view, the OT background centers especially on the word of God.[156] Again, Henry's point here is to emphasize the OT background, not primarily Greco-Roman, that informs what is meant by Jesus as *Logos*.

In summary, Henry's concern here as it relates to evangelism is to draw into focus the central importance of the person and work of Jesus Christ as the manifest, incarnate Word of God. As such, Jesus, reflecting the OT manner in which God's creative Word issued forth in sure action, so too does Jesus the Logos of God come as the embodiment of God's Word, in whom God's message and creative power are fully present. Furthermore, this must be understood as a unique feature of Christ, who alone is preexistent and sovereign God come in the flesh. Plus, nowhere in this section does Henry attempt to make Christ as embodiment of divine Word and deed a model for Christ's followers. That is not to say that word and deed are not both important in the Christian life, but simply that one must not look to the Johannine Logos for support.[157]

---

154. *GRA*, 3:180. Despite Henry's emphasis on the importance of both Jesus words and deeds, he also elsewhere underscores the fact that even in God's revelatory acts, there is a necessary primacy of place given to God's words, because the words of God are the key factor in properly understanding the acts of God in history. In other words, apart from God's intelligible, rational, and written communication, the meaning of God's acts would remain hopelessly obscured. Plus, many biblical passages are independent of any connection to historical events, but are thereby no less important; see *GRA*, 3, 257–271. As Henry says, "without a revealed interpretation of history, we can find no objective meaning in it, since we lack the information necessary for comprehending its meaning normatively"; *GRA*, 3, 261.

155. *GRA*, 3:184.

156. Cf. Köstenberger, *A Theology of John's Gospel and Letters*, 338.

157. In contrast, see Samuel Escobar, *The New Global Mission*, 107; here Escobar specifically cites John 1:14 as a paradigm for missions, even though this passage relates to the unique mission of the Incarnate Son.

The Mediating Logos

The importance of Jesus' role as Logos of God though, lies not entirely, or even primarily, in past events. Rather, Jesus continues to be the mediating agent of God through whom all divine revelation comes. "Jesus Christ is depicted throughout the New Testament epistles as the divine agent in redemption and sanctification, a ministry he still implements through the Holy Spirit (cf. Rev 19:13)." Henry cites at length James Boice's *Witness and Revelation in the Gospel of John* in his emphasis on the contemporary importance of Jesus as Logos of God. As Boice says, "the same Jesus who was active before his incarnation . . . is also active subsequent to that period through the normative witness of the apostles and applying the truths of his ministry to whose who believe through the divinely guided preaching of the Gospel."[158]

The relevance of this to the subject of evangelism cannot be overstated. Apart from Christ as the creative Word and power of God, Christ alone makes God's revelation accessible to human creatures. As Henry says, "the Logos of God as scripturally identified is personal, intelligible communication centered in the transcendent Christ as the sole mediator of divine revelation." Therefore:

> The Logos is the creative Word whereby God fashioned and preserves the universe. He is the light of the understanding, the Reason that enables intelligible creatures to comprehend the truth. The Logos is, moreover, incarnate in Jesus Christ, whose words (*logoi*) are spirit and life because they are the veritable truth of God. Reality has a unified goal because the Logos is its intelligible, creative agent, and on this basis man is called to the reasonable or logical worship and service of God.[159]

Henry's Christology, focusing on the creative Word and power of God, also provides an important corrective to liberation theologies and

---

158. *GRA*, 3: 206–7; See Boice, *Witness and Revelation in the Gospel of John*. Henry also says, "the God of the Bible summons men everywhere to worship Him in Spirit and in truth. As the illuminating light of men, the Logos preserves us before this God in responsible, relational, moral and spiritual relationships"; Henry, *A Plea for Evangelical Demonstration*, 77.

159. Ibid., 3:212. See also Henry's plea for the importance and necessity of rationality as inherent in Christianity in Henry, "American Evangelicals in a Turning Time"; Julian N. Hart stated well the mediatorial role of Christ when he said, "Jesus Christ speaks from within God and from within man"; Hart, *Toward a Theology of Evangelism*, 114.

the influence these theologies have had on the radical discipleship-holistic mission movement. Contra liberation theology's tendency toward a utopian oriented-Christology that places the social over the personal in importance concerning God's redemptive purposes, Henry's understanding of Logos Christology focuses importantly on God's verbal revelation.[160]

Spirit and Church Proclamation

Though Carl Henry has been criticized for not giving proper place to the role of the Spirit in his theological method, he does helpfully develop the role of the Spirit as it concerns proclamation, even if he could have said more than he does.[161] According to Henry, "Rededication to positive and triumphant preaching is the evangelical pulpit's great need."[162] In understanding the preeminence of Christ in evangelistic efforts, one must be careful to not thereby minimize the vital role of the Holy Spirit. It is as "Spirit-anointed couriers carry forward the ongoing task of proclamation" that the message of Christ breaks through.[163] What is required then is both the centrality of Christ and sensitivity to the Spirit. As Henry observes, "the Christian fellowship was born in the context of apostolic preaching. The power of that preaching stemmed from the truth of the biblical message, the centrality of the person and work of Jesus Christ, and the dynamic presence of the Holy Spirit."[164]

Regarding the Gospel's inherent requirement of proclamation, Henry, citing George E. Sweazey, points out that the church is given the message both for our own benefit and so that we may pass it on.[165] Furthermore, Henry points out that proclamation should not be restricted to strictly professional preaching. Public praise of God involving the whole person in individual and personal witness is equally important

---

160. For liberation theology's tendency toward utopianism and toward setting the social over the personal, see Waltermire, *Liberation Christologies*, 22–46. For the radical discipleship/holistic mission tendency toward liberation theology, see Costas, *Christ Outside the Gates*, 67–69, and Kirk, *Liberation Theology*; cf. Hesselgrave, *Paradigms in Conflict*, 145–49.

161. For the critiques of Henry on this point, see White, "Word and Spirit," 185–87.

162. Henry, *Evangelical Responsibility*, 68.

163. *GRA*, 4:476.

164. Ibid; see also Henry's obituary of W. A. Criswell, wherein Henry praises Criswell's Spirit-empowered, expository preaching; Henry, "A Voice of God."

165. Cited in *GRA*, 4:477; see Sweazey, *Preaching the Good News*, 50.

as proclaiming Christ from the pulpit. The truth is, though, this is born along by the fact that "Christian faith is supremely personal."[166] Yet, it would appear, Henry notes, that it is precisely at this personal level that we struggle the most for success. Several factors play important roles in this. There is a linguistic element, in that Christians often speak a language foreign to the modern world. The Christian finds himself in the position of trying to speak to a secular world in decidedly unsecular language. But more importantly, most Christians simply are too busy and thereby fail to engage in significant relationships that might foster evangelism.[167] Add to this that many churches bear a striking resemblance to spectator sports, and the idea of a preacher espousing universal truths seems outdated to the modern mind. Churches though must re-capture the centrality of preaching the Good News and its indispensability, as in keeping with the model of apostolic Christianity:

> The sermon is nothing less than a re-presentation of the Word of God. Sound preaching echoes and reechoes the gospel; by publishing the content of faith, the church shows forth its reason for rejoicing and hope. The preacher no less than the congregation is addressed by the Word of God in the ministry of preaching, for in authentic preaching it is not the preacher alone but God also who speaks, reinforcing his Word given to inspired prophets and apostles.[168]

The preaching portion of the church service must be seen as a "divinely provided opportunity for Spirit and Word to reshape mind and life in the image of Christ."[169] While declaring certainly that preaching should not entirely constitute the church's worship, it, along with sacraments of communion and baptism, summons "the faithful in every facet of life to the adoration and service of God."[170]

In Henry's view, effective preaching depends on the ability of the expositor to link contemporary realities and needs to what Scripture

---

166. *GRA*, 4:478.

167. Ibid.

168. *GRA*, 4:479. As Henry says elsewhere, "if we relate the biblical revelation to the cavernous vacuums in modern life, the Creator-Redeemer God once again can fill our empty-souled generation as a powerful reality; Henry, *Evangelicals at the Brink of Crisis*, 112.

169. *GRA*, 4: 479.

170. Ibid., 4:480.

offers.[171] In doing this though, risks abound, especially as it concerns the danger of the church "promising more than it can deliver and more than is theologically proper."[172] As in the case of Bultmann, the real danger as well lies in overestimating the needs of society and underestimating the authority of Scripture.[173] However, warnings against the faults of Bultmannian kerygmatic approaches to Scripture —wherein the real Christ is the Christ who is proclaimed—should not be interpreted as a warning against theological and philosophical expertise. Many modern churches, in fact, suffer from a dearth of theological depth, and sermons tend only to reduce Christianity's core doctrines to anecdotes and illustrations.

As a corrective, it will be helpful to recall that both Augustine in his *Confessions* and Calvin in his *Institutes* hold forth the necessity of keeping theology and preaching together. "Theology is, as it were, a discipline that preaches to preachers; it teaches them not simply what they can pass along to their congregations, but also the truth indispensible to both preacher and preaching."[174] Furthermore, "through its preaching mission the church brings theology to life in the experience of the gathered community of faith."[175]

Regarding the priority of proclamation, Henry has much to say. Neither political or social activism, nor experiential charismatic experience can ever rightly replace the primary role of proclamation:

> No age of Christian history needs more strongly to be reminded
> of this priority of proclamation than an activist age which

---

171. Ibid. Elsewhere, Henry declares, "the Bible must be known not only for new translations but also for its abiding truth and life-giving power"; Henry, "Evangelicals: Out of the Closet but Going Nowhere?," 21.

172. *GRA*, 4:481.

173. Ibid., 4:482–83. As Henry points out, "The Bultmannian alternative disallows not only transition from past to present in appropriating Jesus, but also transition from present to future. Revelation becomes so internalized and correlated with subjective response that its very reality is imperiled; this bare bones of inner experience cannot long escape being engulfed by the mythological context in which Bultmann sets it"; ibid., 4:484. See also, Henry's warning that "we need, in a nation in peril, to address the conscience of the people. We need to lift God's sure Word into the lively confrontation of beggarly modern notions of the good life and the misguided pursuit of money and sex and world image as life priorities"; Henry, "The Bible and the Conscience of Our Age," 405. See also Henry's comments on cultural relevance vs. cultural accommodation in Henry, "Second Rock Music Church of Boulder"; Henry, "The Church in the World or the World in the Church."

174. *GRA*, 4:487.

175. Ibid., 4:488.

considers political engagement the preferred means of bearing and "doing" the Word. But the reminder is also needed at a time when personal experience, however necessary, tends to take center stage.[176]

Especially dangerous, says Henry, are charismatic tendencies away from a linguistic and intelligible understanding of divine revelation. The emphasis on intelligible preaching is found in Paul, especially 1 Cor 14:1–12; 13–19, wherein the apostle declares that preaching (prophecy) is superior to glossolalia because it is universally understood and "because the Spirit of God can use it to persuade, convict and win the lost." Even Jesus used plain language to convey spiritual truth, "words like birth, water, bread, wind, and light."[177] Furthermore, the Word of God has always stood central to God's redemptive purposes:

> It was the God's creative Word that constituted man in the Creator's likeness. That same Word the renewed sinner harbors in his heart and shares with a fallen race. The Word of God possesses capacities unknown to conventional interchange—not in respect to the rhythm and music of words, or to style and form . . . but rather in its character as God's *logoi* or revealed truth. God's Word is a creative and revelatory Word that expresses his purpose and power (Gen 1:3, 6, 9, 14, 20, 24, 26). Man's fall began with a questioning of God's Word (Gen 3:1). The creation story knows no more fateful moment after the fall than when God spoke to sinful man and received no answer. The covenant of God is linguistically oriented and his commandments are ten words (dabarim). Already in the first eleven chapters of Genesis we see how the words of man reflect a broken relationship to the Word of God and threaten the unity of human language; when at Pentecost alienated man is reunited again across many languages, it is by the Word of God (Acts 2:6–12).[178]

Regarding the tendency among evangelical youth toward social activism, Henry applauds their enthusiasm while affirming the biblical necessity of embodied action. "Evangelical Christianity fully approves

---

176. Ibid.; cf., Henry's declaring that "for good reason we repudiate the inversion of the New Testament by current emphases on the revolutionizing of social structures rather than on the regeneration of individuals; we deplore the emphasis on material more than on moral and spiritual betterment"; Henry, "Facing a New Day in Evangelism," 16.

177. *GRA*, 4:489.

178. Ibid., 4:491.

the demand for deeds, and in fact, sponsors it. It declares that words are worse than useless as a substitute for works."[179] However, in the interest of social action, to neglect the central role of God's word is to be adrift in a sea of meaninglessness. "Action is imperative and indispensible—but action *for what?* Social action for the sake of social activism, or action for action's sake, soon drains into chaotic conflict."[180] Rather, what is unique about Christianity and what must be prioritized is the preaching of God's redemptive word. "Evangelical churches must become voices in the modern babel that recall language to its intended purpose." The lostness of humanity depends on the church fulfilling this function. It is furthermore armed with a powerful, sure Word from God. "What lends power to the Word is . . . that God himself is pledged to be its invisible and invincible herald: he tolerates no fruitless proclamation of his Word; he has ordained fulfillment of its mandated mission."[181]

Given the non-systematic nature of *GRA*, to which we have alluded several times already, it would be unfair to criticize Henry for the obvious fact that this section could have further developed the biblical basis for the role of the Spirit in proclamation. Such a development would include more emphasis on the Spirit and proclamation in the Gospels (cf. Luke 1:41–79; 2:25–35) and especially the many important texts in Acts that relate the Spirit to evangelism (Acts 1:8; 4:1–31; 6:8—7:60; 13:4–12).[182] Otherwise, the importance of preaching is seldom denied in the prioritism-holism debate. Yet when it comes to reaching the lost and edifying the church, as Henry has shown, the verbal proclamation of God's Word remains the primary solution according to Scripture.

Shall We Surrender the Supernatural

Henry strongly argues that in order for the Gospel to really be good news, one must not, despite numerous contemporary attempts to the contrary, discard the biblical understanding of Christianity as a supernatural religion.[183] Following Gordon Clark, Henry affirms that the biblical

179. Ibid., 4:492.
180. Ibid.
181. Ibid., 4:493.
182. Cf. Warrington, *The Message of the Holy Spirit*, 51–56, 121–30.
183. For example, see Henry's declaration that one of the most important religious trends in his day was liberal theology's drift toward secular humanism; "The Concerns

definition of "supernatural" relates especially to God himself, and that God's divine immanence undergirds and holds together every Christian doctrine. The notion of a supernatural God, though, runs contrary to modern empirical notions, and many recent theological trends can be described in terms of their efforts to make the idea of the supernatural more palatable to modern sensibilities.[184] Against this, though, biblical faith is through and through supernatural.[185]

Jesus and Non-biblical Religions

How does Jesus relate, given his unique role as mediator of God's grace and redemption, to non-biblical religions? Some have claimed, based on their supposition of universal salvation, that even non-Christian religious writings ought to be described alongside of and as equal to Christian scriptures.[186]

In response, Henry makes several important points. First, not all non-Christian religions even have sacred writings, as is the case with Confucianism. In fact, some religions such as classical Buddhism even lack the concept of a Supreme Being, rendering impossible the idea of

---

and Considerations of Carl F. H. Henry."

184. *GRA*, 6:27. Henry notes in this regard not only the Enlightenment-influenced liberal Protestantism that "depreciated supernatural transcendence." But Henry also directs his criticism toward Pannenburg and Moltmann, who superimpose the concepts of present and future over the that of time and eternity as well as nature and supernature. He also notes this tendency in the process theology of Shubert Ogden, and that "pantheism, idealism, personalism and then dialectical neoorthodoxy—retreat to make room for later mediating alternatives like Bultmannian existentialism, Tillichian pantheism, and Whiteheadian panpsychism"; ibid., 12, 17–19, 31.

185. *GRA*, 6:34; Henry seeks to hold together both God's immanence and transcendence. He is especially concerned with both liberalism's tendency to exaggerate God's immanence, and neoorthodoxy's tendency toward the opposite extreme of over emphasizing God's transcendence; cf. Henry, "The Nature of God," 90. As Grenz and Olson point out, the quest to properly balance these aspects of Christian theology has proven crucial to Christianity's relevance in the world; Grenz and Olson, *Twentieth Century Theology*, 11.

186. In this, Henry refers to the Indian philosopher and Catholic Ishanand Vempeny who builds on Karl Rahner's theology that places the divine creation of the church over Scripture. Vempeny takes Rahner's divine causality and runs with it, describing it as "not limited simply to the Judeo-Christian Bible." Furthermore, Vempeny asserts "the presence of Christic Grace in the world religions," *GRA*, 6:360; see Vempeny, *Inspiration in the Non-biblical Scriptures*, 190.

sacred texts having an authoritative claim equal to Christian Scripture.[187] Second, the idea of placing all sacred writings on the same plane in terms of their claim to inspirational quality is simply not compatible with what other religions believe about their own writings. And this gets right at the very heart of what Henry believes about universal salvation, "anonymous Christians," and even the idea that other religions might carry implicit biblical truth. "Christ," says Henry, "is not somehow hidden in the non-biblical religions."[188] To claim otherwise is to ignore a great deal of biblical data referring to pagan religions as rejections of the true light. Such claims ignore outright not only the very claims that lie at the center of those religions but also their stark differences with revealed truth in Scripture.[189]

The Ministry of the Holy Spirit

On the subject of the Holy Spirit, Henry acknowledges both a historical neglect of the Person and work of the Holy Spirit in the church, and the dangers of reading into the biblical text assumptions derived from an already existent twentieth-century paradigm. In an effort to overcome these tendencies, Henry proposes five aspects of biblical pneumatology that emerge from the study of Scripture.[190] First, the OT background proves crucial to understanding the role of the Spirit in Christian theology, as there are over one hundred references to the work of God's Spirit in the Hebrew Scriptures. Important to the task of evangelism are the OT emphases on the Spirit's role in guiding and comforting God's people (Isa 63:11, 14), in examining their motives (Isa 4:4), being grieved over their sin and withdrawing (Isa 63:10), and being the source of prophecy

---

187. *GRA*, 6:361; also, Henry points out that even Hinduism cannot be compared to other religions that have a literary basis such as Judaism, Christianity, and Islam. Even Hinduism itself refuses to set its religious writings alongside that of other faiths as equal in status. But more importantly, "no unanimity prevails among Hindus, moreover, over which writings constitute the *Srti* ("what is heard") and over what actually constitutes the content of the *Smrti* ("what is remembered")"; ibid.

188. *GRA*, 6:365.

189. Ibid., 6:367.

190. *GRA*, 6:370–71. In our examination of Henry's writing on this topic, we will not seek to describe all that he says, but rather focus on those aspects directly, or at times indirectly, related to the task of evangelism. See also Henry's comment that "it must be acknowledge that the role of the Holy Spirit is neglected rather than overstated in some Christian circles"; Henry, "The Spirit and the Written Word," 302.

(Isa 48:16).¹⁹¹ Second, in the OT, the Spirit is more precisely the eschatological Spirit:

> The Messiah manifested in the last days will himself possess the Spirit of God (Isa 11:2); God's suffering servant and messianic prophet will bear the Spirit (Isa 42:1) and on him the Spirit will rest (Isa 61:1). "Poured upon us from on high" (Isa 32:15), the Spirit will then become a common heritage, moreover, among the renewed family of God.¹⁹²

Third, in the NT, the giving of the Spirit in full awaited Jesus' exaltation and glorification (John 7:39). Therefore, and fourth, several important aspects of the giving of the Spirit take place before the giving of the Spirit at Pentecost. Among them, the Johannine breathing of the Spirit on the disciples (John 20:21–22), stood as Jesus' commission to the eleven for their evangelistic mandate. It was, either actually or symbolically, a bestowal of the Spirit to the disciples in a way that anticipated what would happen to all of his followers at Pentecost. The evangelistic nature of this Spirit-endowment is made clear in Jesus' declaration, "as the Father hath sent me, so send I you" (John 20:21, KJV).¹⁹³

Fifth, "it is the ascended and exalted Lord who pours out the empowering and enabling divine Spirit upon the people of God."¹⁹⁴ Especially important in the outpouring at Pentecost is the reference to men from every nation (Acts 2:5) that "anticipates intelligible worldwide proclamation of the gospel to every race and people."¹⁹⁵ Denying the notion of a second or subsequent Spirit-baptism, Henry affirms Billy Graham's assertion that the emphasis on the prophetic nature of the Gentile (Acts

---

191. GRA, 6:372.

192. Ibid., 6:373.

193. GRA, 6:374. On whether the Johannine giving of the Spirit is actual or symbolic, Henry believes the account to represent an actual bestowal of the Spirit unique to the apostolic band, given their special and unparalleled role in the creation of the rest of the New Testament. As Henry says, "Perhaps a special advance bestowal of the Spirit attached to this singular role of being inspired interpreters of Jesus' Person and work. On several occasions prior to his crucifixion Jesus had spoken of the Spirit's leading the disciples into the full revelation of God's redemptive work, including, specifically, 'things to come' (John 16:12–13; cf. 14:26)"; ibid., 375.

194. Ibid., 6:377.

195. Ibid., 6:378. Here Henry differentiates therefore tongues at Pentecost from that at Corinth. "Tongues speaking by Corinthians were used in private worship of God; the tongues of Pentecost on the other hand, were employed in public communication of the Gospel to Jews visiting Jerusalem from all parts of the Roman empire, and then to Gentiles beyond"; ibid.

10:44ff) and Samaritan (Acts 8) incidents in which the Spirit is given suggests testimony or proclamation as the central feature.[196]

Prophecy

This in fact is an important feature of the Spirit in the OT. "The Hebrews considered the Spirit of God as essentially the Spirit of prophecy. Transcending the Spirit's working of miracles stood prophetic proclamation as a distinctive work of the Spirit."[197] This same emphasis carries over to the NT. Peter's citation of Joel 2 emphasizes the eschatological and redemptive nature of the now dawning day of the Lord. "While Peter does not stop to define Christian prophecy, its essence is not prediction but rather Spirit-impelled and Spirit-empowered proclamation."[198] Therefore, Henry warns against understanding prophetic utterance within Christianity as anything other than evangelistic and thereby intelligible communication. "At Pentecost the apostles stood forth as interpreters of the Old Testament revelation and of the life and mission of Jesus Christ (cf. John 14:26)." In support of this, Henry cites Paul's instruction in Romans (12:6–7) that prophecy was not to be confused with the gifts of teaching or with the office of apostle. Nor was it to be limited to a select few (1 Cor 14:22–25), or to be considered beyond criticism (1 Cor 12:10; 14:29–33).[199]

Spirit-Baptism

What of the Pentecostal claim that the Baptism in the Holy Spirit as a subsequent endowment of power is essential for Spirit-empowered witness? Regarding his position on this subject, Henry is unambiguous. "The biblical data nowhere teach that the Spirit's baptism of the believer occurs subsequent to new birth."[200] Henry denies that the Damascus road expe-

---

196. Ibid., 6:378–79.
197. Ibid., 6:380.
198. *GRA*, 6:381.
199. *GRA*, 6:381.
200. Ibid., 6:385. For contemporary defenses of the classic Pentecostal position, see Menzies and Menzies, *Spirit and Power: Foundation of Pentecostal Experience*; Stronstad, *The Charismatic Theology of St. Luke*; Stronstad essentially argues that Luke must not be read through a Pauline lense, and when this is done, when Luke is taken on his own terms, it becomes clear that he means something broader than mere conversion initiation. Another important discussion addressing the Pentecostal perspective

rience of Paul should be normative for all believers, given Paul's role as an apostle. "Furthermore, Acts 9:17 states not that Saul was then 'baptized with the Spirit' but rather that he was 'filled with the Spirit,' an experience that Saul later characterizes as a daily repeatable event (Eph 5:18)."[201]

Assessment and Conclusion

There can be no doubt that evangelism remained a central concern for Carl F. H. Henry. So far in this chapter the focus has been to understand, in accordance with the methodology described in chapter one, precisely what Henry had to say about the priority of evangelism, and on what theological-exegetical grounds he defended that notion. The goal of this chapter has been to show the full theological weight that Henry attached to evangelism as the fundamentally necessary component in evaluating his priority model. Having done that, rather than retrace Henry's arguments for the priority of evangelism, which would constitute a lengthy and somewhat pedantic exercise, instead we shall now evaluate Henry's theology of evangelism against his critics within the evangelical community. How have other Evangelicals criticized Henry's approach, and are those criticisms valid?

---

is found in Macchia, *Baptized in the Spirit*, wherein Macchia observes that the current trend among Pentecostal theologians is away from Spirit-Baptism and tongues as initial evidence, and toward a greater focus on eschatology; Macchia, *Baptized in the Spirit*, chapter two, under "Is Spirit Baptism the Central Pentecostal Distinctive?"

201. *GRA*, 6:385. Henry points out the NT understanding of the Spirit in relation to believers. This includes (1) that every regenerate believer has both experienced and continues to be a bearer of the Spirit; (2) the Spirit baptizes believers "into the one body of Christ, the regenerate church" (1 Cor 12:13); (3) the Spirit permanently indwells every believer (John 14:16; 1 Cor 3:16); (4) the fullness of the Spirit must be daily maintained (Eph 5:18); the fullness of the Spirit enables a broad diversity of gifts in the church (Rom 12:6-8; 1 Cor 12:8-10; Eph 4:11; 1 Peter 4:10-11); (6) the contemporary church does not devote as much attention to spiritual gifts as does the NT (1 Cor 12:31); (7) one should be careful to heed Paul's warning about elevating the importance of any gift(s) above others, since all are given by Grace; (8) the fruit of the Spirit, and not specific spiritual gifts, is alone given to all (Gal 5:22); (9) Pentecost, as Feast of Weeks, when first fruits of the harvest were gathered, shows that the Spirit's presence is as Paul notes, the first fruits of the believer's heavenly destiny (Rom. 8:23); (10) contemporary Christians "have difficulty distinguishing in their personal experience between activities of the Father, of the Risen Jesus and of the Holy Spirit"; ibid., 6:384–99.

Henry's Critics

Orlando Costas, a prominent two-thirds world missiologist,[202] faults Henry's understanding of the Kingdom of God, which as we have noted, is a driving force behind Henry's theology of evangelism, as being too narrowly confined to the activity of the church and thereby exhibiting a stunted understanding of salvation that excludes social and political change. Costas, influenced by liberation theology, believes that every activity in human history that promotes and strives for the dignity of persons, for economic equality, and for social solidarity can be rightly understood as signs of God's justice that anticipate God's Kingdom.[203] Such a claim though is wrought with dangers, and Henry's emphasis on the church as the unique means through which the qualities of the Kingdom are manifest seems the far sounder alternative. This is because if every activity which advances social justice in a general sense might be proleptically anticipating the Kingdom of God, even those outside the church, then this would seem to validate whatever theological, atheistic, or non-theistic philosophical presuppositions stand behind those activities, either explicitly or implicitly. Plus, such a paradigm relegates the church to a non-necessary role in God's redemptive plan.

Though Costas does indeed value the unique role of the church as interpreter of God's Kingdom activity in the world, his radical openness to evidence of the Kingdom outside of and apart from the church not only lacks biblical support, but dangerously separates redemptive history from the people of God. To deny that the church is the unique arena of God's Kingdom activity opens the door to universalism and the loss of the Gospel's significance, ultimately proving detrimental to the task of evangelism. After all, what can keep such a perspective from dissolving into the death-of-God approach of Thomas Altizer or the secular theology of Harvey Cox? If God is as much at work outside his church as he is within, then do not all things become valid sources for doing theology?[204]

202. Costas was born in Puerto Rico, but grew up in the U.S. His distinguished pastoral and academic career includes important posts in both the continental United States (Fuller, Eastern Baptist, Gordon Conwell), as well as work with prominent evangelical organizations in Latin America (*Fraternidad Teologica Latinoamerica*, or FTL).

203. Costas, *Christ Outside the Gate*, 30, n.10.

204. See Altizer, who describes as his primary theological sources the works of Hegel, Nietzsche and William Blake; Altizer, *The Gospel of Christian Atheism*, 10; Harvey Cox, *The Secular City*. This is, of course, not to equate the church with the Kingdom, but to highlight the unique relationship between the two.

Costas's effort to define salvation broadly in terms of all that God does in renewing creation ultimately opens the door to the neglect of individual salvation, an important biblical emphasis that Henry has rightly labored to maintain.

In addition, in his efforts to advance the significance of God's revelatory acts, Henry has been criticized for downplaying too much "the mystery and unknowability of God." Trueman especially finds fault with Henry on this issue, claiming that Henry uncritically follows Gordon Clark's thinking on univocity, the idea that words "can be applied to God and humanity in the same qualitative manner." Trueman then proposes that Henry ought to have given more attention to the issue of archetypal/ectypal theology.[205] Trueman's point though is valid only to the extent that it relates to the fact that Henry gives little attention to what it means in a positive sense to attribute to God the quality of "mystery." Henry, though, is far more concerned about efforts to subject the doctrine of revelation to vague notions of "mystery" and thereby move away from clearly defined, specific content. But Henry is not oblivious to the fact that God transcends his revelation, nor does he believe, as we have shown, that God's revelation exhausts the content of God's nature. Henry, rather, is especially concerned to guard against reductionist approaches to special revelation, and thereby the loss in importance of the task of preaching. Henry's primary concern is the doctrine of revelation, and its focus on the unveiling of God's redemptive will, nature and purposes. If that doctrine is reduced to subjectivity or undefined experiential notions, then lost humanity is without hope.

Conclusion

While there are certainly lacunas in Henry's theology of evangelism, these must be considered in the context of his goals. None of his works that address evangelism lay out a comprehensive or systematic theology. Therefore, one can wish that Henry had developed a more explicit ecclesiology and more fully articulated the theological foundations for

---

205. Trueman, "Admiring the Sistine Chapel," 57–58; as Trueman points out, "*archetypal theology* is the knowledge of God which he has about himself, which is, by definition, infinite exhaustive and perfect; *ectypal theology* is that knowledge of God which he has made available via revelation to humanity, by definition, finite but fully adequate"; 57.

the primacy of the local church in the evangelistic task.[206] But one cannot fault Henry for this, especially in *GRA*, which is concerned especially with the doctrine of revelation. Evangelism emerges primarily in the context of discussions that relate to that topic. It is also this very reality, moreover, that makes Henry's discussion of this issue so intriguing and worthy of attention. Henry's theology of evangelism evidences a robust understanding of the doctrine of revelation that underscores the regenerational emphasis in both God's own nature and in his self-disclosure. When fully considered, this foundation legitimately justifies prioritization, as has been amply shown. God's nature, his purposes, along with his actions in Christ and through the Holy Spirit, are run through with evangelistic impetus deriving especially from the verbal and personal nature of God's self-revelation.

Looking in some depth at the doctrine of revelation as it relates to the mission and purpose of the church proves a crucial component in understanding the theological weight attached to the priority of evangelism. And, it is this component that is almost always missing in contemporary discussions of this topic. In fact, none of the texts that address evangelism and social concern referred to in this study (other than Henry's) come close to considering the full weight of the doctrine of revelation as a vital theological concept in this discussion. While the concept of the Kingdom of God proves central for understanding that both evangelism and social concern are vital to a biblical faith, it is the doctrine of revelation and the necessary and unique correlation between this doctrine and the verbal proclamation of the Gospel that gives evangelism priority. Therefore, the relationship between evangelism and social concern cannot be properly understood without taking into account the importance and weight of this doctrine. Henry was right to say as he did that the doctrine of the Bible controls all other doctrines. The profound biblical understanding of God's self-revelation as especially verbal activity rightly necessitates for Henry that evangelism, though it may include a social component, begins with a spoken word.

---

206. Gabriel Fackre has criticized Henry on his ecclesiology as well, although especially as it relates to Henry's doctrine of inspiration and inerrancy. Yet, Fackre it seems, is guilty of also faulting Henry for not doing what Henry did not set out to do, that is formulate a systematic theology; Fackre, *The Doctrine of Revelation*, 174.

— 5 —

Henry and Social Concern

> Whether acknowledged or not, no one lives for a moment without theologico-ethical commitments, however superficial.[1]

Introduction

HARDLY ANYONE QUESTIONS HENRY's contribution to evangelical social concern. Yet, as mentioned in the introduction, references to his contribution in this area almost always begin and end with the publication of *The Uneasy Conscience*, and the acknowledgement that in writing that text, as Henry himself puts it, he was "out ahead of the pack."[2] Beyond that, though, this chapter will show that Henry said much more about evangelical social concern than what was contained in that early work. In fact, *The Uneasy Conscience* was but the veritable tip of the iceberg. In examining the larger corpus of Henry's writings on the topic, also, the reasons Henry gives for prioritizing evangelism and for yet considering social concern as non-negotiable will become even clearer.

The Danger of Neglect

In the introduction to *Baker's Dictionary of Christian Ethics*, which Henry edited, he issues a warning about neglecting social concern. "It becomes all too easy for the Christian, knowing the blessings of personal redemption, to concentrate on evangelistic and eternal matters, and to neglect other concerns that bind him to all mankind on the basis of a common

---

1. *GRA*, 1:19.
2. Henry, *The Ministry of Development*, 96.

humanity."³ But Henry also warns that though evangelism alone cannot fulfill the obligations of God's people, the neglect of evangelism cannot be abided either. Rather, the church is called to both emphasize the necessity of individual conversion and the need for social justice. A just society, though, apart from regeneration ultimately leaves a person destined for damnation. "Hell is the only society now possible where all structures are sound but all citizens are unconverted; requisite to an ideal society on earth are both personal religion and social justice."⁴

In addition, Henry also acknowledges that Evangelicalism by and large "has carried the burden for evangelism more than it has carried the burden for social justice."⁵ In this neglect, nothing less than God's own reputation is at stake. "Evangelicals know that injustice is reprehensible not simply because it is anti-human but because it is anti-God." Therefore, "Evangelicals must make God's Word and ways known because it is the divine will and demand that is flouted by social injustice."⁶

The Credibility of the Gospel

Furthermore, Henry believed that there was an inherent connection between the receptivity of the Gospel in society and the degree to which Christian social concern was present. To the extent that the latter is

3. Henry, *Dictionary of Christian Ethics*, vii.
4. Ibid.
5. Henry, *A Plea for Evangelical Demonstration*, under "preface," n.p; although, Hunter notes that as early as 1987, a rising generation of Evangelicals were already showing signs of change, with fifty-four percent of evangelical college and seminary students placing evangelism and social concern on an equal footing; Hunter, *Evangelicalism*, 43. This trend has continued, as evidence shows that giving among churches to relief and development type work is increasing, and consequently giving to evangelistic ministries is declining; for example, between 2001 and 2008, giving to evangelistic and discipleship missions efforts decreased by over ten percent, while giving to relief and development work increased by nearly three percent; Weber, *Mission Handbook*, 52.
6. Ibid., 14; cf. Henry's statement that "theology devoid of social justice is a deforming weakness of much present day evangelical witness"; *GRA*, 4:551; also cited in Thornbury, *Recovering Classic Evangelicalism*, 152; similarly Leung points out, "Henry warned of two threats to the vitality and witness of the church if evangelicals remained lingering at the fringes of the public realm. One if the misrepresentation of Christianity in the eyes of non-evangelicals as socially impotent and countening injustices." The other was the co-opting of public morals by "ungodly cultural forces"; Leung, "With What is Evangelicalism to Penetrate the World?," 229. It is furthermore, worth noting that on both accounts Henry has been proven right.

lacking, the former will be diminished. Furthermore, to neglect either or both is to short-circuit the full power of the Christian message. As Henry says, "we have not applied the genius of our position constructively to those problems which press most for solution in a social way. Unless we do this, I am unsure that we shall get another world hearing for the Gospel."[7] Elsewhere, he says, "the public power of evangelism itself is seriously curtailed wherever God's will for society is not known."[8]

Henry acknowledges that there exists in modern society the loss not only of God's truth, expressed in the Bible, but also of the very concept of truth itself. "God's very existence, and with this the objectivity of truth, has been submerged, alas, in tidal waves of modern doubt."[9] The recovery of this loss of truth depends on a three-fold understanding of the nature of Gospel truth: namely, its divinity, its demonstration, and its destination. In elaborating these, Henry makes several note-worthy points. First, regarding the divinity of the truth, Henry argues that the truth of the Gospel is of primary importance, not its usefulness.[10] Second, Henry believes that the demonstration of the truth constitutes a vital component of the biblical paradigm. The primary way in which the Gospel is demonstrated is in its saving power, "in resurrection might, as well as by its power of logical conviction."[11] That is, the Gospel is credible all by itself in that it is the proclamation of God's mighty acts in Jesus Christ. Furthermore, the supreme demonstration of Gospel truth centers on the Person and work of Jesus. "Jesus of Nazareth who 'went about doing

---

7. Henry, *The Uneasy Conscience*, xvii.

8. Henry, *A Plea for Evangelical Demonstration*, preface, n.p.; cf. Miles, who, though differing from Henry on the precise relation between evangelism and social concern (Miles sees the two solely as partners), speaks of social concern also as adding credibility to evangelistic efforts; Miles, *Evangelism and Social Involvment*, 162.

9. Ibid., 74.

10. In support of this claim, Henry cites Jesus' unique use of "amen" to signify the truthfulness of his words, his claim to have direct knowledge of the Father, and to truthfully reveal that knowledge (Matt 11:27; John 5:19; John 8:26). Plus, Henry cites the numerous references in the NT to truth that define the Christian calling: "true life" (Luke 21:19); "true justice" (James 3:18); "true faith" (1 Tim 2:7); "true doctrine" (Titus 1:9); "teaching the truth" (2 Tim 3:16); taking "firm hold on the deep truth of our faith" (1 Tim 3:9); et al. (NEB). Thus, "the power of this truth is what the church proffers to a doomed and decadent world." Thus, by "divinity of the truth" Henry refers to his previously stated position that all truth depends on God and is accessible by Him and confronts sinful men in their fallen state; ibid., 76–79.

11. Henry, *A Plea for Evangelical Demonstration*, 80; cf. Rom 1:16.

good' (Acts 10:38) is the Truth of God enfleshed."[12] That said, and after warning of "deverbalizing" the Christian message, Henry then declares that this same message loses its potency when it is divorced from "a living breathing faith."[13] The need for this embodiment of the truth rings aloud throughout the NT.[14] "Let us show the world what life made whole truly is."[15] As Henry explains:

> Such demonstration manifests and proves the transcendent power of the gospel-truth. All who believe, it lifts to a new order of existence in the midst of human history, shaping them into a new race of men who reflect the fellowship of the twice-born in a new society, and who exhibit the standards of the Kingdom of God.[16]

This eudemonistic view of salvation is one that finds frequent expression in Henry's thoughts on this topic. As such, the church in embodying the love and justice demanded of it, reflects its eternal destiny with anticipatory joy, inviting sinners to join the chorus of saints:

> While the day of decision remains, the church of Christ must in life and word be the global echo of the Risen Christ's invitation to turn from judgment to joy. This address to the world is not only in audible words, but also in a compassionate demonstration of the gospel truth; enfleshed goodness and justice are the church's special fashion, a style of life that mirrors heaven as her proximate abode.[17]

In other words, a distinctively different lifestyle should characterize how Christians live in the world. Without this, the evangelical message rings hollow. Thus, "if we are ambiguous about modeling the evangelical lifestyle, if we have no heart to die to self, no longing for Christ's return because that would end our privileged comforts, then what right have we to judge the world?"[18] This call to live authentically before the world includes both personal holiness and social action. That said, the church must closely guard her evangelistic mandate. "Vital as they are, however,

---

12. Ibid., 81.
13. Ibid., 82–83.
14. 1 Cor 1:6; 8:2; Eph 4:14; 17-24; 1 John 3:8; 3:19; 4:20.
15. Henry, *The Christian Mindset in a Secular Society*, 21.
16. Henry, *A Plea for Evangelical Demonstration*, 84.
17. Ibid., 88.
18. Henry, *The Christian Mindset*, 21.

social concerns must not obscure the need of personal conversion and the importance of holy living."[19]

Surveying the Landscape

In order to best understand Henry's perspective, it will prove helpful to set his thoughts in the theological context of his day as it relates to Christian social concern. That setting includes the fundamentalist-modernist controversy, as well as neoorthodox approaches to the issue. In the midst of these, Henry championed an evangelical social ethic that reflected a bibliocentric perspective.

The Fundamentalist-Modernist Controversy

It is widely acknowledged that much of the present-day confusion over the relationship between evangelism and social concern in biblical faith has been a by-product of the fundamentalist-modernist controversy.[20] As it relates to social concern, this issue, which Henry addresses in *The Uneasy Conscience*, led fundamentalists to mostly withdraw from social concern in reaction to the liberally oriented Social Gospel. As Henry observes, within much of fundamentalism, "the Gospel was often narrowed to personal and pietistic religious experience, in which the spiritual role of the intellect is disparaged, and the social and cultural imperative of Christianity evaded."[21] Henry points this out somewhat in defense of Fundamentalists, though acknowledging their actions lacked a biblical basis. As he says, "if evangelicals came to stress evangelism above social concern, it was because of liberalism's skepticism over supernatural

---

19. Ibid., 23; elsewhere Henry says, "If the church preaches only divine forgiveness and does not affirm justice, she implies that God treats immorality and sin lightly. If the church proclaims only justice, we shall die in unforgiven sin and without the Spirit's empowerment for righteousness. We should be equally troubled that we lag in championing justice and in fulfilling our evangelistic mandate"; "A Summons to Justice," 40.

20. See especially Brown, "Evangelicals and Social Ethics," 263; see also Hunter, *Evangelicalism*, 41; Marsden, *Understanding Evangelicalism and Fundamentalism*, 30–31; Collins, *The Evangelical Moment: The Promise of an American Religion*, 35; Quebedeaux, *The Young Evangelicals*, 8; Dollar, *A History of Fundamentalism in America*, 69; Gill, "Christian Social Responsibility," 87–102.

21. Henry, *Evangelical Responsibility*, 46.

redemptive dynamisms and its pursuit of the Kingdom of God by sociological techniques only."[22]

Christian Theology and Social Change

The divide over social issues continued well into the later half of the twentieth century. Despite this, "many evangelical leaders who are thoroughly committed to evangelism as the primary task of the church affirm the need also of a social witness."[23] In other words, many who take a prioritist position, do so without neglecting social concern. We shall return to this topic later in the chapter. For now, though, it will be helpful to examine Henry's belief that "an overview of novel perspectives" will show the superiority of the Evangelical position that prioritizes evangelism and simultaneously necessitates social concern.

First, the Social Gospel, dependent as it was on the ideas of Hegel and Darwin, "subverted the historic Christian assertion of transcendent divine redemption." Through the progress of both history and evolutionary process, humanity was expected to reach a utopian state, defined as the Kingdom of God. In this view, justice was made subservient to love, and in fact was dissolved into an all-encompassing concept of divine benevolence. On Henry's view, this corrupt understanding of justice is evident, for example, in Christian advocacy of pacifism and the rejection of capital punishment, both of which, according to Henry, ignore the divinely ordained role of government in establishing and upholding justice.[24]

Hegel's theology emphasizing divine immanence, and its optimistic outlook for human history suffered a serious blow after WWII. This facilitated the rise of Henry's second novel view in the twentieth century, namely Nieburhian ethics, after Reinhold Niebuhr. Niebuhr, in good neoorthodox fashion, sought to recover some of what liberal theology had given up on, namely the transcendence of God and the reality of

---

22. Henry, *The God Who Shows Himself*, 59. For a useful discussion of liberal ethics, see Jellema, "Ethics," 112–18. For a seminal study of the development of the social gospel, see Visser'T Hooft, *The Background of the Social Gospel in America*.

23. Henry, *A Plea for Evangelical Demonstration*, 28.

24. Ibid., 29. Important here is Hegel's dialectical view of history, in which Spirit—defined as "the principle of rationality in the universe," engages in a process of progressive unfolding; Hegel, *The Philosophy of History*; Gonzalez, *A History of Christian Thought*, 3:362–363. The leaders of the social gospel movement were Walter Rauschenbusch (1861–1918) and Washington Gladden (1836–1918), among others.

sin. Although, on the latter, he did not understand sin or other tenets of Christianity in the orthodox sense. As Henry says, Niebuhr "elaborates these tenets in the context of a permanent dialectical tension between the eternal and the historical."[25] In sum, "Niebuhrian ethics reasserted divine transcendence and human sinfulness, the inadequacy of agape social ethics and the indispensability of the state's coercive role in preserving order and justice in a fallen society, and emphasized the limitations of a purely rationalistic approach to the problems of human life and destiny."[26] Though wrought with many problems as attested by critics from across the theological spectrum, Niebuhr's views concerned Henry, and Evangelicals at large, especially on the issue of individual regeneration. "And for evangelical Christianity also, the Niebuhrian dismissal of the social significance of individual regeneration and sanctification signaled an unjustifiable defection from the primary task of the church in the world, that of the spiritual evangelization of unregenerate humanity."[27]

The third problematic approach Henry describes is that of revolutionary ethics. This approach emerged as a distinctly secular model, scorning supernaturalism and individual regeneration in preference for "swift, revolutionary social change."[28] Building on Niebuhr's socialist tendencies, and the socialist commitment inherent in the Social Gospel,

---

25. Henry, *A Plea for Evangelical Demonstration*, 32. One of the defining characteristics of neoorthodoxy, was its dialectical approach to theological method. The term dialectical has its roots in Socratic method, and relates to the process of questions and answers to arrive at new heights of truth and awareness. In neoorthodoxy, though, this process results in crisis, wherein apparent opposites are held together in tension, without attempting to resolve that tension. Or, "the neoorthodoxy, in summarizing their methodology, used dialectics in relation to the paradoxes of the faith which precipitated crisis which in turn became the situation for the revelation of truth"; R. V. Schnucker, "Neo-orthodoxy," in Elwell, *Evangelical Dictionary of Theology*, 755; in Niebuhr's view of sin is hubris, or, pride and self-centeredness. Though Augustinian in lineage, Niebuhr developed this though in a contemporary manner: "Niebuhr's view does not require him to treat self-centeredness as total; life itself presupposes some dependency upon a center outside the self. Nevertheless, sin is sufficiently universal that we can presuppose it to be an important factor in the life of every person"; Wogaman, *Christian Ethics*, 219.

26. Henry, *A Plea for Evangelical Demonstration*, 33.

27. Ibid., 34. Importantly, Niebuhr also distinguished Christ as an ideal from Jesus of Nazareth; ibid. Niebuhr's social ethic sought to dialectically take account of the sinful self-interest of humanity and the ideal of the Kingdom of God. Concerning the Cross, Jesus embodied the counter to human self-interest through self-giving love, or *agapē*; see Niebuhr, *An Interpretation of Christian Ethics*; Niebuhr, *Moral Man and Immoral Society*; Werpehowski, "Reinhold Niebuhr," 204–11.

28. Henry, *A Plea for Evangelical Demonstration*, 38.

ecumenically minded thinkers became increasingly disposed toward "rapid social change" of the revolutionary type. This method bypasses, though, government's role in justice in favor of mob violence shrouded as loving acts. Furthermore, this method exists without grounding in metaphysical realities, but rather under a corrupt understanding of eschatological fulfillment that ignores the plight of the unregenerate. This stands in direct opposition to the orthodox Christian view, which insists "that the social context in relation to God's purpose in creation is frustrated by the fall, but renewable by redemptive grace."[29]

In responding to these various approaches, each of which neglects the need for a redemptive focus, Henry issues a strong warning about ignoring social concern. "The temptation to stress evangelism only as 'the Christian answer' and to withdraw from social confrontation is dangerous and one that Protestant orthodoxy had best avoid."[30] His primary reason for this is that in doing so, Christians would thereby surrender the social arena to non-biblical social agendas. Furthermore, by looking to the NT, several helpful realities emerge regarding the way early Christians engaged social issues.

First, the first-century church never lost sight of its eternal destiny, and consequently never made temporal things ultimate things (Phil 1:23; 1 Cor 15:14). "Loss of the supernatural world in which righteousness reigns and redeemed sinners share endless glory would have meant for them that the Christian religion is a tragic illusion."[31] Second, a personal relationship with Christ and participation in his church was paramount. "Nowhere did they encourage those outside of Christ and of the fellowship of the redeemed to think that they could find abundant life and a permanently rewarding existence apart from new life in Christ and outside the Christian community."[32]

Third, the early church tenaciously held both justice and justification together. "The church's message was not simply that God wills justice for and by all, but that God in mercy offers justification to sinners otherwise exposed to divine condemnation."[33] Fourth, the NT church empha-

---

29. Ibid., 40–41, 42. Also, Henry cites as an example, Harvey Cox, who bases a secular revolutionary ethic in an evolutionary rather than a redemptive view of history; ibid., 41.

30. Ibid., 43.

31. Ibid., 45.

32. Ibid., 46.

33. Ibid.

sized individual regeneration over the church's broader role in society. "The New Testament nowhere declares the current view that the church's role in society takes precedence over her inner life—of worship, study, and holiness—and that only after altering the social structures can she discover how to be renewed."[34] Fifth, the early church demonstrated its unique character by boldly declaring the will of God, for both men and nations, and by living in exemplary obedience to the will of God. "The church had no revelational solutions to secular specifics; nonetheless it encouraged all Christians to fulfill their duties as citizens of two worlds in devout obedience to the commandments of God."[35] Sixth, the NT never advocates civil disobedience, except when authorities attempt to suppress the proclamation of the Gospel. Rather, "the early Christians relied on proclamation, persuasion, and example." Finally, the NT roots social stability in God's ideals for marriage and the family, work and economics, and government.[36]

As with his discussion of evangelism, Henry's articulation of these aspects of NT social concern provides a necessary corrective to some evangelical alternatives that tend to flatten out too much the relationship between evangelism and social concern by not distinguishing clearly enough the proclamational aspect of evangelism from the social aspect, and by not fully distinguishing the importance of individual repentance. For example, when Kirk says that "evangelism and social concern are one task, not two," he overlooks this emphasis that Henry has helpfully

34. Ibid. cf. Henry, *The God Who Shows Himself*, 71. Here, Henry says on the question of whether a "new breed" of socially conscious evangelicals are emerging, that Evangelicals are indeed a new breed; but, not because they "are switching from proclamation of the good tidings to pronouncements, picketing, and politicking as sacred means of legislating Christians sentiment on earth. Rather, evangelicals are a new breed because redemptive religion seeks first and foremost a new race of men, new creatures in Christ"; ibid. For an excellent discussion of evangelism in the early Christianity, see Green, *Evangelism in the Early Church*.

35. Henry, *A Plea for Evangelical Demonstration*, 46–47. Here Henry clearly echoes the Augustinian theme found in *City of God*, in which regenerate humanity lives both in the Kingdom of God and amidst the kingdoms of the world. As Pearcey observes, for Augustine, "we help build the City of God when our actions are animated and directed by the love of God, offered up to his service. We build the city of Man whenever our actions are motivated by self-love, serving sinful purposes"; Pearcey, *Total Truth*, 40.

36. The specifics of how Henry understands Evangelical political action can be found especially in his dialogue with Lewis B. Smedes in Cerillo and Dempster, *Salt and Light*. Because we are concerned especially with theological foundations, these specific discussions, though important and interesting, lie beyond the scope of this study.

articulated that takes note of the primacy of a personal relationship with Christ, something only attainable through evangelism in the verbal, proclamational sense.[37] Also, Henry's measures presented above, which he derives from the first-century church, prove helpful guards against erroneous views of social concern. This is evident, for example, when Henry notes the distinction the early church maintained between the temporal and the eternal, even though it never lost sight of the temporal relevance of social action.[38]

The Problem of Morality

At the very heart of social concern lies the issue of moral obligations and ethics. The issue of morality raises important questions for regarding social action. For example, what provides the basis, the means, and the objectivity of moral obligation when it comes to issues of justice?

The Loss of Morality

Carl Henry believed moral relativity to be one of the great encroaching dangers in American culture.[39] He also held that the moral problem in the world is first and foremost a spiritual problem deriving from human sinfulness. "The world of human decision and relations is a fallen world in revolt against the holy will of the Creator-God. The image of God in man

---

37. Kirk, *The Good News of the Coming Kingdom*, 103; Mott makes a point similar to that of Henry when he argues that "while evangelism is extremely important for social responsibility, it is not synonymous with it. Evangelism is aimed at the basic allegiance of the person; it operates only through freedom, never by compulsion; it is addressed to the individual or to individuals in a group. To become a child of God through faith in Christ is an end in itself of utmost worth. While a great variety of nonverbal means can contribute to the communication of the Good News, the spoken and written word is essential, since the content is a past event, which ultimately must be communicated with language"; Mott, *Biblical Ethics and Social Change*, 110.

38. This proves a crucial corrective to those who, like Kirk, attempt to downplay any distinction between the temporal and eternal; see Kirk, *Good News of the Coming Kingdom*, 91–92. This is not to deny that there is new life in the present for those who trust in Christ, but to, along with the apostle Paul, as Henry has noted, affirm that this present life pales in comparison to what is yet to come.

39. Henry, "The Concerns and Considerations of Carl F. H. Henry," 21.

is sullied. Man is a moral rebel who is threatened with divine wrath."[40] In other words, immorality and human sin are opposite sides of the same coin. Thus, contra the tendencies of liberal and neoorthodox theologies, apart from commitment to the realities of sin, Satan, and the fall of humanity, there can be no legitimate discussion of morality, or thereby of social concern based on moral imperatives. This is evident in that Scripture often links ethical disobedience with the work of Satan.[41] But not only sin, but also equally the consequences of sin, especially death, factor into a biblical understanding of morality. This is because of the unique redemptive focus of Christianity itself. "Redemption is directed toward fallen men who stand always under the shadow of death."[42] But death itself is not what is so dreadful. Rather, the real cause for concern is judgment, not the grave, *per se*. As such, only the redemptive assurance of eternity offers genuine hope and moral impetus. "Only an experience of 'eternal life' gives indication of the spiritual and moral tone fit for eternity to come."[43] By being united with Christ and empowered by the Spirit, "the redeemed enjoy in this life a spiritual and moral union with the exalted Redeemer."[44] Here again Henry's redemptive focus is evident. Moral obligations are necessarily dependent on God's redemptive purpose and nature.

All of this is especially important because, as Henry observes, spiritual regeneration is necessary for moral good:

> Christian ethics also espouses the biblical view that man's moral predicament may be traced to a corrupt nature that cannot be conformed to the right apart from spiritual rebirth. In both the teaching of Jesus and the epistles this estimate of the sinners moral plight is foremost. "Make the tree good and the fruit will be good" (Matt 7:17; 12:33ff.). "Except a man be born again he cannot see the Kingdom of God" (John 3:3). Jesus found the key to true morality in the new birth. The Pauline expressions carry forward the same theme. Men are "by nature the children of wrath" (Eph 2:3), but "if any man be in Christ he is a new

---

40. Henry, *Christian Personal Ethics*, 172.

41. Ibid., 175. Matt 13:38; John 8:44; Eph 2:2; 2 Cor 4:3; cf. Houlden, who observes that sin in the writings of Paul "is a religious category before it is a moral category. It is a force which beguiles and enslaves man (Rom 7), not simply wrongdoing"; Houlden, *Ethics and the New Testament*, 32.

42. Ibid., 178.

43. Ibid.

44. Ibid., 179.

creature; old things are passed away, behold all things are become new" (2 Cor 5:17).[45]

Thus, as Henry says in conclusion, "salvation ethics," that is, ethics grounded in the reality of Satan, the facticity and implications of the fall, and the redemptive hope offered in and through Christ, provide the only solution to the loss of morality in modern culture. "There just is no other way out."[46]

Henry's focus on individual salvation and its correlation with moral virtue is important. This is true especially because the central problem in some expressions of the social gospel as well as various expressions of the holistic mission/mission as transformation movement directly relates to properly understanding how to best understand salvation. The tendency in both of these has been to move away from a focus on the individual with the claim that an individualistic focus is rooted in Western thought and a perversion of the biblical Gospel. But salvation in Scripture *is* individualistic and to de-emphasize that in favor of the social results in a loss of the redemptive focus of Scripture.[47]

---

45. Ibid., 184; see also Matt 3:8, wherein "fruits" represents behaviour in keeping with repentence; 12:33, where the reference to fruit points to one's true allegiance; 13:8, 23, and the linking of one's lifestyle with reception of the preached word; France, *Matthew*, Accordance, n.p. Regarding John 3:3, it will also be helpful to note the connection between this verse and John 3:21, wherein Jesus emphasizes the importance of deeds reflective of new life: "But he who practices the truth comes to the Light, so that his deeds may be manifested as having been wrought in God," (NASB95).

46. Ibid., 187.

47. Cf. On the tendency in holistic mission away from individualism, see for example, Chris Sugden, who says, "wholistic evangelism was about sharing the gospel with communities and groups of people at that point that the good news of the kingdom challenged the group in view"; Sugden, "Evangelicals and Wholistic Evangelism," 37; on the emphasis in Scripture on salvation as especially focused on the individual, see Acts 2:38, and Peter's admonition there, "Repent and be baptized, *each* of you . . . ", and Rom 1:16–17, where one should note the requirement of faith and the reality that individuals, not communities or groups, are in view. This is of course not to deny the importance of the church as a community, but to say simply that regeneration and the Gospel call to repentance is directed toward individuals; cf. also Leitch, "The Primary Task of the Church," 12. The point here is not to suggest that Sugden or other proponents of holistic mission have turned a blind eye to the need for individual salvation, but that they wrongly elevated the social dimension to a level plane with the individual, and that this is contrary to Scripture; cf. Costas, who questions liberation theology's tendency to elevate the social plane, by asking "but is [Christianity] not also a personal faith? Is not the personal (not the private) dimension of faith equally worthy of theological inquiry?", *Christ Outside the Gates*, 129.

Morals and the Modern Mind

In his text, *Remaking the Modern Mind*, originally published in 1946, Henry directly addresses the challenges of modern philosophy as they relate to Christianity. The most crucial chapter in *Modern Mind* relating to our present discussion is chapter nine, "The Problem of Morality." Here Henry shows the futility of attempting to construct objective morality in the absence of Christian theism.[48] In this text, Henry argues that moral obligations require not only a theistic basis, but ultimately a basis in special revelation. Even more so than the Platonic or Aristotelian philosophies, "The Hebrew-Christian mind" demands an even greater emphasis on the non-animalistic, spiritual nature of man, by positing that humans, created in God's image were destined for a personal relationship with God.[49]

The modern concept of humans, however, has tended away from these ideas and toward the animalistic nature of human beings. "Modern thought, in its prevailing mood, discovers man's difference not in rationality so much as in complex animality."[50] Henry's main objective in discussing modern man's approach to being human is to show the incoherence and circularity of a view of morality that denies the transcendent, and to bring the reader around again to the importance of morality centered upon Christian revelation. He traces the modern approach to morals through Locke and later Bertrand Russell and others who developed Darwin's theory into an entire philosophical worldview. The result is that:

> The modern man has outmoded reconciliation to God only to find that man cannot now be reconciled to himself; he cannot make himself feel as he thinks (that rationality is an unforeseen accident of nature) nor make himself think as he feels (that the universe is morally and purposively constituted).[51]

---

48. For a discussion of claimed objective alternatives to this approach (e.g. ethical naturalism), see Craig and Moreland, *Philosophical Foundations for a Christian Worldview*, 401.

49. Henry, *Remaking the Modern Mind*, 244; see also Soper's review, "Remaking the Modern Mind," 184–85. Though charging Henry with the vague notion of "literalism," Soper affirms that Henry has cogently argued for the cultural relevance of Christianity as it concerns the modern moral dillema.

50. Ibid., 245.

51. Ibid., 257.

Of critical importance for Henry is the necessity of special revelation and the special place afforded humanity in creation. Not only does Christianity supply the ontological necessity, namely God, in order for morals and ethics to be objective, but it also provides the power to make them livable through God's redemptive acts. "The demand of God and the redemption of God stand together in any effective attack on the problem of morality."[52] Again, this redemptive focus proves the key to Henry's evangelistic and moral understanding of the church's mission.

The Bible and Morality

Against the backdrop of this tendency to downplay the uniqueness of human persons in favor of an evolutionary schema, Henry points out that the God of the Bible has long informed Western values and moral considerations. As Henry says:

> Among these are the convictions that God is intrinsically moral and the sovereign source of all ethical distinctions; that a comprehensive moral purpose pervades all human history; that the articulately-revealed will of the Creator embraces all matters private and public (including human relationships to fellow humans, to the state, and to the cosmos); that agapē is both the nature of God and the prime human virtue; that life even in the womb is God's gift, and that human existence gains its fixed worth from creation in the *imago Dei*; that Jesus of Nazareth incarnates the very life, truth and holy love of God; that the Kingdom of God and its blessings are mercifully accessible to sinful humanity through the crucified and risen Jesus who controls the sluice gates of eternity; and that through its unyielding call to the justice and justification of God; the regenerate church as the New Society is to reflect worldwide the joys and privileges of the Kingdom of God through its witness to redemptive good news and new life.[53]

In fact, it is the loss of the Bible's place in Western culture that accounts for its moral uncertainty. Yet, amidst that uncertainty, non-Christian approaches to ethics, such as naturalistic humanism, cherry-pick Christian virtues apparently unaware of how these virtues conflict with

---

52. Ibid., 261.

53. Henry, *Christian Countermoves in a Decadent Culture*, 9–10.

their philosophical presuppositions.[54] Contrary to this, though, "only in the context of the living God and of his moral purpose in the universe do we find the reason for man's being."[55]

As such Henry commends a divine command view of ethics and morals, noting its ancient lineage not only in Augustine, Duns Scotus and the Reformers, but more importantly in the Judeo-Christian heritage. "What distinguished ancient Israel from her pagan neighbor nations in the Near East was her knowledge of the revealed will of Yahweh and her commitment to live responsibly in view of his divine commandments."[56] This means, of course, that Scripture plays a central role in knowing what God wills:

> God makes known his character and will not only in general or universal revelation, but specifically in his salvific disclosure to his covenant people; this he does, moreover, both in redemptive historical acts and in the inspired and inscripturated prophetic-apostolic interpretation of those acts, and supremely so in the divine incarnation in Jesus Christ.[57]

Henry points out that attempts to locate ethics in the will of God but apart from special revelation have resulted in complete lack of

---

54. Ibid., 11.

55. Ibid., 12.

56. Ibid., 13–14. In *Twilight of a Great Civilization*, Henry laments the loss of "divine-command morality," and citing the warning of G. E. M. Anscombe, Henry declares, "if obligation statements are to make any sense, morality must be coupled with a divine-law conception of ethics"; Henry, *Twilight of a Great Civilization*, 170. The concept of a divine command theory of ethics has its lineage in Calvin and Augustine, and focuses generally on "theological voluntarism," or, the idea that something is right because God wills it, and this having its roots in God's own moral integrity. Furthermore, Scripture plays the key role in divine command ethics, in that it provides the specifics of God's moral commandments, and in that it also provides general principles that guide ethical and moral behavior; cf. Reuschling, "Divine Command Theories of Ethics," 242–46. Also, as Craig and Moreland point out, this does not mean that God's moral decrees are arbitrary but are located in his own character as the objective source of goodness; Craig and Moreland, *Philosophical Foundations for a Christian Worldview*, 532.

57. Henry, *Christian Countermoves in a Decadent Culture*, 15. As Henry says elsewhere, "biblical behavior is not based solely on human values and ideals. Its fountainhead is the will of God. It is received in the Divine confrontation of man by commandments, statutes and laws, and face-to-face in the incarnation"; Henry, *Christian Personal Ethics*, 193.

agreement.[58] Also, the precise nature of biblical compassion centers in the idea of *agapē*, that is, "an outgoing affection that confers upon the needy an unmerited benefit." The Father's giving of the Son to redeem humanity provides the supreme example of this kind of love, that contrasts worldly, self-serving love, or what the Greeks called *eros*. From the impetus of Christ's atoning sacrifice, the example *par excellence* of self-giving love, "biblical theism has stimulated an unprecedented manifestation of compassionate concern for the weak, the needy, and the helpless."[59]

Also important though, is that for the Christian, it is not only God's commands that make his moral imperatives necessary, but his Spirit that makes them possible. "According to the New Testament, the Holy Spirit as an inner, renewable, divine resource is the wellspring of virtue and of the virtuous life."[60] Thus, the Christian's moral obligations are not left to the will power or self-sufficiency of the individual. Rather:

> Christian morality is not merely conformity to a set of rules inferred from ethical principles, although the Risen Lord does in fact rule over the church in the world through the propositional teaching of the Bible; Christian morality participates also in the extension of divine sovereignty over the world through the Son's moral energizing of believers by the Spirit.[61]

We should carefully note here the emphasis on regeneration as necessarily preceding moral ability. Also, one must understand the Christian moral duties within the context of the kingdom or reign of God. As this proves crucial to Henry's entire understanding of biblical social concern, his thoughts are worth quoting at length:

---

58. Henry, *Christian Personal Ethics*, 237.

59. Henry, *Christian Countermoves in a Decadent Culture*, 18. In the NT αγαπη is always used to denote God's love for man, even though at times φιλέω is used interchangeably when referring to love in a more general sense; cf. "αγαπη" in *NIDNTT*; for an accessible study of the social impact of Christianity upon civilization, see Schmidt, *How Christianity Changed the World*. Henry also carefully points out that the liberal tendency to prefer *agapē* as the center of Jesus' ethics, and to simultaneously deny the supernatural element of Christianity results ultimately in the loss of the biblical meaning of the word; Henry, "Evangelicals in the Social Struggle," 8–11; see also Anders Nygren's important text, *Agape and Eros*.

60. Ibid., 23.

61. Ibid., 24; cf. Gal 5:22; 1 Cor 12–14; Houlden, *Ethics and the New Testament*, 27.

Jesus focused not simply on God's transcendent eternal rule (Matthew 25:34ff.), but also encouraged the view that his own earthly life and ministry constituted God's final redemptive act (Matthew 10:7; Luke 10:9ff.) and that the eschatological kingdom had already dawned in his own conquest of sin, death, and Satan. He focuses as well on a climatic future consummation when he, the Son of Man, would return in universal power and glory (Matthew 26:29). In the present interim, God anticipatively extends his kingdom rule through repentance and new birth (John 3:3, 5). Jesus' disciples constitute earth's new society; they are light and salt to the world, a regenerate ecclesia that the Risen Lord rules as living head of a body encompassing both believing Jews and Gentiles. His followers are to model a character and behavior exceeding that of Pharisees and scribes (Matthew 5:19ff). While not itself the kingdom, the church is the kingdom's most vital approximation and manifestation in the present age. Its ongoing mission is to extend the King's victory over the hostile forces of sin and evil, injustice and oppression; this it does by proclaiming the gospel, declaring and exemplifying the standards by which the King will judge mankind at his return, and witnessing to the present privileges and joys of serving the Risen Lord to whom all humanity must ultimately bow.[62]

This is especially important to understand, because as Henry observes, secular moral theories are almost invariably a corruption of the biblical concept of the Kingdom of God. The concept of the biblical Kingdom, Henry says, was taken over and thereby "was metamorphosed into a secular doctrine of the kingdom, one unrelated to supernatural redemption and regeneration and linked instead to a supposed comprehensive law of evolutionary development."[63] The only hope, though for Western civilization, lies in the recovery of the Bible as its sure foundation for moral truth and obligation.[64] Especially important here is the

62. Ibid., 25–26. For contemporary advocacy of evangelical Christian ethics grounded in the Kingdom of God, see especially Stassen and Gushee, *Kingdom Ethics: Following Jesus in Contemporary Context*. Also, Chilton and McDonald, through a study of Jesus' kingdom parables, also emphasize the ethical demands of the Kingdom of God; Chilton and McDonald, *Jesus and the Ethics of the Kingdom*. See also, Newbigin, *The Open Secret*. Also a relevant discussion of repentance as "the great reversal," or turning around, in consequent to Jesus' Kingdom demands and call to Kingdom living can be found in Verhey, *The Great Reversal*, especially 15–17.

63. Henry, *Christian Countermoves*, 26.

64. Ibid., 29; cf. Dempster, "The Role of Scripture in the Social Ethical Writings of Carl F. H. Henry," 3.

emphasis on the link between special revelation and the proper understanding of the Kingdom of God. Even in articulating the importance of Christian moral obligations, Henry sets the doctrine of revelation as it pertains to Scripture at the forefront as essential for knowing God's moral requirements.

Morality and the OT

How can one make the claim that only God serves as the proper foundation for knowing and doing "good?" To this, Henry answers, "what God has revealed in the inspired Scriptures defines the content of his will."[65] Therefore, Scripture provides the sure answer to moral ambiguities and longings. Apart from divine revelation, attempts to ground ethics, as is commonly done, in a vague and undefined ideal of "love" ends ultimately in a content-less notion mired in subjectivity. As Henry puts it, "in personal ethics no less than social ethics, love as a formal principle detached from authoritative external content gained a fallible internal direction."[66] Even though both the OT and NT affirm that moral law is etched upon human hearts (e.g., Rom 2:14), and that human beings possess a moral intuition, the specifics of moral obligation still yet must depend on divine revelation. Even before the fall, there was a need for God's specific instructions regarding moral duties (Gen 1:28; 2:15ff; cf. 3:3, 11, 17). So, even though by virtue of the *imago Dei*, humans may have a sense of moral obligation, that alone is insufficient. Instead, "man desperately needs an authoritative external revelation of the moral law."[67]

This need of special revelation forms then the backdrop necessary for exploring the OT understanding of the moral life. Specifically, the Decalogue stands as the centerpiece of OT righteous expectations, and highlight that within national Israel, religion and morality went hand in

---

65. Henry, *Christian Personal Ethics*, 264.

66. Ibid., 239.

67. Ibid., 239–45. Regarding Romans 1:14; see also Moo, who notes that generally three interpretations have historically been proposed: "(1) Gentiles who fulfill the law and are saved apart from explicit faith in Christ; (2) Gentiles who do some part of the law but who are not saved; (3) Gentile Christians who fulfill the law by virtue of their relationship to Christ." Like Henry, Moo prefers the second position on the grounds that the passage appears to speak of those who have a general sense of moral right, but since they lack "the" Law, have no concept of their culpability before God, and thus, as vs. 15 states, judgment is their fate; Moo, *The Epistle to the Romans*, Accordance ed., n.p.

hand. Also important for understanding OT moral obligations though, is the progressive nature of God's revealed ethics, accounting for the realities of both temporal and enduring obligations.[68] The ten commandments, though, are not temporal, but "are valid for all men in all places and at all times."[69] As Henry summarizes them:

1. Thou shalt have no other gods before me.
2. Thou shalt not make unto thyself any graven image.
3. Thou shalt not take the name of Jehovah thy God in vain.
4. Remember the sabbath day to keep it holy.
5. Honor thy father and mother.
6. Thou shalt not kill.
7. Thou shalt not commit adultery.
8. Thou shalt not steal.
9. Thou shalt not bear false witness.
10. Thou shalt not covet.

Henry points out that the commandments feature four primary themes—*imago*, labor and rest, marriage and procreation, and coveting—that reflect something of the moral condition of humanity before the fall.[70] Though not every commandment can be explicitly linked in such a way, several connections are readily apparent. For example, the first three commandments focus on elements of the *imago Dei*, and are as such designed to guard the unique dignity of human persons and their responsibility to reflect the divine image. The prohibition of taking God's

---

68. Ibid., 266–69. The Decalogue, or Ten Words (from the Gr. *deka logoi* in the LXX), are found in Exod 20:1–7; and the giving of them is reiterated in Exod 31:18 and Deut 4:13; 10:4. Their significance is underscored by this three-fold reference in the Pentateuch, and by the fact that they are the only commandments uttered directly from God in the hearing of the congregation of Israel, rather than through Moses' mediation; cf. Lapsley, "Ten Commandments," 775; for a discussion of whether these should properly be called "commandments" see Hamilton's argument in favor, in Hamilton, *Exodus*, 313.

69. Ibid., 269.

70. Ibid., 272. That is, each of these elements can be related to either the condition of humanity, or the commandments given to humanity in Eden prior to the fall. Also, as House observes, the central issue with the giving of the ten commandments is Israel's covenant relationship: God first redeemed Israel, and then issued the moral obligations required by the covenant; House, *Old Testament Theology*, 111.

name in vain furthermore warns of the severity of blasphemy, as the divine name stands for God's own will and character.[71]

The fourth commandment reflects both the importance of work and of rest, as in the creation account these go together (cf. Exod 20:8–11). The fifth commandment emphasizes family and its foundational relationship to society. "Hence the Decalogue underwrites the soundness of the thesis of social ethics that a well-ordered nation has its roots in a well-ordered home."[72] Furthermore, this commandment anticipates the seventh commandment, prohibiting adultery, based on the Genesis account of creation of male and female (Gen 2:24). This commandment then provides "a permanent spiritual and moral basis for monogamous marriage."[73]

Especially important, says Henry, the sixth commandment contains the standard of neighbor love upon which much of biblical ethics rests. "The sixth commandment, as does the whole law, gains its fuller meaning only when the law is perfectly summarized by the law of love."[74] What Henry means by this is that a connection runs through these last commandments, whose understanding depends on the narrative of the fall. In that context, the inner life, and not just external actions, comes clearly into view. This is evident in that Genesis describes Eve's temptation in terms of desire, or covetousness in Gen 3:6. "The woman saw that the tree . . . was *to be desired* to make one wise and she took of its fruit and ate, and gave to her husband by her, and he did eat."[75] In conclusion Henry says, "hence, the central importance of all desire and motive, of a genuine love that stands sentinel against lust after the illicit, appears as the summarizing emphasis of the Decalogue."[76] Thus, the Ten Commandments

---

71. Ibid. Cf. chapter four of this study; cf. House's observation that von Rad is correct in declaring that Israel's whole religious history can be understood as a struggle to keep the first commandment; House, *Old Testament Theology*, 111–12.

72. Ibid., 274.

73. Ibid., 273.

74. Ibid., 274. Also, Lapsley confirms that the Hebrew text here cannot precisely be stated either as simply murder or killing, but rather the word *rasah* carries the connotation of not just forbidding murder, but "also the prior emotions and attitudes that feed them." Therefore, the emphasis on internal attitudes by Jesus in the SOM was already inherent in original source; Lapsley, "Ten Commandments," 774.

75. Henry, *Christian Personal Ethics*, 275. Emphasis Henry's. Henry points out that the Hebrew word "*chamad*," is used both in the Decalogue and the fall account in Genesis 3.

76. Ibid; as House says of this injunction against coveting, that coveting ultimately is what leads one to break all of the other commandments, adding that the word

inform all OT ethical and moral requirements and stand at the center of its prophetic pronouncements, both harkening back to a pre-fall era, and looking forward to a messianic new age. In this, the Hebrew prophets never divorced ethical demands from personal religion.[77]

Moral Foundations in the NT: The Sermon on the Mount

The Sermon on the Mount (Matt 5:1–7:29) is widely regarded as the standard for Jesus' ethical teachings.[78] As Henry sees it, while the Decalogue constitutes the center of OT ethical standards, the Sermon on the Mount (SOM), fulfills this role in the NT. Of seven possible interpretations, Henry identifies firmly with the traditional Reformed view.[79] In what follows, the main contours of Henry's Reformed approach to the SOM will be explored. First, Henry sums up the Reformed approach as follows:

"covet" means especially to desire, not just a house, or a wife, but one's neighbor's house or wife; House, *Old Testament Theology*, 114.

77. Ibid., 277.

78. As Stassen points out, "The Sermon on the Mount (Matt. 5:1–7:12) is the largest block of Jesus' teaching in the NT and the most referred to teaching in the church's early centuries"; Stassen, "Sermon on the Mount," 714; Houlden, 53. Verhey, following Jeremias, says that the Sermon reflects the ethic of Matthew more than it does that of Jesus, even while claiming that it is dependent upon the ethics of Jesus. But this seems unfounded, and attributes to Matthew a greater latitude than he would have likely taken; Verhey, 85.

79. The other interpretations are (1) humanistic, (2) liberal, (3) dispensational, (4) interim-ethic, (5) existential, and (6) Anabaptist-Mennonite. The essential problems with each are as follows: First, humanistic approaches rooted in anti-supernaturalism and denying humans sinfulness, believe the ethical demands of Jesus hypothetically possible but largely irrelevant to the complexities of modern man. Henry points out that this is more a non-approach than an actual approach to the SOM, but one that exists as humanists interact with the church. Second, the liberal approach equates the fulfillment of ethical demands in the SOM with salvation, either individually as with Harnack, or societally as with the Social Gospel. Third, dispensationalists view the SOM as relating solely to the millennium, and having no relevance to the present age. Fourth, interim-ethical views, such as that of Albert Schweitzer and Johannes Weis, read the SOM as built on Jesus' false expectation of an immanent cataclysmic end-time. Fifth, the existential view holds the Sermon as not bearing concrete instructions, but as reflective of a desired inner disposition. Finally, the Anabaptist-Mennonite view holds that the SOM is to be radically binding on believers in both their personal and official or public lives. This view holds to a natural literal sense of the Sermon holding that the teachings contained therein are absolute; cf. Henry, *Christian Personal Ethics*, 278–304.

The historic Reformed view is that the Sermon is an exposition of the deeper implications of the moral law, and hence a statement of the practical way in which *agapē* is to work itself out in daily conduct here and now. The Sermon expresses therefore the only righteousness acceptable to God in this age or in any. As such, the Sermon condemns the man in sin, is fulfilled by Christ's active and passive obedience, and serves as the believer's rule of Christian gratitude in personal relations.[80]

As such the SOM stands in direct lineage with the Torah, and provides in propositional form the moral demands placed upon the believer. The inability to fulfill the demands of the SOM derives from sinfulness. Salvation, however, is consistently linked in both the OT and NT to obedience to God's will (Lev 18:5; Rom 10:5; Gal 3:12).[81] Though Henry argues that the SOM does not contain the entirety of Jesus' ethical teachings, he argues that it does essentially demonstrate Jesus' "profound regard for the authority of the Decalogue."[82]

As to the evidence for a connection between the Decalogue and the SOM, Henry makes several points. The focus on the inner life that Henry says is evident when one considers the fall narrative alongside the Ten Commandments, becomes even more explicit in Jesus' Sermon. More importantly though, is the idea that within the Reformed view, there lies "the unity of the Divine covenant with man." In other words, though there is progressive revelation as it relates to moral obligations, the differences are more of degree than of substance.[83]

Crucial to Henry's understanding of the SOM, is his declaration regarding the connection between the OT Law and the SOM. "It is clear that Jesus understood the law to be the will of God in propositional form. He so interpreted it in the Sermon."[84] As to the specifics of how the

---

80. Ibid., 308. According to Moore, there is little disagreement today about whether the Sermon applies to the present church age; see Moore, "The Uneasy Conscience of Modern Fundamentalism," 182.

81. Or, as Dietrich Bonhoeffer has said of the Sermon on the Mount, "the only proper response to this word which Jesus brings with him from eternity is simply to do it. Jesus has spoken: His is the word, ours the obedience"; Bonhoeffer, *The Cost of Discipleship*, 197; cited in Burridge, *Imitating Jesus*, 209.

82. Henry, *Christian Personal Ethics*, 310.

83. Ibid., 309–10.

84. Ibid., 299. There does seem to be legitimacy to the claim that the Decalogue and SOM stand in continuity with one another, in that "the Sermon's setting (a new Moses delivering a new law from a new Sinai), certainly suggests continuity (cf. Matt

Decalogue and SOM relate to one another, Henry argues that the Lord's Prayer especially underscores and elaborates on the first commandment:

> The Lord's Prayer crowds out all other reference points for this world and the next (6:9ff.); it is God's kingdom that will prevail (6:13);, and that men are to seek above all else (6:33); their perfection is to mirror his (5:48), their works are to glorify him (5:16), and they are to hunger and thirst for the righteousness he prescribes (5:6); he sees them in secret (6:4, 6, 18), and rewards sincerity in almsgiving, prayer, fasting, while denying a reward to ostentation (6:1ff.).[85]

Furthermore, Henry believes the commandment against graven images to be implied in the opening of the Lord's prayer—"our Father which art in heaven" (6:9). The prohibition against taking God's name in vain finds embodiment in the warning against taking oaths (5:33; cf. Lev 5:4; 19:12). Regarding the Sabbath, Henry points out that neither can the Sabbath be dismissed as belonging to only the ceremonial law. Rather, Jesus' discussion of the Sabbath uphold its basic purpose, emphasizing as with the other commandments, its inward spiritual importance. Henry also concedes that there is no inherent reference to honoring one's parents; although, it does emphasize caring for children (7:9f.).[86] However, Jesus elaborates on the commandments against both murder and adultery, again emphasizing the internal aspect of disobedience to these commandments. Though stealing and bearing false witness are not explicit in the SOM, Jesus certainly alludes to them (6:19; 5:22; 7:1ff.). Neither is coveting directly dealt with, though the inward focus of the SOM brings this into view as well in discussing other issues which covetousness can be said to stand behind, such as issues related to riches and poverty, wealth and property (5:3; 6:19ff.; 6:24–25ff.).[87]

5:17–18), while the 'antithesis formula' ('It has been said . . . But I tell you') may suggest something more radical than a break with the law's acknowledged teachers. Jesus' claim to 'fulfill' the law helps to resolve the tension. He brings out the law's full meaning by highlighting the inward attitudes which underlie behavior and by exposing hypocritical motives"; Field, "Sermon on the Mount," Kindle, n.p.

85. Henry, *Christian Personal Ethics*, 310.

86. Here, Henry points out that Jesus does, later in Matthew's Gospel specifically address the issue of honoring one's mother and father, especially in Matt 15:3ff. Also, Henry argues that Jesus' use of "Father" for God implies "that an earthly father is a responsible authority deserving of obedience"; ibid., 311.

87. Ibid., 299–315.

In summary, Henry again emphasizes the connection between the Ten Commandments and the Sermon. "The Sermon itself provides, as we have noted, its own broad contact with the ethical teaching of the Old Testament in Jesus' declaration that he came not to destroy but to fulfill the law and the prophets (5:17)." Furthermore, the SOM underscores Jesus' teaching that moral impurity is essentially an internal issue flowing from neglect of the law of neighbor love. In the story of the rich young ruler, the difference between legalistic and spiritual obedience to the law is highlighted. Furthermore, "the ethic of Eden and the ethic of Sinai and the ethic of the Mount of Beatitudes and the ethic of the future judgment of the race stand in essential unity and continuity."[88] In conclusion, Henry is careful to point out yet again that the ethical teachings of Jesus have both an inner and external quality. That is, the moral standards God sets relate especially to the human heart, but also find expression in real life:

> The inner life is a unity; God the Father is the center of the spiritual life; moral and spiritual values have primacy over the material; love is the fundamental social law; righteousness has its roots in the inner man; fulfillment is the final test of life—these are the principles which the Sermon upholds.[89]

Henry acknowledges that both an Anabaptist-Mennonite and Reformed approach to the SOM emphasize the need for regeneration.[90] However, Henry also admits that the Sermon does not address how one possesses such a righteousness, rather only argues for its indispensability.

---

88. Ibid., 315; cf. also Sanders, who observes of Matt. 6:14 that "clearly, Matthew has here related an ethical norm to something other than the command to love—the character of eschatological judgment"; Sanders, *Ethics in the New Testament*, 43. Although, it must be noted that Sanders holds that "Jesus does not provide a valid ethic for today"; Sanders, *Ethics*, 29.

89. Ibid., 301. cf. also ibid., 298, where Henry says, "Jesus is assuredly dealing with a righteousness of doing as well as a righteousness of being, even though the latter is fundamental." Cf. Jesus' statement, "A good man brings good things out of the good stored up in his heart, and an evil man brings evil things out of the evil stored up in his heart. For the mouth speaks what the heart is full of" (Luke 6:45; NIV).

90. Again, Henry differentiates these two positions by noting the Anabaptist-Mennonite tendency to apply these to civic organizations as well and as a basis for formulating the ideal government. Against this, Henry says, "in the Sermon, Jesus recognizes only what must be rendered to God, not what must be rendered to Caesar"; ibid., 324; also, as France observes, the SOM is concerned not with general moral obligations but with discipleship, that is, with the moral response of those who are the people of God; France, *Matthew*, 107.

Thus, the SOM only implicitly anticipates the Pauline development of the doctrine of justification and imputed righteousness.[91]

It will be helpful here to carefully trace the progressive elements in Henry's understanding of Christian moral imperatives. First, these imperatives are divinely revealed and therefore the doctrine of revelation features first and foremost in obedience. Following the emphasis on revelation, Henry then states the primary and essential theological components in moral virtue: the sovereignty of God, the nature of God, the nature of humanity, the Incarnation, the Kingdom of God, the redemption of sinners, and the purpose of the church. Most advocates of holistic mission rightly emphasize the Kingdom of God, but their neglect of the doctrine of revelation, which again is Henry's starting point, results in a misunderstanding about how evangelism and social concern relate to one another. To say that evangelism and social concern are both Kingdom activities, true as that is, actually says nothing about how these two mandates relate in the mission of the church, because this fails to consider what other theological weight may stand behind these activities by way of other doctrines. By virtue of his thorough study of the doctrine of revelation, Henry has shown how this necessitates some degree of prioritizing, based on the relationship outlined above between revelation and divine moral imperatives.[92]

---

91. Ibid., 320–23.

92. Kirk is representative of this neglect, when he asks how the social and individual aspects of the Gospel go together, and responds that the key is the Kingdom of God: "The kingdom sums up God's plan to create a new human life by making possible a new kind of community among people, families, and groups"; Kirk, *Good News of the Coming Kingdom*, 47; see also Wagner, *Church Growth and the Whole Gospel*, especially chapter one, "The Church, The Kingdom, and the Cultural Mandate." Sider comes close to articulating the importance of the doctrine of revelation, although he never really develops the idea beyond a passing reference; see Sider, *Good News and Good Works*, 111, 124. Also, even though Flemming takes a Scripture-centered approach and looks to revelation to advance his thesis that being, doing, and telling are equal parts of the mission of God's people, he seems to ignore the fact that it is only by revelation, that is, God's revealed and proclaimed will, that the biblical mandate is known; see Flemming, *Recovering the Full Mission of God*. Similarly, Miles identifies three "theological motifs" which unite evangelism and social concern (creation, sin, and *agapē*), but makes no reference to the doctrine of revelation; Miles, *Evangelism and Social Involvement*, 55–67. Also, Mott argues that Christian ethics is the proper response to God's actions, glossing over the fact that God's actions are explained only via his Word(s); Mott, *biblical Ethics and Social Change*, 28–29.

Challenging the Status Quo

The Uneasy Conscience of Modern Fundamentalism (1947)

Carl Henry, following WWII, expressly challenged the fundamentalist community for its tepid approach to social concern.[93] This is the precise objective of Henry's *The Uneasy Conscience of Modern Fundamentalism*.[94] In this text Henry chastises the Fundamentalist withdrawal from social concern, and the resultant negative impact on Christianity's ability to witness to the love of God in a world wrought with suffering and need. As Henry later said, his goal in this book was "to enlist evangelicals for cultural involvement no less energetically than for their dedication to evangelism."[95]

While pointing out that there were elements (especially those with Reformed lineage) within Fundamentalism that maintained active involvement in social issues, Henry acknowledged that much of the criticism directed against Fundamentalism's lack of social concern was *apropos*. Essentially, as Cerillo and Dempster have observed, Henry believed the Fundamentalist non-approach to social concern to be "apologetically fatal."[96] Furthermore, Henry noted that the current (1947)

---

93. Cf. Cerillo and Dempster, "Carl F H Henry's Early Apologetic for an Evangelical Social Ethic, 1942–1956," 368. But also, as Thornbury points out, the text was not only directed at fundamentalism, but also at theological liberalism; Thornbury, *Recovering Classic Evangelicalism*, 135.

94. Henry, *The Uneasy Conscience of Modern Fundamentalism*. The importance of this text, as already noted, is widely agreed upon across the Evangelical spectrum; cf. Moore's observation that "one of the few matters of evangelical historiography that all sides of the evangelical debate can agree on is the role of Carl Henry's 1947 manifesto *The Uneasy Conscience of Modern Fundamentalism* in shaping the theological definition of the founding era; Moore, "Leftward of Scofield: The Eclipse of the Kingdom of God in Post-Conservative Evangelical Theology," 424.

95. Carl F. H. Henry, "The Uneasy Conscience 45 Years Later," 475; Henry later predicted that Scripture's relevance and receptibility within culture would continue to be a pressing issue for evangelical theology; "The Concerns and Considerations of Carl F. H. Henry," 19.

96. Cerillo and Dempster, "Carl F H Henry's Early Apologetic for an Evangelical Social Ethic, 1942–1956," 369. Also, as Wirt has pointed out, evangelicals, in the broad sense of that term, including fundamentalists, had labored for social good in society. However, "historical judgments are based upon total effect," and in that regard, "the social impress of evangelical Christianity between 1860-1960, apart from missionary outreach, must be judged a failure"; Wirt, *The Social Conscience of the Evangelical*, 49–50. It is also noteworthy, though, to observe that around 1950 there was a resurgence in the belief that social concern was dependent upon individual regeneration. Furthermore, this resurgence fostered the cooperation by mainline churches with Billy

evangelical efforts regarding social issues "has been spotty and usually of the emergency type."[97] However, Henry also acknowledged that Fundamentalism was right in its insistence upon the sinfulness of humanity and of the need for salvation through Christ. That said, Fundamentalism's rejection of social concern because of liberalism's social emphasis was uncalled for, since "historically, Christianity embraced a life view as well as a world view; it was socially as well as philosophically pertinent."[98] Henry also observed that to the extent that social concern was absent in historical Christian eras, that it correspondingly lost its apostolic and missionary fervor.[99] Where Christianity has been most successful is precisely where it has kept evangelism and social concern closely tied together. As Henry says:

> Hebrew-Christian thought, historically, has stood as a closely-knit world and life view. Metaphysics and ethics went everywhere together, in biblical intent. The great doctrines implied a divinely related social order with intimations for all humanity. The ideal Hebrew or Christian society throbbed with challenge to the predominant culture of its generation, condemning with redemptive might the tolerated social evils, for the redemptive message was to light the world and salt the earth. No insistence on a doctrinal framework alone was sufficient; always this was coupled with the most vigorous assault against evils, so that the globe stood anticipatively at the Judgment seat of Christ.[100]

Though clearly believing that social transformation started with individual regeneration, Henry took a more proactive stance than fundamentalism at large and went far beyond this first step. Henry believed firmly that Fundamentalism needed to recapture the ethos of the early church regarding social transformation, and as mentioned previously, held that the two could not be divorced one from the other within a biblical framework. He wrote:

Graham's crusades; cf. Berg, "Proclaiming Together," 53.

97. Henry, *The Uneasy Conscience*, 3.

98. Ibid., 18; cf. Marsden, who observes "Fundamentalists confused social reform with humanistic secularism and so abandoned drives for social reform. They thus confined themselves to the task of preaching personal salvation, which, crucial as it was, by itself made the gospel otherworldly"; Marsden, *Reforming Fundamentalism: Fuller Seminary and the New Evangelicalism*, 80.

99. Henry, *The Uneasy Conscience*, 28.

100. Ibid., 30.

> A globe-changing passion certainly characterized the early church, however much it thought within a redemptive pattern centering on Christ's substitutionary death and bodily resurrection. Had it not been so, Christianity would not have been the religion of the then-known world within three centuries. Some sort of world passion had made the Christian message pertinent enough for rulers to want to bring their subjects to subjection to it. A Christianity without a passion to turn the world upside down is not reflective of apostolic Christianity.[101]

In explaining this, Henry points to a "theologico-ethical" emphasis that "runs through the Hebrew-Christian outlook."[102] He notes that in both the Old and New Testaments, redemption and ethics were closely tied together. In the OT, as previously noted, this is apparent in the Ten Commandments, which directed Israel to a right relationship with God and one another. In the NT, John the Baptist both declared Jesus as the sacrificial Lamb who takes away sins, as well as directed his hearers to the inherent ethical implications of the coming Kingdom. "Persons with two coats were to give to those without any. Those with abundant provisions were to share with the needy. Publicans were not to extort. Soldiers were not to commit violence nor to accuse individuals falsely."[103] When John the Baptist sent an inquiry concerning Jesus, Henry observes that Jesus replied in a most significant way:

> Jesus endorses a particular expectation about the Messiah which the Baptist had doubtless gleaned from the Old Testament: "Go and show John again those things which ye do hear and see: the blind receive their sight, and the lame walk, the lepers are cleansed, and the deaf hear, the dead are raised up, and the poor have the gospel preached to them" (Matt. 11:4-5; Luke 7:22). In view of so central a passage, it is difficult to find room for a gospel cut loose entirely from non-spiritual needs.[104]

---

101. Ibid., 16.

102. Ibid., 31.

103. Ibid., 34. As Mark D. Baker observes, "God's covenants in the OT had both formal and familial characteristics. Within a covenantal context, people are not considered just or righteous based on an abstract standard or legal code; they are considered just or righteous if they are faithful to their covenantal obligations to other people and to God." In the NT, Jesus' atoning sacrifice frees God's people, and along with the bestowal of God's Spirit, enables them to enter into right relationship with both God and others; Baker, "Atonement," 81–84.

104. Henry, *The Uneasy Conscience*, 34–35. Henry points out that though there is a tendency to see this passage in purely spiritual terms, and that indeed, the concept

That said, Henry argues that "the methodology of Jesus is a redemption methodology." As such, "it is offered as the only adequate rest for world weariness, whether political, economic, academic, recreational. It stands in judgment upon all non-Christian solutions."[105] In addition, Henry notes that the apostle Paul, like Jesus, kept social concern and the gospel together. "The apostle to the Gentiles thus proclaims a social, as well as a personal, Christianity.... He was spiritually aflame to bring the world to the feet of Jesus."[106] Yet, "this does not mean that early Christianity charted the course for social reform; rather, it furnished the basic principles and the moral dynamic for such reform, and concentrated on regeneration as the guarantee of bettered conditions."[107]

Henry also notes that much of the Fundamentalist hesitancy about social concern relates to ideas about the Kingdom of God. Liberals have tended to emphasize the possibility of a present, earthly utopia ushered in by human effort. In response, Fundamentalists have tended to lay their focus on future expectations of the Kingdom, and have even become reluctant to refer to the kingdom at all because of its wrongful interpretation by theological liberals. Even among conservatives there was widespread disagreement on the nature of the Kingdom of God. In the midst

---

of the deaf hearing, the blind seeing, and the dead being raised are often employed in the NT for spiritual rebirth, the same cannot be said of the lame walking and lepers being cleansed; ibid., 35. On the claim that Jesus' reference to the poor indicates only or primarily spiritual poverty, see Joel B. Green, who says, "Jesus' mention of good news to the poor, located in the final, emphatic position in this register of salvific activity. Collocated with these other persons who stand in need of divine intervention and appearing at the conclusion of the list, "the poor" interprets and is amplified by these other designations of those who stand on the margins of respectable society yet are the unexpected recipients of salvation. As in 4:18–19, "the poor" include but are not limited to those who are without material resources; the centurion of 7:1–10, for example, is wealthy enough to underwrite the building of a synagogue in Capernaum, yet is a religious outsider who becomes a recipient of divine benefaction"; Green, *Luke*, Accordance ed., n.p. See also Calvin's comment, "By *the poor* are undoubtedly meant those whose condition is wretched and despicable, and who are held in no estimation. However mean any person may be, his poverty is so far from being a ground of despair, that it ought rather to animate him with courage to seek Christ. But let us remember that none are accounted *poor* but those who are really such, or, in other words, who lie low and overwhelmed by a conviction of their poverty"; Calvin, *Calvin's Commentaries*, Accordance ed., n.p.

105. Henry, *The Uneasy Conscience*, 36.
106. Ibid.
107. Ibid., 37.

of this, consensus seemed far off, if not impossible.[108] Henry advocates that, for a proper biblical understanding of social concern, one must hold in tension the already and not-yet aspects of the Kingdom. He calls upon contemporary Evangelicalism to recapture this balanced understanding of what God is doing now and will do in the future in order to avoid theological errors regarding the function of the church in society and in the world. Nothing less than the relevance of Christianity amidst world suffering hinges on this very issue. Henry thus proposes four crucial issues related to reawaking evangelical social concern:

> Contemporary evangelicalism needs (1) to reawaken to the relevance of its redemptive message to the global predicament; (2) to stress the great evangelical agreements in a common world front; (3) to discard elements of its message which cut the nerve of world compassion as contradictory to the inherent genius of Christianity; (4) to restudy eschatological convictions for proper perspective which will not unnecessarily dissipate evangelical strength in controversy over secondary positions, in a day when the significance of the primary insistence is international.[109]

Henry illustrates this reality by calling upon Fundamentalists to reflect on the thief on the cross. "'Today shalt thou be with me in paradise.' The message for decadent modern civilization must ring with the present tense. We must confront the world now with an ethics to make it tremble, and with a dynamic to give it hope."[110]

Henry also points out that to a large degree Fundamentalism has not been given a fair shake. The movement has been lampooned by liberals in such a way that even Fundamentalists hardly recognize the picture painted of them, when in fact the movement is grounded in many solid

---

108. Ibid., 43–45. As Moore observes, "In 1947, an evangelical consensus on the Kingdom—and its implications for the whole of life—seemed nearly impossible. After all, the evangelical coalition was agreed on the "fundamentals" of biblical inerrancy, substitutionary atonement, bodily resurrection, personal regeneration, and so forth. But the coalition was badly divided on the Kingdom itself between dispensationalists and covenant theologians. Remarkably, the past generation has seen evangelical theology coalesce around a consensus view of the Kingdom as "already and not yet"—with both dispensationalists and covenant theologians moving toward one another." Furthermore, that division has more recently been replaced "by a more biblical portrait of the Kingdom and its relationship to the future reign of Christ, the present reality of the church, and the cosmic scope of salvation"; Moore, "The Uneasy Conscience of Modern Fundamentalism," 182.

109. Henry, *The Uneasy Conscience*, 53–54.

110. Ibid., 55.

biblical convictions, such as a personal God, a moral and purposive universe, and the centrality and sufficiency of Scripture in leading people to Christ as Redeemer, among other things.[111] And so Fundamentalism inherently contains a valid message. However, the corrective that Henry advocates is that this message must also be one of temporal relevance if it is to gain a hearing in today's world and be faithful to orthodoxy.[112]

Henry also challenges Fundamentalism for its "religious escapism" that took the form of retreat from social concern. In defining what precisely evangelical social action ought to look like, Henry proposed three general guidelines. He says Evangelicalism offers a unique response to social ills because it (1) is redemptively centered and globally relevant, (2) addresses evil in any realm, whether societal or personal, and (3) offers more than ethical uplift, but through Christ leads to the highest morality.[113] Also, Henry says Evangelicals should not cooperate with social reform programs that deny the need for personal redemption.[114] Evangelicals must also avoid linking their social programs with their politics. We are to seek not a "Republican victory, or a labor victory, but the Kingdom of God and his righteousness."[115] While it is not the church's

---

111. Ibid., 58. And indeed, Henry critiqued Fundamentalism as something of an insider; cf. Weeks, "Carl F.H. Henry's Moral Arguments," 90.

112. Henry, *The Uneasy Conscience*, 63.

113. Ibid., 75.

114. Ibid., 81, 87.

115. Ibid., 85; When asked if there ought to be a "Christian or Evangelical Party," Henry declared no. "To take the route of a Christian party is, in my view, a mistake. But neither is it right to commit oneself unreservedly to one of the existing major parties. Better yet, why not forge a moral majority in which evangelicals join forces locally with their townspeople on crucial issues?" At the same time, Henry took umbrage with the approach of Jerry Falwell's Moral Majority, claiming that they should never have promoted a "Christian litmus test" to specific issues and as a means of vetting candidates. He further criticizes this movement for its poor connection between specific actions and general biblical principles; "The Concerns and Consdierations of Carl F. H. Henry," 22–23; for a defense of the Moral Majority see also Falwell, *The Fundamentalist Phenomenon*, 193–94; see also Nash, *Evangelicals in America*, 88–89; Henry, "Private Sins, Public Office," 28. It is interesting to point out that Henry has been criticized with the same charges he laid at the feet of Jerry Falwell, namely that his move from biblical moral principles to specific applications is unjustified. For example, Murray Dempster claims that there "is simply no axiomatic connection between Henry's biblical principles and his specific prescriptions." This perhaps more than anything attests to the difficulty involved when it comes to the application of Scripture to the social and political arena; cf. Dempster, "The Role of Scripture in the Social Ethical Writings of Carl F. H. Henry," 10. In fact, Henry himself admits to this

primary task to bring about social, moral, or political reform, the church must confront evil wherever it is found with the redemptive hope of Christ as revealed in Scripture. Thus, "Christian ethics will always resist any reduction of the good of the community to something divorced from theism and revelation."[116] It becomes apparent then that Henry proposed a solution that took seriously the doctrine of sin, and thus saw individual regeneration as the necessary first step in social reform. He wrote:

> The evangelical task primarily is the preaching of the Gospel, in the interest of individual regeneration by the supernatural grace of God, in such a way that divine redemption can be recognized as the best solution of our problems, individual and social. This produces within history, through the regenerative work of the Holy Spirit, a divine society that transcends national and international lines. The corporate testimony of believers, in their purity of life, should provide for the world an example of the divine dynamic to overcome evils in every realm.[117]

Thus, in the end, Henry advocates a redemptive-focused social agenda that gives primacy of place to the church's evangelistic task.[118] Yet, it does so in such a way that the social mandate, properly understood, cannot be divorced from this task nor deemed non-essential. By way of analogy, one might even say that the redemptive focus is the vessel in which evangelical social concern must be carried. Take away the vessel and the contents run everywhere and nowhere at the same time. The vessel thus becomes the essential container to give meaning, shape, and clear redemptive focus to the social emphasis. Perhaps Marsden best sums up Henry's approach in *The Uneasy Conscience*, when he says:

---

very problem; Henry, *Conversations With Carl Henry*, 111. For a helpful study of the Evangelical left, see Swartz, *Moral Minority*. On the difficulties of this task and on some of the unfortunate excesses of conservative evangelicals, that include support for the "highest levels of military spending" as a litmus test for Christian politicians, see Wallis, "A Wolf in Sheep's Clothing: The Political Right Invades the Evangelical Fold," 136. Helpful also in this discussion is Hindson, "Religion and Politics: Do They Mix?," 139–43.

116. Ibid., 88.

117. Ibid.

118. Cf. Thornbury's observation that in this text, "Henry confronts critics on all sides by arguing that evangelicalism is intrinsically linked to the redemptive energy of the Christian evangel in the active and practical opposition of social and spiritual evils"; Thornbury, *Recovering Classic Evangelicalism*, 165.

Henry worked out more clearly than did most of his evangelical colleagues the puzzling question of how social and political efforts could be kingdom work while the kingdom could never be equated with social, political, or national programs. his solution was essentially a version of Augustine's two cities conception, which sees a distinction between the city of God and the city, or civilization, of earth. Kingdom principles can influence the earthly city, but can never be fully realized there in this age.[119]

The Uneasy Conscience, Revisited

At two points in his career, Henry took the opportunity to reflect back on the impact of *The Uneasy Conscience*: once in the final chapter of his 1988 text, *Twilight of a Great Civilization*, and a second time four years later at a speech given to the Southern Baptist Convention.[120]

In the first of these reflections, Henry identifies the crucial issues as lack of Evangelical unity, academic malaise, social activism apart from an emphasis on individual sin, and an uncritical bent toward physical satisfaction in American culture. The latter plays out, says Henry, often in spiritual laziness and prayerlessness. "We may be rich in this world's goods, but spiritual vitality we have not because we ask not."[121] In remedy to this, and especially so in light of an increasingly secular and amoral society, Henry believes the local church plays the crucial role. "The day has come when local churches, whose congregations are known by upright lives and neighbor-love, are once again decisively important witnesses to Christ and his Kingdom."[122] In addition, Evangelicals must stand ready to unapologetically confront non-Christian religions as well as secular philosophies.[123]

In his 1992 reflection, Henry noted that some significant gain had been made by Evangelicals on the issue of social concern. Citing the

---

119. Marsden, *Reforming Fundamentalism*, 81. Cf. Henry, who says, "Whereas once the redemptive gospel was a world-changing message, now it was narrowed to a world-resisting message. Out of twentieth century Fundamentalism of this sort there could come no contemporary version of Augustine's The City of God"; Henry, *The Uneasy Conscience of Modern Fundamentalism*, 18.

120. Henry, *Twilight of a Great Civilization*; Henry, "The Uneasy Conscience 45 Years Later," 475–80.

121. Henry, *Twighlight of a Great Civilization*,173.

122. Ibid., 175.

123. Ibid., 175–81.

examples of World Vision, the Moral Majority, Operation Rescue, and others, Henry declared "the evangelical movement has therefore passed far beyond its initial stages of an uneasy conscience to a stance of political participation and aggressive confrontation and lobbying."[124] Yet, despite these efforts, the increasing tendency in American culture toward naturalistic or humanistic outlooks cannot be denied. This Henry attributes to a social agenda that has been more horizontally and symptomatically oriented than vertical and centered on the will and purposes of God. Plus, the accommodation of most evangelicals to culture has stunted the potential of evangelical efforts. "The real reason evangelicalism has still not deeply penetrated the reigning culture is that the culture—whether on its right or on its left—has too much penetrated the evangelical movement."[125] To rectify this, Henry calls for a social program that is overtly Christ-centered and forward looking to the Kingdom of God as fulfillment of its hope.[126]

Even Henry's critics applaud his efforts in *The Uneasy Conscience*. Though disagreement exists over Henry's application, as is evident in Henry's dialogue with Lewis B. Smedes, the need for Evangelicalism to adhere to a socially relevant Christianity is fundamentally correct and broadly agreed upon.[127] It is vital for a culturally robust Christianity to maintain the biblical injunction to stand for and embody God's own justice as part of its mandate in the world. Yet, even as the contemporary church shows increasing signs of interest in compassion and social issues, the need to maintain a redemptive focus is a warning that deserves a fresh hearing. Plus, Henry's warnings of the cultural captivity of the American church to materialism and self-comfort still stand as a potent challenge to a church that often appears woefully ignorant of its own affluence and poor stewardship.[128]

124. Henry, "The Uneasy Conscience 45 Years Later," 476.
125. Ibid., 477.
126. Ibid., 479.

127. See for example, Smedes, who says, "No single person has done more to awaken the fundamentalist conscience on the score of social ethics than has Carl Henry"; Smedes, "The Evangelicals and The Social Question," 41. The Henry/Smedes debate is a central focus of Cerillo and Dempster's *Salt and Light*.

128. For example, it is uncertain if the seemingly ever increasing passion among young evangelicals for justice issues stems from an understanding of the biblical mandate, or if this trend is culturally driven. If the latter, this proves highly problematic, even as Henry observes, for it eventuates in the church taking its instructions from culture; Henry, "What Social Structures," 75; also, only about twenty-five percent of

Aspects of Christian Social Ethics (1964)

Henry's *Aspects of Christian Social Ethics* began as the 1963 Payton Lectures at Fuller Theological Seminary. In these lectures-turned-essays, Henry explores the ways in which vocational calling (i.e., a theology of work), legislation and civil authority, and an evangelical understanding of the importance of God's justice and love all relate to the church's role in society. Henry sets the stage for his discussion in the opening paragraph of the first chapter:

> In seeking a better social order, to what extent shall we rely on law and to what extent shall we rely on grace? How much shall we trust legislation and how much shall we trust regeneration to change the social setting? What should we expect the State to contribute, what should we expect the church to contribute, if we are seeking a society ruled by justice and love?[129]

Before answering these questions, Henry compares and contrasts competing strategies for social change. Specifically, he examines approaches he terms *revolution*—defined as "the radical change of social patterns . . . through violence and compulsion," *reformation*—the "gradual but pervasive ethical amendment of particular abuses which secures a decisive improvement of prevailing social character and forms," *revaluation*—"a fresh intellectual comprehension and direction whereby social life and structures are critically reassessed in light of transcendent moral norms," and *regeneration*—defined as "transformation through supernatural impulse in individual lives whereby the social scene is renewed through divine spiritual motivation."[130] Henry finds the first three of these wanting, and advocates a "strategy of regeneration" when it comes to social change.[131] This means he sees ethics as closely tied to the effects

---

missionary personnel from North America are involved in evangelistic efforts, while seventy-five percent focus on compassionate type ministries; see Yohannan, *Come Let's Reach the World*, 63. On American Christianity and materialism, or "affluenza," see also Blomberg, *Christians In an Age of Wealth*, especially chapter one, "What Are We To Do With All Our Stuff?"; also Stassen and Gushee, *Kingdom Ethics*, 426.

129. Henry, *Aspects of Christian Social Ethics*, 15.

130. Ibid., 16–17.

131. Ibid., 24–25. Some have criticized Henry here for basing this view on "nineteenth century economic individualism," but I would argue that Henry's concern lay more on the issue of preserving the necessity of individual responsibility for sin and the need for personal regeneration. See Peachey, "Aspects of Christian Social Ethics," 175.

of regeneration. This is because only a strategy of regeneration derives its "social message from divinely revealed principles."[132] Here the connection between evangelism and social concern emerges, as the dependence of a regenerational strategy upon the revelation of Scripture proves crucial for Henry. Henry makes an astute observation in his critique of the other models, especially noting their lack of basis in revelation:

> But capitalizing on the social and minimizing the personal message of Christianity, and thereby obscuring the special framework of revelation and redemption on which both depend, has serious consequences. By divorcing the social from the personal, it deals with human rights in abstraction from human responsibilities, or rather, from the divine obligation of man.[133]

Thus, Henry says, "Evangelism and revival remain the wellspring of evangelical humanitarianism and social awakening."[134] He further avows that social change should not be thought of as running "alongside" evangelism and mission as though it might be separate from it, but rather "in and through."[135] His point here is to stress the inherent connection between evangelism and social concern and to point to the "Gospel's relevance and indispensability to the whole of the church's work, including its mission to society."[136]

In his chapter on "The Christian View of Work," Henry explores one of the ways in which Christian social ethics might be expressed in the workplace. He points out that Scripture especially underscores the value of work as part of a believer's witness in the world:

---

132. Henry, *Aspects of Christian Social Ethics*, 21. Henry has been especially criticized on this point for taking too narrow view of God's purposes, and for too individualistic of an approach to morals. This appears, however, to be based on a misunderstanding of what Henry is saying. He does not mean that Christian social ethics begin and end with individual relationships, but rather that they must start there; for criticism of Henry's approach see Rasmussen's review, 178–79.

133. Henry, *Aspects*, 22.

134. Ibid., 26; Smedes, though not responding specifically to *Aspects*, criticizes Henry on this point, claiming that this amounts not to a genuine social ethic, but rather to simply a call for more preaching; Smedes, in *Salt and Light*, 43. Henry though contends that the church's primary calling is not the setting up of just social structures, but of "ordering its own life" in accord with divinely revealed principles, in such a way that its life stands in stark contrast to the world; Henry, ibid., 52.

135. Henry, *Aspects*, 22.

136. Ibid., 27.

> A distinctive feature of New Testament ethics is its call to every believer to serve God and neighbor. Within family and community redeemed man stands in social relationship to both divine and human society. This dual relationship motivates his social responsibilities and by it he is linked to the whole enterprise of civilization.[137]

Henry goes on to describe how "work for the believer is a sacred stewardship, and in fulfilling his job he will either accredit or violate the Christian witness."[138] Henry believes that Christianity gives unique meaning and value to the concept of work as a "divinely appointed sphere where man as a worker is ordained to glorify God, and in his name to serve his fellow man."[139]

Henry maintains that it is absolutely crucial for a religion to speak to the relevance of the workplace, since it is the arena where most people spend most of their time. Unless Christianity can give meaningful interpretation to people's work it risks fostering the false notion of a secular-sacred divide and denying the all-encompassing demands of the Gospel. This is highly relevant to the present study for it underscores yet another way in which Henry aims to show the holistic demands (though he never uses that term) of the Gospel. This portion of this text represents one of Henry's strongest admonitions for the church to avoid unbiblically dichotomizing various aspects of life as sacred while relegating others as secular.

> If the church yields [one's] work and leisure to secularism, and asks him to reserve only prayer meeting or Sunday services for God, then it erodes the biblical concept of Christian commitment that encompasses the vast oceanfront of secular concerns to but a tiny, inadequate beachhead of private devotion.[140]

Henry's discussion of work then proceeds in regards to three subtopics. First, he further explores "The Recognition of Work as a Calling." Here Henry traces the demise of the biblical notion of work as a sacred calling through Roman Catholicism's determination that only the priestly office could rightly be considered as a calling. The Reformers denounced

---

137. Ibid., 31.

138. Ibid.

139. Ibid., 32; cf. Blomberg, *Christians in an Age of Wealth*, chapter seven, under "Work as Vocational Stewardship."

140. Ibid., 34. For a contemporary evangelical text that addresses labor and the Kingdom of God, see Witherington III, *Work: A Kingdom Perspective on Labor*.

this notion though, and returned to the scriptural teaching that all work is sacred. Luther and Calvin both advocated a return to the scriptural view teaching that any vocation might be understood as a calling (see Exod 31:2–11; Isa 22:20; 1 Thess 4:11; Rom 11:29; 1 Cor 7:20, et al.). Henry also characteristically takes Fundamentalism to task for not recognizing this, and for fostering the notion that only ministerial work properly fits that bill. Henry concludes of work:

> Every time the Christian worker leaves his home for work, he moves from the private social sphere of the family to the public sphere of labor and economics. Through the Christian on the job the world meets the church. But it meets far more: it meets the Divine Worker.[141]

Second, Henry looks at "The Bible and the Dignity of Work." Here he observes that "biblical religion stresses the dignity of work in various ways."[142] First, it affirms that the dignity of work is maintained in God's purpose, especially the biblical mandate to exercise dominion over the earth, in God's example as Creator, Sustainer, and Redeemer, in the example of Jesus, the carpenter from Nazareth, and in the example of the early church.[143] Henry's points here are important. First, God's mandate to the human race regarding creation is precisely to subject creation to the moral purposes of God, "to lift the physical and animal worlds to their proper function under God."[144] Second, it must be understood that labor is not a product of the fall, but an invitation for man to join the creative work of God. "Work is permeated by purpose; it is intended to serve God, benefit mankind, make nature subservient to the moral program of creation."[145] Also, Christianity, uniquely among the world's religions, affirms the value of the material world and of labor. "Man as a worker finds his archetype in God the mighty Worker."[146] God's work reflects God's character, as "Planner, Preserver, and Lover"—as "thinker, willer, and redeemer." So too then human work should reflect these qualities of the God who entreats his people to work on his behalf.[147] Jesus the carpenter

---

141. Henry, *Aspects*, 45.
142. Ibid., 47.
143. Ibid., 47–53.
144. Ibid., 47.
145. Ibid., 48.
146. Ibid., 50.
147. Ibid., 51.

himself especially models for believers that it is possible and desirable to "glorify God at a factory bench or on the assembly line."[148]

Though Henry has much more to say about work in relation to the Christian calling, it will suffice to note that in all of this Henry endeavors to advocate that the workplace is one of the primary arenas of life in which the attentive Christian can affectively influence and transform society. Because of the unique value that Christianity places on the notion of work, workers in any field have an inherent obligation to bring to the workplace their Christian commitments, and to allow those commitments to shape their personal and professional relationships, as well as their own productivity. "To say 'I'm a soul-winner, but I cobble shoes to pay expenses' is both right and wrong: while Christian witness is always a believer's responsibility, the work he does involves far more than a means of livelihood and carries tremendous spiritual overtones."[149] In other words, Henry aims to show that when it comes to social ethics, most Christians already have by virtue of their work environment an avenue through which they can be salt and light in the world. The church then should endeavor to affirm the value of all work, and to affirm the biblical teaching on vocational calling as extending to every type of work.

Henry's approach to Christian involvement in legislation is one that emphasizes preservation over transformation. That is, he believes transformation only comes about by regenerate individuals, but that the church must strive for the preservation of that which is good and noble.[150] This of course raises an important question, and one that Henry never answers, namely what of the society in which nothing is left worth preserving? It is precisely on this point that Henry has been sharply criticized by Smedes, who also rightly notes that Henry has not sufficiently articulated why economic rights only extend to what one already has.[151]

---

148. Ibid., 52.

149. Ibid., 70.

150. Ibid., 72.

151. Smedes, in *Salt and Light*, 54. As Smedes points out, Henry's notion of "preservation" is somewhat vague and seems to presume a society in which government is functioning at least minimally in the interest of the people. But Henry has not worked out though what the idea of preservation should look like in a society in which government has abandoned the interest of the people all together, as for example, in North Korea. Smedes point regarding economic rights appears to refer to the issue of those who lack even basic necessities, and the question of whether they have a right to such. Also, as Stassen and Gushee note, the issue of property rights among Christians has been variously interpreted, including the idea that such a notion is foreign to biblical

That said, Henry's position on economic rights is to be preferred over that of Padilla, who exaggerates Jesus' political agenda.[152]

Henry's ensuing argument, however, about the role of the church in society can be traced via several key points. First, historically the church within a short period of time after its inception moved away from the idea that "the company of the redeemed constitutes a new society" and toward "the larger ecclesial ambition to Christianize the outside world."[153] This program would ultimately lead to the disastrous union of church and State, of which the negative consequences are well known. That union would ultimately lead to the isolation of religion from the public sphere as skepticism of religious contributions mounted. Despite this, Henry comes back again to the importance of "the revealed will of God" regarding the relationship between church and State. That is, Scripture has something vital to say to the exercise of government. "The church must expound the revealed will of God for the political order no less than for the other spheres of life, for all are answerable and subject to divine judgment."[154] But what precisely should this look like, and what principles should the church follow?

First, Henry points out that the church can demand moral acquiescence from its members, but not from society at large. "To impose a particular theory of society and Christian moral ideals upon unresponsive masses both abuses ecclesiastical influence and breeds resentment

---

Christianity (e.g., Tolstoy). Against this and the opposite extreme which may be seen as an uncritical endorsement of capitalism, Stassen and Gushee propose "a qualified right to private property subordinate to the primary norm of economic justice as an aspect of God's reign"; Stassen and Gushee, 420.

152. Padilla says, for example, "no justice is done to the evidence provided in the Gospels in any reconstruction of Jesus' death that disregards the political charge implied in the *titulus* written on the cross: 'This is the king of the Jews.' He did not die as a religious teacher who had become an unbearable annoyance . . . but as a political rebel"; C. René Padilla, "Politics of the Kingdom of God," in *Proclaiming Christ in Christ's Way*, 188. But Padilla overlooks that it was the charge of blasphemy, a charge associated with his religious claims, not his political subversion, that got Jesus arrested and then crucified. As Newbigin points out (though not referring directly to Padilla), this view, often rooted in attempts to identify Jesus with the Zealot movement cannot be sustained; Newbigin, *The Open Secret*, 98; see also Henry et al., *The Ministry of Development*, 98; cf. also Burridge, who says that to associate the biblical concept of the Kingdom of God with a political state is highly problematic, given that the term should be understood as especially "the reign of God," wherein the emphasis on not on locality, but on Deity; Burridge, *Imitating Jesus*, 41.

153. Henry, *Aspects*, 72.

154. Ibid., 76.

of church interference in government."[155] With Karl Barth, Henry avows that the church's aim is not "to achieve a Christian society through political action."[156] Instead, the church is to focus on the moral obligations of believers. "Through government of its own members, the church promotes the welfare of society as a whole."[157] However, this should not be understood to mean that the church must remain silent regarding society at large. Not only is the church called to pray for its civic leaders, "but also, as part of the whole counsel of God, to proclaim publicly the divinely intended role of civil government."[158] Furthermore:

> this proclamation involves more than preaching political duty and morality to its own members . . . . The church must lead men to understand government as guardian of justice, must condemn legal infractions as crimes against the State, and must emphasize the culpability of offenders and their need to repent.

But the church must not stop even there. It has the right and duty to call upon rulers, even pagan rulers, to maintain order and justice. It must stress the divine responsibility of government, condemn every repudiation of divine answerability, and challenge the State's neglect of its duty.[159]

In Henry's discussion of the "practical considerations" of Christian involvement in legislation, he hones in on the key problem around which most errors regarding social concern have centered. Time and again Henry locates the neglect of "scriptural principles" as the root cause of both excess and neglect in the church's social calling.[160] Theological liberals in setting aside the demand for personal regeneration and thus by disconnecting social engagement from the Christ of Scripture became subject to a number of other, non-scriptural controlling forces, such as political powers and parties. Conservative Christians, on the other hand, who ought to have been at the forefront of the race and civil rights movements in the southern U.S., instead remained (mostly) on the sidelines because of confused priorities. "Indignation over statute-breaking ran deeper in the Bible Belt than a sense of guilt concerning the injustice of

---

155. Ibid., 78.
156. Ibid., 79.
157. Ibid.
158. Ibid., 81.
159. Ibid., 81–82.
160. Ibid., 107; 108; 123; 129.

their own local laws."[161] Because of this, "in shaping a climate of public opinion, the ministry and the laity need the firm guidance of scriptural principles more than sentimental ideals championed by modern social reformers."[162] Again, those guiding principles are minimally described:

> the divine source and sanction of human rights; the accountability of men and nations to objective justice and transcendent moral law, and the servant-role of the State as a minister of justice and order in a fallen society; the permanent significance of the social commandments of the Decalogue; the inclusion of property rights as human rights; and so on.[163]

Finally, in closing, Henry draws attention to "The Nature of God" and "Social Ideals" in order to emphasize the inherent relationship between God's character and the people he begets. This is actually a very crucial piece of Henry's take on Christian social involvement and an essential component for getting it right: "How the theologian defines and relates God's sovereignty, righteousness, and love actually predetermines his exposition of basic positions in many areas—in social ethics no less than in soteriology and eschatology."[164]

In this section Henry underscores the necessity of distinguishing between the justice of God and the love of God, which though related and at times overlapping, are not identical with one another. The failure of liberal social programs has been the equivocation of justice with love, and thereby minimizing one of justice's inherent attributes in God, namely God's wrath. Despite attempts by Barth and others to conflate God's love and justice, Henry points out that Scripture disallows for such a move. By confusing the two, the roles of church and State become equally confused since, as Philip Schaff has observed, the State exists to administer justice and the church to administer love.[165] The solution to maintaining justice and its attenuating concept of God's wrath, along with God's love and benevolence and its components in grace and redemption, Henry points again to the primacy of Scripture:

---

161. Ibid., 123. See also the ensuing discussion in this study regarding Henry's notion of "a moment of protest." Oddly, Henry himself expresses "personal reservations about some aspects of civil rights legislation"; Henry, in *Salt and Light*, 51.
162. Ibid.
163. Ibid., 124.
164. Ibid., 146.
165. Ibid., 170.

the Bible unmistakably states the spiritual foundation of the world order. Justice belongs to the very being of God, whose righteousness is the sure source of law. He commands justice among his creatures; he will judge human justice eschatologically by divine justice. The Bible, moreover, discredits any theological maneuver that would demote either the righteousness or the love of God to inferior status by viewing divine love either as a matter of necessity or of caprice, or divine righteousness as a mere differentiation of love. Scripture warns against so fusing and confusing righteousness and love that the dominance of either nullifies the other. The Bible stands sentry against speaking of God's love as the foremost or conditioning divine attribute; it discredits fitting God's justice to love's convenience.[166]

Despite the fact that Henry's treatment of social ethics requires further clarification at points, especially as it relates to moving from principles to specific applications, and delineating more clearly the issue of rights and how far they extend, his call to greater social action that included political involvement and serving the poor has been welcomed and celebrated. More importantly, his regeneration model offers greater fidelity to Scripture than some expressions of holistic mission, for example, that tend to overstate Jesus' supposed revolutionary agenda. Also, Henry's emphasis on work provides an important element essential to human dignity, and related closely to the *imago dei*, that is often missing in holistic missions discussions.[167]

Theological Foundations

Up to this point we have noted Henry's fundamental assessment of the moral problem (deviation from biblical foundations) and his basic

---

166. Ibid., 169.

167. Texts advocating a more holistic approach to evangelism and social concern in which a theology of work as part of social transformation is noticeably absent, are Sider's *Good News and Good Works* and Escobar's *New Global Mission*, regarding the latter, especially 153–54. A few other texts do minimally refer to the value of work, such as Tizon's citation of Vinay Samuel's "ten aspects of personhood," which includes "a vocational self"; Tizon, *Transformation After Lausanne*, 146; Kirk also critiques the tendency to associate the Protestant work ethic uncritically with capitalism, but this turns into more of a criticism of the excesses of capitalism than a positive development of a theology of work. In addition, the volume *Jubilee Manifesto*, edited by Michael Schluter and John Ashcroft, features a chapter on case studies that addresses employment strategies as part of social concern, but again, not a theology of work.

declaration of the fundamental solution (the application of scriptural principles). Now we turn to his more fully developed theological agenda. Typically, theological defenses of evangelical social concern focus on the Kingdom of God and the various and many other doctrines informed by this theme in Scripture. These other themes include the imago Dei, soteriology, ecclesiology (i.e., the purpose of the church), and the biblical concepts of justice, righteousness, and shalom, as indicated in the introduction.[168] What makes Henry's discussion of each of these topics unique, is that he unpacks them within the overall context of the doctrine of revelation, as that is the central issue he addresses in GRA. And so while Henry shares some of the same concerns about the loss of a social agenda, divine revelation and its supreme importance for Christian thought and practice is always paramount, and none of these other theological topics can be rightly understood outside of that overarching doctrine.

The Image of God and Social Concern

Just as the biblical concept of the *imago Dei* informs Henry's view of evangelism, as demonstrated in the previous chapter, so too does it inform his understanding of social concern. Specifically, Henry's thirteenth thesis relates to the *imago* as, in Henry's words, "Bestower of spiritual life, the Holy Spirit, enables individuals to appropriate God's truth savingly, and attest its power in their personal experience."[169] His point is that the work of the Holy Spirit in God's children causes the truth of God's message to manifest in concrete ways within the contours of everyday life.

Henry argues that, owing to the image of God, people as well as "inspired books" proclaim the will of God. Both Scripture and the lives it shapes testify to God's will for humanity. To show this, Henry argues that the NT everywhere points out that to be saved is to exhibit a radically transformed moral life. Paul for instance, likens what God does in the believer to the original act of creation (2 Cor 4:6). Furthermore, "Only a wickedly apostate pseudochurch, or theologically ignorant church can and would neglect as a central preaching theme God's life-transforming

---

168. Cf. Kirk, *Good News of the Coming Kingdom*, 46–47, 48–58; Costas, *Christ Outside the Gate*, 16; Sider, *Good News and Good Works*, under chapter 3, "The Dawning Kingdom"; et. al.

169. *GRA*, 4:494.

plan of salvation."[170] The church then as a community of redemption and transformation must hold fast to two convictions, so as not to confuse its purpose: "first, that God ordains civil government to preserve justice and restrain disorder in fallen society, and second, that he commissions the church to exhibit in word and deed the moral standards by which Christ at his return will judge all mankind and all nations."[171]

With that understanding regarding the church's mandate, the church is to exhibit a radical new lifestyle in a fallen world. The evangelical believer should endeavor then to see the world and humanity through the eyes of Christ (Phil 2:5). As such, God has both "a special eye for the poor, a special duty for the rich." Specifically, "Christians are to stand on the side of the poor against exploitation, injustice and oppression; sensitive to human needs, they are to respond generously as God has enabled them." In doing so, they "manifest what it means to be the people of God."[172]

This is abundantly evident in the NT, which frequently links together "the truth of God's revelation with the transforming power of divine redemption." Paul clearly has this idea in mind when he speaks of

---

170. Ibid., 495.

171. Ibid. Elsewhere Henry says, similarly, "the church is not only to proclaim the gospel at the edges of history, but she is to exemplify the standards by which at the end of history Christ will judge the world and is in fact already even now judging it. She is to herald the availability of salvation for all who repent and receive and follow Christ. The church must leave no doubt that she serves a supernatural, self-revealing God, and that she is entrusted with the very Word and will of God, proclaims divinely revealed truths and commands, and offers a divinely vouchsafed redemption. To perceive the church only in terms of ethical and salvific probabilities, and not as the bearer of moral absolutes and soteric imperatives, is to eclipse her transcendent Ground"; Henry, *Twilight of a Great Civilization*, 32; cf. Dyrness, who observes that the imago is especially relational, and that as such it relates do human activity, what humans are called to do as God's covenant partners; Dyrness, *Let the Earth Rejoice*, 31–33.

172. *GRA*, 4:496. Henry's phrasing, "a special eye for the poor, a special duty for the rich" seems preferable to "a preferential option for the poor," as in liberation theology. This phrase, originating with Gustavo Guitérrez, one of the early founders of Latin American liberation theology, is problematic because it has the appearance of an unqualified association of poverty with piety. Henry's way of stating this avoids the implication that the rich, or riches *per se*, are necessarily looked upon less favorably by God. The better view though is to understand neither the rich nor riches as necessarily objects of judgment, unless the rich demonstrate neglect of the poor and greater love for money than for God. This seems to be the lesson of the rich young ruler (Luke 18:18–23), and was a frequent concern of preaching by the church fathers; for example, see Basil, *On Social Justice*, Kindle edition, Introduction, under "Holy Simplicity: Basil as Priest and Homilist." On liberation theology, see also Costas, *Christ Outside the Gate*, 123–33.

being a new creation in Christ (2 Cor. 5:17). In addition, this coherence and unity between the word of truth and a transformed life is echoed at several points in 1 Thessalonians (1:5, 9; 2:13). In Ephesians Paul stresses the transforming Spirit that produces "good works" in those in Christ (Eph 2:5, 10). Even when declaring the divine origin of Scripture, Paul is careful to point out that it issues in good works (2 Tim 3:16–17). In sum, "the goal of God's truth is godliness. Toward this end God has given the transcendent revelation of his Word as a teacher to escort us to 'the crown of righteousness' (2 Tim 4:8)."[173] Or, as Henry says elsewhere, "the good news requires visibility no less than audibility."[174]

Despite the fall having marred the image of God in humanity, God's redemptive plan especially includes the full restoration of the image of God in humanity. And this is especially a work of the Holy Spirit. "To the regenerate family of God the transforming Holy Spirit imparts virtues and powers that characterize the eternal age (Eph 1:14)." In fact, the very term "Holy" as it concerns the Spirit (Luke 11:13; Eph 1:13; 4:30; 1 Thess 4:8), must be understood in terms of the Spirit's work in bringing about "an ethical transformation of life in which love (*agapē*) is the forefront virtue."[175] As Henry observes regarding Romans 8, "the Spirit shapes a new mindset that prizes God's truth and stimulates wholehearted obedience to his will." Also, Hebrews especially highlights the present moral imperative based on God's new covenant, at the center of which lies a new mind and new heart for the believer (Heb 8:10). Also in Hebrews, the church stands proleptically between the OT and the promised new age. In the just cited Hebrews 8:10, which quotes Jeremiah 31:31–34, "the righteousness of God is a preeminent concern of the community of the faithful." As such, "the covenant focuses not upon human physical phe-

---

173. Ibid.

174. Henry, *A Plea for Evangelical Demonstration*, 82. Henry is quick to point out here that deeds are revelatory only when accompanied by a Gospel word; ibid., 83.

175. Ibid., 501; see also Austin, who argues that being made in the image of God necessitates that biblical compassion be understood as a matter not of charity, but of justice. He says, "we reflect and represent who God is as human persons made in his image. God is the locus of ultimate value, and we, as human beings created in his image and to reflect his character share that value. This has important implications for ethics generally and, and for the virtue of compassion specifically. Given that all humans are made in the image of God, all human beings possess a basic dignity, a fundamental value such that they have a conditional right to have their basic needs met"; Austin and Geivett, *Being Good*, Kindle ed., under part three entitled "Love," and the chapter therein titled "Compassion."

nomena—such as speaking in tongues or bodily miracles—but on welding man's inmost self as a psychophysical unity to the holy will of God."[176] In fact, not only Hebrews, but the whole NT resounds with this theme:

> The Old Testament had promised forgiveness of sins and had enjoined moral obedience, but did so in anticipation of the earthly life, sacrifice, and heavenly ministry of Jesus Christ the High Priest after Melchizedek's order. Now with the realized substitutionary death and resurrection of the promised Redeemer (1 Cor 15:3–4), the outpouring and indwelling and infilling of the Spirit enliven ethical attainment and nurtured the expectation of Christ's return, to whose righteous image the godly shall be eschatologically conformed.[177]

After his conversion, the apostle Paul reflected in his own life this eschatological perspective. He ceased viewing others by "worldly standards" (2 Cor 5:18) and emphasized the new life in the Spirit for those in Christ (Gal 5:25). Even though he also stressed the intimate relationship between God and believer (Rom 8:15–17) and the "universal accessibility of the truth of God mediated through the prophets and apostles and illuminated by the Holy Spirit (2 Tim 3:16; 1 Cor 2:9–14)," along with the dramatic freedom inherent in being once-and-for-all forgiven through Christ's atoning sacrifice, Paul also insisted that present transformation requires an emphasis on future consummation. Only then shall we know even as we are known (1 Cor 13:12).

Henry's emphasis on the priority of redemption here should not be overlooked. The righteousness of the believer flows from being justified in Christ and conformed to his image. Thus, as Moore observes, "individual regeneration is not the sum of the message of the lordship of Christ," but rather biblically results in an active social concern. Yet, wherever the priority of redemption is lost, one runs the risk, as is evident in the Social Gospel, of minimizing the need for individual salvation and an elevation of humanity's supposed innate goodness, as opposed to goodness that flows from a transformed life. This is the key to Henry's regenerational model.[178]

---

176. Ibid., 501–2.

177. Ibid., 502.

178. Moore, *The Kingdom of Christ*, 127; for the essence of the social gospel, see Visser't Hooft, *The Background of the Social Gospel*, 169–87; see also Ferguson who says "the person who has been justified by God then pursues righteousness (1 Tim 6:11; 2 Tim 2:22). Righteous living includes . . . the doing of charitable deeds (Matt 6:1–2; 2 Cor 9:9). Human righteous conduct is the consequence of God's justifying activity in Christ"; Ferguson, *The Church of Christ*, 158. See also Nicole's statement

Good News for the Oppressed

Henry's fourteenth thesis states that "the church approximates God's kingdom in miniature, mirroring to each generation the power and joy of the appropriated realities of divine revelation." Echoing his earlier statements about the content of the Gospel, he adds, "into the morass of sinful human history and experience the gospel heralds a new order of life shaped by God's redemptive intervention." In this new order Christ overturns all the works of the enemy in every arena of human life. "Christ's gospel is comprehensively liberating."[179]

The church then functions as "the sign of God's redemptive presence in the world." As such, the church provides evidence of God's redemptive work. "The church evidences that in fallen history a new humanity and a new society can arise where reconciliation and righteousness, hope and joy replace the rampant exploitation and oppression of fellow humans and their despair of survival."[180] This theme of God's restorative work for the poor and needy is a common theme in Scripture. The book of James reminds the church of the travesty of neglecting the poor, who occupy a place of special concern in the eyes of God. James also warns against wrongly giving special attention to the rich. As Henry observes, "To direct the good news only to a preferred company and to divert it from those who stand in direct need of it because they are sunk in physical as well as spiritual poverty is scandalous." To understand this biblical imperative, the church must turn its gaze upon the Mosaic Law's "special provision for the poor" and note that the "prophets sternly condemned oppression of the weak and destitute by the rich of the land."[181]

---

that "Christianity is essentially and pre-eminently a redemptive religion"; Nicole, "The Nature of Redemption," 193–222.

179. Ibid., 542. Though no longer as contentious as it once was, the issue of relationship between the Kingdom of God (eschatology) and Jesus' ethical teachings has long been the subject of theological debate. A excellent summary of this debate, tracing the development especially in Henry Cadbury, Albert Schweitzer, C. H. Dodd, E. Käsemann, and more recently, Robert W. Funk, see Sanders, *Ethics in the New Testament*, 1–11.

180. Ibid., 543; cf. Ott and Straus, who say similarly, "The church as God's kingdom people manifests the character of the kingdom in its common life as redemptive community of love and its public life as salt and light in the world"; Ott and Strauss, *Encountering Theology of Mission*, 196.

181. *GRA*, 4:544; cf. Isa 3:14–15; 10:2; 11:4; 58:7; Jer 2:34; 5:4, 28; 39:10; 40:7; 52:15–16; Ezek 16:49; 18:12, 17; 22:29; Dan 4:27; Amos 4:1; 5:11–12; Zech 7:10; see also Wright, *Old Testament Ethics for the People of God*, Kindle edition, under chapter

Henry also muses about Christ's frequent interest in social outsiders. "At all times, he placed himself in the service of others in the moment of their need." And in fact, Jesus himself was something of an outcast, as H. Cecil McConnell observes, given Jesus' migrant parents and suspicious birth. Even so, "he persisted in associating with the worst people and justifying himself."[182] To not understand God's concern for the disenfranchised and downtrodden is to misunderstand the very mission and purpose of the church. The church therefore must exercise great care regarding the causes with which it aligns itself. "The Christian world mission dare not be labeled sympathetic to ongoing domination and oppression when its true mission encompasses new freedom and new life."[183] The present Evangelical malaise in this regard "is one not simply of knowledge, but rather of irresponsibility and lovelessness—of people who know better, but do not care and do not act, of persons who affirm God with their lips but not with their lives."[184]

As to what precisely then Christian concern for the poor and needy should look like, Henry makes several important points. First, he points out that identifying with the poor must go beyond merely moving in among them, as some missionaries have tended to do. Such strategies are ineffective, according to Henry. "The poor sometimes regard such missionary migrants as 'kooks.'" Instead, the church as Christ's earthly representative, is "called now, to challenge and contain the powers of evil." And in fact, here Henry presents a rather integrated understanding of the church's proclamational and social tasks:

---

five, "Economics and the Poor." Regarding the book of James, Marshall points out that wealth and poverty is one of five dominant themes in James (the other four being temptation and maturity, faith and action, sins and speech, and patience and prayer), as evident in the following passages: Jas 1:9–11; 2:1–13; 4:8–10, 13–16; 5:1–6). Marshall also points out that the references to God championing the poor refers not to the poor in general but the poor who believe in Him (Jas 1:12; 5:10–11); Marshall, *A Concise New Testament Theology*, 253–55.

182. *GRA*, 4:544; McConnell, cited in Henry, 544.

183. Ibid., 545; see also Henry's observation that "the ascended Lord wants to extend his victory over sin and evil through us, the new society, and enjoins us to be salt and light to the world. We are to have an illuminating and preserving role, one that includes the ministry of compassion, the benevolent ministry of the church throughout history"; Henry et al., *The Ministry of Development*, 99; on Jesus' concern for the marginalized and oppressed, see Burridge, *Imitating Jesus*, 261–68; plus, it is widely acknowledged that the Gospel of Luke especially emphasizes Jesus' concern for the oppressed and marginalized.

184. *GRA*, 5:545.

as the living Body of its living Head the church is now to resist the Evil One, now to indict rampant injustices and support the afflicted and oppressed, now to sensitize moral conscience against wrong and for the right, now to exhibit the purpose of God in a new life and a new community while it proclaims the revealed truth and will of God.[185]

In addition, the responsibility to care for the poor and needy falls on all people everywhere, not just Christians. Everyone is capable of offering something to the less fortunate, "even it if need be only a kind word, a sympathetic tear, or a prayer." Furthermore, the biblical story of the Good Samaritan calls all people to understand themselves as "stewards of God's gifts and to respond to the needs of his neighbor." That said, however, God ultimately requires more than words for the church. "If words are all we have, they will choke us in judgment: 'By your words you will be justified and by your words you will be condemned' (Matt 12:37)." Not only that, but Christian social concern must focus on development issues, and move beyond mere relief, "to determine the root causes of social need and to cope with the conditions that perpetuate problems in an ongoing way." Even so, he applauds the work of the *Salvation Army*, and *World Vision*, especially, which has tended to be more of a relief nature.[186]

In a manner that likewise reflects some of his earlier thought on the subject, Henry notes the value of a Christian view of both work and life itself.[187] But ultimately all Christian social concern must be governed by a scriptural framework. "The gospel can achieve what neither speculative philosophy nor secular ideology can accomplish, that is, nurture an evangelical renaissance in which God sovereignly shapes a new creature in a new society."[188]

The Bible notes two forms of poverty, material and spiritual. Among these, spiritual poverty is by far the greater affliction in part because those in physical poverty can do something to change their condition. Henry goes on to point out how Christians sometimes misuse Jesus' statements about the poor such as that in Matt 26:11—"the poor ye always have with you" (KJV)—as an excuse to neglect the poor. But the Markan parallel

---

185. Ibid.

186. Ibid., 548. Recent texts that address the need for Christian social concern to focus on development rather than strictly disaster relief, include Lupton, *Toxic Charity*; Keller, *Ministries of Mercy*; but especially Corbett and Fikkert, *When Helping Hurts*.

187. See Henry, *Aspects of Christian Social Ethics*, especially chapter 2.

188. *GRA*, 4:549.

explicitly prohibits such an interpretation. "Ye have the poor with you always, and whensoever ye will ye may do them good" (Mark 14:7). Plus, John 13:29 shows that Jesus commonly gave alms to the poor.[189]

In terms of specifics, Henry warns the church against spending money on extravagant buildings while the needs within their community go unmet. "When believers speak of the church with pride only in terms of costly buildings that stand idle much of the week, while multitudes lack shelter and warmth, the distance between Christians and the needy seems needlessly multiplied."[190] He proposes therefore that church properties must be used to serve the community during the other six days a week when they mostly sit empty. Possibilities include literacy training, teaching sewing, nutrition, crafts, or even art skills. He also calls for two sorts of programs to be offered by the church: those that might be characterized as "rescue operations" and "remedial programs." Both he says are "implicit in redemptive religion."[191]

When Henry does directly address the relationship between evangelism and social concern in this section, Henry's unique perspective begins to emerge:

> In and through its evangelistic mission to the world, the church is to enunciate and implement the revealed principles that God addresses to the human race by exemplary Christian leadership to the whole realm of public affairs. Social justice is not, moreover, simply an appendage to the evangelical message; it is an intrinsic part of the whole, without which the preaching of the gospel itself is truncated. Theology devoid of social justice is a deforming weakness of much present-day evangelical witness.[192]

To say, as Henry does here, that social justice is "an intrinsic part of the whole" and that "without it the preaching of the gospel is truncated" seems to require some nuancing regarding his notion of the priority of

---

189. Ibid., 550. Carson observes of this passage, "it was customary to give alms to the poor on Passover night, the temple gates being left open from midnight on, allowing beggars to congregate there. On any night other than Passover it is hard to imagine why the disciples might have thought Jesus was sending Judas out *to give something to the poor*: the next day would have done just as well"; Carson, *The Gospel of John*, Accordance electronic, n.p. Also in the context of John 13:29 is the very important reality that the NT emphasizes that shared life ought to be a prominent characteristic of God's people; cf. Flemming, *Recovering the Full Mission of God*, 122.

190. *GRA*, 4:550.

191. Ibid., 551.

192. Ibid.

proclamation. This statement suggests that Henry's sees social concern as vital concerning the function of the church in society. Thus it seems clear that for Henry, contra Bosch's claim otherwise, priority and integration are not mutually exclusive concepts. This is evident in that Henry goes on to explain that Christian social engagement is endemic to the very nature of Christianity itself and an essential part of one's Christian witness:

> The Christian should know himself by spiritual birthright to be in the fallen world as a member of the already existing "new community" which is not only called "out of the world" but also disperses through it as "salt" and "light." In this social engagement the fellowship of the faithful bears witness to the living risen Head of the Body and to the coming King before whom every knee must bow.[193]

Elsewhere, Henry makes a similar statement about the interrelated nature of the church's evangelistic and social mandates. He says, "The God of justice *and* the God of justification, these two emphases stand together."[194] However, Henry also gives priority in this to the need for justification:

> If all we have is the declaration that God wills justice, we'll all pass each other on the road to hell. For a race of fallen sinners, there is no ultimately good news in just that. There is no hope apart from the message that God forgives sins and offers new power for righteousness.[195]

The great tragedy of the contemporary evangelism-social concern debate is that it polarizes various sides against one another. Because of this, Henry's call for a socially relevant Gospel deserves a fresh hearing. Perhaps the greatest contemporary perversion of Christian social concern finds expression in the advent and self-centered tendencies of the modern-day prosperity gospel, wherein the acquisition of material goods is held up as a sign of God's favor or blessing. Even beyond this extreme, though, many western Christians have failed to properly understand the biblical injunctions that ought to compel believers to less materialism and greater generosity directed toward the less well-off. Such concern is

---

193. Ibid., 553.

194. Henry et al., *The Ministry of Development*, 102. Emphasis Henry's. This theme finds frequent repetition in Henry's discussions of Christian social concern, as evident in the next section.

195. Ibid.

all part of the church's role as a sign pointing to the qualities and reality of God's already/not yet Kingdom. So, while Christopher Little is right to say that the church does not usher in the Kingdom of God, he is less correct when he, in agreement with DeYoung and Gilbert, denies that the church engages in Kingdom work.[196] As Henry has shown, the church does indeed engage in Kingdom work, so long as one is careful to define what that means and not overstate the essence of that work.

The God of Justice and Justification

Regarding the biblical concept of justice, Henry argues that this is rooted in God's own character. In Scripture, the "Hebrew nouns *tsedeq* and *tsedeqah* and the Greek noun *dikaiosune* are properly translated either as "righteousness" or as 'justice.'" Though there is a slight nuance in meaning between the two, and the church has at times tended to emphasize one to the neglect of the other, while "the fact is that the God of the Bible requires attention to both." [197]

Scripture furthermore emphasizes God's non-preferential treatment. He is no respecter of persons (Acts 10:34; Rom 2:11; Eph 6:9; Col 3:25; 1 Pet 1:17).[198] Furthermore, "Scripture locates the supreme precedent for human justice in the fact that the God of justice grants each person his due."[199] This notion lies behind Jesus' "golden rule" of Matt 7:12, which he declared to be a summary of the law and prophets. The Bible also stresses God's retributive justice, or judgment according

---

196. Little, *Polemic Missiology*, chapter 1, "The Contours of Christian Mission." As Snyder observes, the church as Christ's body shares his reconciling work, and this includes concern for the poor and needy; Snyder, *The Community of the King*, under chapter four, "The Church in God's Plan"; cf. Moore, *The Kingdom of Christ*, 173. This is not to deny the church's role as the entry point to the Kingdom, as indicated by the giving of the keys of the Kingdom (Matt 16:19), but to instead say that this is simply not all there is. Also, Bockmuehl's criticism of Henry on the role of the church in relation to Christ's victory over oppression might have been avoided had Bockmuehl paid attention to Henry's other works. Instead, he looked solely at Henry's argument at Lausanne I, which Henry based on Isa 61/Luke 4; see Bockmuehl, *Evangelicals and Social*, 11.

197. Henry, *GRA*, 6: 404; cf. Henry's observation that "it is interesting to note that the words justice and righteousness in our Old Testament often come from the same Hebrew word; each goes hand in hand with the other"; "A Summons To Justice," 40.

198. Ibid., 405.

199. Ibid., 406; also, John 3:16 attests to the extension of God's love to all of humanity based on his non-preferential treatment; ibid.

to works. This theme runs throughout the OT and NT alike.[200] What is missing in Henry's analysis of the concept of justice from the OT to the NT, however, is a much needed discussion concerning the abundance of references to social justice in the OT, and the noticeable lack of explicit references in the NT.[201]

Even though Scripture emphasizes God's "special concern for the poor," one must be careful in expressing this. That is, the Bible does not associate wealth necessarily with injustice and poverty necessarily with justice. "It reflects the fact, rather, that the poor are often helpless against their exploiters."[202]

Once again, Henry warns against conflating God's justice and love as some (e.g., Barth, Brunner) have done. Henry's main point is that justice belongs to the realm of government and love to the realm of interpersonal relationships. When love and justice are conflated, it diminishes the fact reality that God's justice involves also his wrath and judgment. Rather, God takes up the cause of the poor precisely on account that he stands over creation as the final judge of all. Oppression of the poor and answering their distress represents a fundamental perspective of the Hebrew outlook (Exod 23:6; Ps 82:3), since "oppression of the poor is an affront to the Creator (Prov 17:5)."[203] Therefore, God's judgment of human works intends not with an eye toward works righteousness or the earning of God's favor, but in view of God's omniscience, justice and power.

Thus, in Scripture God's justice and mercy go together. "The God of covenant is the God of justice and salvation" (cf. Isa 45:21). Thus, "the Psalmist can say of Yahweh: 'The Lord loves righteousness and justice; the earth is full of his unfailing love" (Ps 33:5, NIV). The justice of God

---

200. Deut 32:15–43; Ps. 28:4; 78; 62:12; Job 34:11; Jer 25:14; Hos 12:2; Matt 16:27; Luke 12:45-48; Rom 2:2-16; 6:23; 2 Cor 5:10; 11:15; Col 3:24ff; 2 Thess 1:8ff; Heb 2:2ff; 10:26-31; Rev 20:12.

201. Some of this can be explained owing to the fact that Greek word *dikaiosunē*, usually translated "righteousness," at times can mean both righteousness and justice; even so, as Dempster observes regarding the construction of a Pentecostal social ethic, "church leaders will find it necessary to look to the Old Testament moral tradition to discover the biblical injunction for God's people to pursue social justice. Social justice is not an explicitly articulated ethical category within New Testament moral theology, although it is certainly implied"; Dempster, "Pentecostal Social Concern and the biblical Mandate for Social Justice," 129. The problem in Henry's account is that he gives insufficient attention to this discussion, which is a major point of tension in the prioritism-holism debate.

202. *GRA*, 6:408.

203. Ibid., 6:409.

"vindicates his people from their oppressors (Deut 32:4; 35ff; Hos 2:19; Mic 7:9).

Henry's concern to hold together justice and justification emphasizes that the neglect of either produces an imbalanced theological understanding of the Christian faith. In Scripture judgment and justice go together—God judges because he is inherently just. In his love and mercy though, he also offers grace and salvation. These are not the same and cannot be collapsed one into the other. Rather, "there is hope in the sinner's appeal to justice only if he lays claim by grace to the Just and Holy One whom God set forth a propitiation for sin that he might remain both 'just and the justifier of him that believes in Jesus' (Rom 3:26)."[204] Henry's point is that if one upholds the justice of God that demands righteousness and action on behalf of the poor, that one must also simultaneously uphold the judgment of God over sin, for it is the same God and same Judge who in his sovereignty and righteousness condemns both.[205] Furthermore, none of this can be known apart from Scripture. "Not from ourselves, but only from the just and justifying God known in his revelation . . . only from the objective literary deposit of Scripture can we gain both this bad news and good news about ourselves."[206]

Justice and the Kingdom of God

Henry points out that Jesus' parable of the unjust judge (Luke 18:1–8) underscores the reality that God ultimately judges all injustice and stands as "the supreme and heavenly trustee of justice."[207] That is, justice belongs to God. This leads Henry to discern four salient points regarding justice and the Kingdom of God.

First, justice only fully and entirely resides with the coming new heaven and new earth, "the home of justice" (2 Peter 3:13). Second,

---

204. Ibid., 6:414.

205. In this section Henry observes not only the theological shortcomings of Barth and Ritschl, but also of evangelicals on the issue of justice. He notes for instance, that in *The New International Dictionary of New Testament Theology* (ed. Colin Brown) that there oddly exists no article on justice and even seems to deliberately avoid reference to this in its article on righteousness. Furthermore, Tenney's five volume *The Zondervan Pictorial Encyclopedia of the Bible*, contains an extended essay in justification but nothing on justice, ibid., 6:411.

206. Ibid., 6:414.

207. Ibid., 6:419.

"justice has its very foundation and structure in the Kingdom of God." That is, "the source, content, and sanction of justice exist exclusively and uniquely in the nature and will of God." This is evident from OT passages such as Ps 11:7—"because Yahweh is righteous his law is righteous." Also, "to set oneself against the law of God is to challenge the divinely ordained course of creation and history (Jer 8:7)." In this, Henry does advocate the priority of God's self-revelation as it relates to justice. "Justice in the biblical view is grounded in the self-revealing God who stipulates its nature and content." Plus, "from the biblical point of view, social injustice is related to apostasy from the living God; injustice stems from false conceptions of duty that deny that Yahweh is Lord."[208]

Henry's third observation centers on Jesus as the fulfillment of divine love and justice. "Justice . . . steps dramatically into fallen history in the holy person of Messiah, Jesus Christ." This follows from the OT, which speaks of the Messiah overtly in terms of righteousness (Jer 23:5-6; 33:15; Zech 9:9). Furthermore, the NT "repeatedly applies to Jesus the term *dikaios* which means both righteousness and justice (Matt 27:19, 27:24; John 5:30; Acts 3:14, 7:54, 22:14; Rom 3:26; 1 John 1:9; 1 Pet 3:18; etc.)." As such, Jesus is "the living bulletin of God's incomparable justice and mercy." He models for a fallen humanity the enduring and binding nature of God's eternal laws and righteous character.[209]

This leads Henry then to his fourth and final observation, which gets directly at the church's task in the world. Here Henry says that Christians have an inherent responsibility in the social and political arenas. He first agrees with Schenk's observation that in apostolic Christianity, "the Christian is the one who fulfills the law." He says that Christians fulfill the law both by accepting Christ's substitutionary atonement, but also in "prayerful yearning and active working for the extension of God's kingdom (Luke 1:17)." This understanding he derives from the Lord's

---

208. Ibid., 428–29; cf Stephen C. Mott, who, as previously mentioned, says, "the reign of God is a central biblical concept which incorporates the imperative for social responsibility into God's goals in history. Rather than merely an ethical principle, justice is made part of the story of God's provision—the fall of humanity, the coming of Christ, the final reconciliation of all things under the sovereign rule of God"; Mott, *Biblical Ethics and Social Change*, 82; cf. Witherington, who argues that the phrase "Kingdom of God" is not the best tranlation of *basileia tou theou* "for the very good reason that the phrase often does not refer to a place, but rather an event or the result of an event, or to a state of being"; Witherington, *The Problem With Evangelical Theology*, Kindle edition, under "Jesus, Paul, and the Dominion of God."

209. Ibid., 6:431, 432.

prayer: "Thy kingdom come. Thy will be done in earth, as it is in heaven' (Matt 6:10, KJV)." Thus Henry declares that since the time of Jesus, his followers have taken great care to maintain a close connection between their inward faith and their outward lives.[210] As Henry says elsewhere, "to proclaim the criteria by which the Coming King will judge persons and nations, to exemplify those standards in the church as the new society, and to work for their recognition by the world—these are irreducible aspects of the Christian summons to the forgiveness of sins and new life, and to the lordship of the risen and returning King."[211]

The embodiment of Kingdom ethics can especially be found in the life of Jesus, who serves as the example of Christian morals, *par excellence*. Though evangelical theology has not always rightly emphasized this, the command to do so is amply attested in Scripture.[212] That said, Henry strongly warns against equating biblical justice with unbiblical socialism.[213]

The idea of the praxis of the Kingdom has wide support among Evangelicals who champion a socially relevant Gospel.[214] What Henry uniquely contributes to this discussion though is especially his argument that concern for justice within a biblical understanding of the demands of the Kingdom of God depends on the priority of revelation, since revelation alone provides the basic means by which to know God's just demands. Thus to deny that there is a certain priority to the proclamation of God's revelation as the means for making known God's will is not only problematic, it runs counter to the fact of Scripture itself, which is verbal-linguistic in nature. Furthermore, Henry's argument both here and in this entire chapter refutes the claim that to assign priority to one aspect of the church's mission serves only to excuse neglect of other tasks

---

210. Ibid., 6:434.

211. Henry, "American Evangelicals in a Turning Time," 1062.

212. Henry, *Christian Personal Ethics*, 398–418; cf. 1 Pet 2:21; 1 John 3:16; Heb 12:3; Phil 2:5; also texts which emphasize Christ as image on which believers are to model their own life, e.g., Rom 8:29; 1 Cor 15:49; 2 Cor 3:18; Col 3:10; other texts advocate that believers are to "put on Christ," e.g., Rom. 13:14; Gal 3:27; Eph 4:24; Col 3:10; ibid., 408; cf. Hesselgrave's discussion of incarnationalism vs. representationalism, in *Paradigms in Conflict*, 141–65.

213. At the center of this concern is the loss of central Christian doctrines, such as individual sin and the need of salvation; Henry, "Evangelicals in a Turning Time," 1060.

214. Cf. Stassen and Gushee, *Kingdom Ethics*, 21; Flemming, *Recovering the Full Mission of God*, 260–61; Padilla, "Politics," in *Proclaiming Christ in Christ's Way*, 190.

the church might carry out. As Henry has shown, there is simply no necessary correlation.[215]

The Church in the World

Any understanding of Christian social concern, especially in relation to evangelism, must deal with the general topic of ecclesiology, and more precisely with the purpose of the church in the world. Henry frequently deals with this issue, and in doing so often references both evangelism and social concern. For example, he says, "ideally, the purpose of the church is to preach the Gospel and to manifest unmerited, compassionate love."[216] In this though, Henry, as he does throughout his works, maintains the priority of the church's evangelistic mandate. "Surely evangelical Christianity has more to offer mankind than its unique message of salvation, even if that is its highest and holiest mission."[217]

The Church and the Christian Worldview

The need of a Christian worldview capable of overcoming unbiblical dualisms, especially between the secular and the sacred and between nature and grace, was a hallmark of the Reformation.[218] For both Luther and Calvin

---

215. Among those who claim that prioritism leads to neglect are Mott, *Biblical Ethics and Social Change*, 127 and also Bosch, *Transforming Mission*, 405; on the tendency to equivocate evangelism and social action, see Arias's declaration that healing ministry, whether "through prayer, medicine, pastoral counseling, group therapy, nutrition and mental health services, rehabilitation from drug addictions, or social reconciliation and the defense of human rights," is "an inseparable part of the announcement of the good news"; Arias, *Announcing the Reign of God*, 75; Wagner also admits that this claim is historically false, as many evangelicals who prioritized evangelism have also done much to advance social concern; Wagner, *Church Growth and the Whole*, 112–13.

216. Henry, *The God Who Shows Himself*, 60.

217. Ibid., 61.

218. As Nancy Pearcey observes, "the Reformers were eager to banish any form of dualism that denigrated God's creation, and so they argued that God created human nature as good in itself. Grace was not a substance added on to human nature," (i.e., *donum superadditum*), "but was God's merciful acceptance of sinners, whereby he redeems and restores them to their original perfect state"; Pearcey, *Total Truth*, 81. This issue, of course, gets at the very core of Henry's attack on natural theology, dependent as it was on Aquinas's borrowing of an Aristotelian view of nature; cf. ibid., 79. See also Kuyperian theologian Henry Van Til, who observes also that Calvin rejected Aquinas's

this especially took shape in their theology of work. However, according to Pearcey, the Reformers did not sufficiently provide their followers with the philosophical resources needed to defend this holistic emphasis against non-Christian alternatives. "As a result, the successors of Luther and Calvin went right back to teaching scholasticism in the Protestant universities, using Aristotle's logic and metaphysics as the basis of their systems—and thus, dualistic thinking continued to affect all the Christian traditions."[219] Key figures in reversing this trend, though, were Abraham Kuyper and Herman Dooyeweerd, two Dutch neo-Calvinists who especially emphasized "the formative impact of worldviews themselves and the need to evaluate them as unified wholes."[220] Like Henry, these thinkers sought to return not only to the ideals of Calvin in applying Christianity to all of life, but also to recapture "the Augustinian interpretation of

---

nature/Grace dichotomy, and sought to apply the Christian faith to all of life; Van Til, *Calvinistic Concept of Culture*, Kindle edition, under Chapter VII, "Calvin's Impact on Culture."

219. Pearcey, *Total Truth*, 82; Mark E. Roberts points out that a Christian worldview dominated western civilization prior to the Enlightenment, first in Augustinian form, and in the middle ages in Aristotelian-Christain form. Roberts traces the loss of a Christian worldview to a shift from "knowledge based on trust in God, to knowledge based in doubt, and to the actual loss of knowledge owing to the growing influence of naturalism; Roberts, "How the West Lost Its (Christian) Mind and Can Find it Again," 76.

220. Ibid., 313. Again, this is not to suggest that Arminian-Wesleyan traditions have been without concern for applying the truth of Christianity to all of life. There can be no doubt that Wesley himself did so. But both revivalism and liberalism tended to focus religion inwardly, and often this narrowing of Christianity can be traced to false notions about the Kingdom of God. For example, as Moore observes of the kingdom consensus that Henry helped advance, "a holistic view of redemption necessitates the cultivation of a rigorous worldview theology. In the emerging Kingdom theology of evangelical consensus, salvation as a matter of the 'heart' is not reduced to social justice (as in Social Gospel liberalism), nor is it a matter of personal ethical piety as in other forms of Protestant liberalism. Neither is it, however, the pietistic-world denying 'heart' religion, disconnected from matters of public justice and order, as in some forms of conservative revivalism"; Moore, *The Kingdom of Christ: The New Evangelical Perspective*, 125. Also, it might be argued that Protestantism itself is somewhat hardwired toward a belief-centered vs. a worldview centered understanding of Christianity, that is, a tendency to emphasize orthodoxy over orthopraxis. As Hunter observes, "the history of conservative Protestantism in twentieth-century America has, in large measure, been the history of the effort to maintain the purity and integrity of its theology." Furthermore, this has been the primary concern not only of theologians and ministers, "but the vast number of people calling themselves Evangelicals or Fundamentalists"; Hunter, *Evangelicalism: The Coming Generation*, 19; cf. Thornbury, *Recovering Classic Evangelicalism*, 159–64.

culture" portrayed in *City of God*.²²¹ As previously mentioned, Kuyper was especially influential of Henry's own work in this area.

When it comes to the social mandate of the church, Henry carefully articulates the importance of a Christian worldview as a necessary foundation in addressing social evils. In this, the church has a two-fold mandate. "The Christian task in the world includes that of calling to account the cultural milieu in view of God's revealed Word, and that of exhibiting the New Society's regenerate community life reflecting the wisdom, righteousness, and joy of serving the one true God."²²²

Henry argues that the church has a countercultural mission in two senses. First, it must "dispute not only the corrupt practices but also the alien beliefs about God and ultimate reality that inspire non-biblical perspectives on life and the world." Second, the church "challenges the notion that a good society and just state can in fact be permanently sustained by unregenerate human nature."²²³ In this regard Henry calls for a balanced approach to cultural engagement, one that rejects being overly optimistic about the prospects of societal improvement, and the opposite extreme that abandons all concern for culture. Also, Henry says this means not that there exists "*a* Christian culture" but rather, Christian culture in more general terms, wherein "the Christian community should seek to elaborate Christian culture vis-à-vis the antichristian or subchristian culture that engulfs it, and it should moreover seek to permeate secular society with the ideals and vitalities and realities of Christian culture."²²⁴

Furthermore, "it makes a critical difference whether or not one thinks and acts Christianly." What one believes about God's sovereignty, about being made in God's image, about God's design for marriage and sexuality, and so forth, informs our actions and gives Christians a

---

221. Vanhoozer, "The World Well Staged?" 16.

222. Henry, *Twilight of a Great Civilization*, 117; cf. his comment elsewhere, that "the Christian world-life view embraced heaven and earth from creation to end time and enlisted a fellowship of redeemed and regenerate humans in a salvific mission of interpersonal and public duty and functioning as a channel of God's love and of social justice"; Henry, "Fortunes of the Christian Worldview," 163. Henry's thoughts on worldview and its relationship to Christianity and culture invites comparison with Francis Schaeffer, who took a similar approach; see Schaeffer, *Christian Manifesto*. Noteable differences though between the Henry and Schaeffer include Schaeffer's apologetic method being more open to evidences, and perhaps combining the best of a presuppositional approach with the best of evidentialism.

223. Henry, *Twilight*, ibid.

224. Ibid., 118.

distinctive outlook that sets them apart from the rest of culture. "If one believes that God commands us to love our neighbors as ourselves, one will not leave a neighbor in need or trouble to fend for him or herself, but will treat the neighbor as extended family."[225] Such an approach though to culture must move beyond simply expounding biblical particulars and in fact apply the Christian outlook to every arena of life. Furthermore, prior to expounding a Christian view of art, culture, education, media, entertainment, philosophy, and science, these values must be evident in the Christian community. "It counts little when a vanguard confronts secular society with demonstrations and calls for options that in fact are not widely entrenched in the community of faith."[226] In sum, "there is not a sphere of learning and life that should fall outside the Christian vision."[227] Furthermore, the possibility of thinking Christianly about all of life depends, as does so much of Henry's theology, on God's own intelligible attributes, and the *imago Dei*.[228] Yet this vision has, to date, not materialized. That is, the failure of Henry's socio-cultural program, as Leung points out, was directly the failure of the evangelical community to as a whole appropriate a worldview orientation to its Christian faith.[229]

Evangelism and Social Justice

If we recall Hesselgrave's categories, since he defines traditional prioritism as relegating social concern to a second order task of the church, this cannot therefore be true of Henry's position, as should be evident from much of the above study. Therefore, Henry would fall into the second category of restrained holism, upholding the priority of evangelism and simultaneously the necessity of social concern.[230] That said, the very term itself, "restrained holism," carries with it the connotation of excess—thus,

---

225. Ibid., 119–20.

226. Ibid., 122.

227. Ibid., 123. Elsewhere, Henry says, "Christianity is no scientific theory, nor speculative philosophy. Rather, as a consequence of special divine revelation, it stands committed to its world view, its own interpretation of the whole of reality and existence. It refers the natural, the moral, and the historical orders to one ultimate principle of explanation, namely, to the self-revealing God who defines the content of religion of redemption"; Henry, *The God Who Shows Himself*, 78.

228. Henry, "Fortunes of a Christian Worldview," 175.

229. Leung, 236; also Wells, *No Place for Truth*, 293.

230. cf. Bockmuehl, *Evangelicals and Social Ethic*, 8–12.

as referring to something (holism in this case) in need of being reigned in. Henry, though, would surely admit of no such thing. Perhaps then a better term for Henry's position would be "a regenerational model," in keeping with Henry's own description in *Aspects of Christian Social Ethics*.

In his *Plea for Evangelical Demonstration*, Henry declares that Scripture declares, "both individual conversion and social justice to be alike *indispensible*."[231] This is so because the vision of Scripture is not merely of individual salvation, but also of the dawning of a new age. "The Bible envisages nothing less than a new man, a new society, a veritable new heaven and earth in which universal righteousness prevails."[232] Henry compares the evangelical tendency to focus solely on evangelism with the tendency in national Israel in Scripture to strive for social justice apart from an emphasis on personal conversion. By contrast, Scripture gives superior place to spiritual realities, and applies these realities to the material world. "By impressing the ethical aims of the Creator upon the universe, the Christian community brings the physical world into the service of the spiritual. Man's thoughts and plans are dedicated in love, righteousness and hope, and in expectation of God's own final realization of his holy purpose in creation."[233] Notice that in this, though, theological reflection precedes social concern as a necessary first step. As McGrath observes of the Evangelical Affirmations conference led by Henry and Kantzer, "the commitment to social justice is placed after the laying of a solid theological foundation for such action, thus ensuring that social action is seen as the consequence of theology, rather than as something that is independent of theology or takes priority over theology."[234]

Henry also warns against making social concern a platform for evangelism, or simply a means to an end. Rather, the reasons for social concern lie in the holiness of God and in the church's role in calling humanity to recognize God and his purposes, and to conform "culture and cosmos" to God's holy will:

231. Henry, *A Plea for Evangelical Demonstration*, 107. Emphasis added.
232. Ibid., 108.
233 Ibid., 111.
234. McGrath, *Evangelicalism and the Future of Christianity*, 166; or, as Sweazey points out, there is a need to distinguish between understanding how Christians live their lives as not evangelism, but rather as pre-evangelism and post-evangelism. The point is that the well-lived life of a Christian can make one open to consideration of the truth claims of Christianity, but it cannot make one a Christian; Sweazey, *The Church as Evangelist*, 32–33.

> The new man and the new community called into being by the gospel of redemption anticipate the new creation as the climax toward which God is daily moving history and the cosmos. Where the church is truly the church, she mirrors that coming new society of the Kingdom of God in miniature. She reflects the joy of life of a Body whose Head is the Exalted Lord himself and whose identity as future judge of all mankind has already been published by his resurrection from the dead (Acts 17:31).[235]

In his argument that the concept of the Kingdom of God provides the necessary framework for understanding both social concern and evangelism, Henry denies the claim of some that passages such as Matthew 25:31-46 provide the necessary foundations.[236] Even the story of the Good Samaritan must not be employed to deny the necessity of verbal witness. Rather, "social action must not be viewed as an independent and detachable concern, nor may the preaching of the gospel be aborted from the whole counsel of God."[237] In conclusion, Henry says:

> Jesus was neither a social reformer nor a political activist; his message, rather warned of apocalyptic judgment on the world. The Kerygma preached by his followers was related to this warning. For all that Christ sent his disciples in the present world as salt and light. Never do his followers serve more truly as preserving salt than when they undergird the righteousness of God, and never more truly as radiant light than when they present the gospel with joy and holy power.[238]

---

235. Henry, *A Plea for Evangelical Demonstration*, 113; elsewhere, Henry states, "the church is to be light of the world and salt of the earth. It illumines earth's bleak problems, and extols Christ as the light of the world, and in a degenerating cultural climate preserves whatever is meritorious. Christ is extending his kingdom in the world in and through the church's victories over sin and Satan. These victories are both personal and social"; Henry, "The Purpose of God," 29; cf. Henry's comment that "the church is not the Kingdom of God in its completeness, but she is nothing if she is not the nearest approximation to God's kingdom which the earth has"; Henry, *New Strides of Faith*, 99.

236. For an example of this position, see Sider, *Good News and Good Works*, Kindle edition, 144.

237. Henry, *A Plea for Evangelical Demonstration*, 120.

238. Ibid., 123-24.

A Moment of Protest

When Henry talks about social concern, he expresses caution about the degree to which the church engages in public protest. Therefore, it is necessary to keep in mind one of the distinguishing characteristics of his understanding of this issue. As Henry sees it, though the church is called to address social evil and take a stand against injustice, this should not be the defining essence of the church. First of all, it is imperative for the church to clarify why, according to biblical standards, an injustice is wrong to begin with, and to then offer a solution. Without the "why," the "what" becomes rather meaningless. "The realm of evangelical enterprise in social morality should be to identify why a situation is wrong, when and why it demands public confrontation, and precisely what the right alternative is."[239] The clear failure of most ecumenical attempts at social concern centers especially on its incapacity to articulate the biblical standard.

In its efforts for social action, though, the church is called to engage in "a moment of protest." That is, public protest should not define the mission of the church. However, nor should it be absent in its mission. As Henry says:

> Notice, I speak of a moment of protest, because I do not think the Christian community is called simply to a day or to a life of protest. It is called above all to proclaim the truth and the righteousness of God, to proclaim on the public scene what God says and wills. Nor am I proposing a division of the churches into those that are social activists on one hand and the prayer warriors on the other. At the moment of identification, let the church bells ring to remind the community that forgiveness of sins and the offer of a new life is sounded by the churches.[240]

Summary and Conclusion

Most criticisms of Carl Henry's call to evangelical social action focus not on his theological foundations, but on specific applications. Since this study has focused especially on the former, those critiques, though

---

239. Ibid., 18.

240. Henry, "The Tension between Evangelism and Christian Concern for Social Justice," 9.

interesting, are not particularly relevant here.[241] Our concern has been, rather, to determine how Henry's views contribute to the ongoing debate regarding the relationship between evangelism and social concern in Evangelical theology.

Looking back, a few important points emerge in Henry's approach. First, he avoids the error of some (e.g., Kirk) who dangerously minimize the difference between evangelism and social concern, and others (e.g., Sugden) who move away from an individualistic understanding of salvation in favor of a more social or community-oriented view. To say as Kirk does that evangelism and social concern are "one task" implies that to do one is to do the other. This risks an unbiblical equivocation of the two. Since, as Henry points out, Scripture plays the key fundamental role in understanding God's revealed will, then the doctrine of revelation provides the necessary corrective to other paradigms that too closely associate these two mandates of the church. Also, as we have noted, references to this doctrine are almost entirely missing in most other discussions of evangelism and social concern and this accounts for not prioritizing evangelism. When social concern is seen as part of the evangelistic mandate then one's actions might easily be seen as somehow revealing God's will for society. But unless verbally articulated, the precise content of the Divine will cannot possibly be known, especially given that it is verbally revealed. Furthermore, at the center of God's will lies God's redemptive purposes. Since redemption in Scripture depends on an acknowledgment of the truth (John 8:32), and since truth can only be agreed upon or rejected if known cognitively and propositionally, then social concern can never substitute for evangelism. The equivocal status afforded to evangelism and social concern in many holistic models runs the danger of moving in this direction. This, though, by no means diminishes the importance of social concern as an outflow of the redeemed life.

Because God commands moral obedience and requires that the redeemed life reflect God's own concerns for the poor and needy, social concern can never be thought of as optional. Marsden rightly points out that Henry has succeeded where others have not because he has, borrowing from Augustine, kept the Kingdom of God from being defined by an overly ambitious social agenda or from abiding too lofty a view of human progress. At the same time, Henry avoids the Kingdom hesitancy exhibited by Fundamentalists and more recently by some strict

---

241. For example, see Henry's dialogue with Smedes and others in Cerillo and Dempster, *Salt and Light*; also Weeks, "Carl F. H. Henry's Moral Arguments," 83.

priority advocates (e.g., Little). The regenerational emphasis of Henry's understanding of the Kingdom of God allows Henry to define the social mandate as being "in and through" yet not equal or tantamount to evangelism. Again, as mentioned previously, this seems highly preferable to models that would define the two as "partners," "two sides of the same coin," or "two wings of the same bird," as these analogies fall short by minimizing important differences in favor of a few minor similarities. Though the similarities would include the fact that both evangelism and social concern are (1) necessary and (2) commanded by God, the differences are striking. These differences include the fact that redemption requires assent to the truth, and that the truth of God's redemptive plan requires verbalization. Plus, if social concern is to have any revelatory aspect, as it should since all are lost apart from the knowledge of God, then it must be accompanied by word or proclamation.

— 6 —

Conclusion

THE ARTICULATION OF AN Evangelical theology of evangelism and social concern cannot proceed primarily on the premise of limited resources, prior failures of either denominations or individuals, the tendency to err, the potential for abuse, the varieties of spiritual gifts, or the diversity of callings within the church. To be authentically Evangelical, a theology must begin with the question, "what does the Bible say?" Furthermore, this constitutes no naïve approach, but rather one rooted in the Augustinian tradition of *crede, ut intelligas* (believe, in order to understand), which itself takes as a starting point the biblical axiom "Thus sayeth the Lord." In this, Carl Henry has led the way in the modern era.

Carl F. H. Henry articulates and defends a model of evangelism and social concern that prioritizes evangelism in order to underscore the profound implications of divine revelation for the task of evangelism, and the church's unique role in proclaiming God's redemptive purposes. The doctrine of revelation, which is rarely discussed in understanding how evangelism and social concern relate to one another, provides the fundamental support for Henry's priority model. Furthermore, he simultaneously upholds the absolute necessity of evangelical social concern, as requisite to the church's embodiment of God's ethical ideals reflective of the dawning Kingdom. Thus, the key ingredients in both of these mandates for the church are (1) God's redemptive purposes, made known through God's revelation in Scripture and in Christ, and (2) the Kingdom of God as the interpretive framework. But to say that the doctrine of revelation and the Kingdom of God inform both evangelism and social concern is not to thereby say that on that account these are on the same footing. Through God's gracious self-revelation one is offered a place in God's Kingdom. This is the essence of evangelism. Once in the Kingdom, one is exhorted to practice and embody the qualities of the Kingdom, or, put another way, to live faithfully according to the concerns of the King. There is therefore a necessary and logical order that requires the prioritizing of evangelism concerning the church's redemptive focus.

Advocates of a holism approach should find Henry instructive at several points. First, Henry avoids the tendency among holistic mission advocates (e.g., Sugden) to decry the emphasis on individual salvation as an unbiblical western corruption. Just because western individualism has run rampant and made individual autonomy a supreme virtue, does not therefore mean that Scripture is unconcerned or even minimally concerned about the plight of individuals. Second, though the Kingdom of God has present tense implications, these implications by no means erase the biblical distinction between the present age and the age to come, or between the temporal and eternal. Third, while holistic mission advocates have rightly pointed to the prominence of justice in Scripture, they have not always avoided divorcing it from justification. The God who demands justice also will one day judge all people. These emphases must be kept together.

Especially instructive in Henry's model is the prominent place he affords the doctrine of revelation. As we have noted on several occasions, this emphasis is virtually absent in every other discussion of this topic, and yet proves crucial to properly balancing evangelism and social concern. As we saw in chapter four, self-revelation lies at the center of God's nature, as is evident in the Divine Names given in Scripture, and in the terms used to define/describe God's revelatory acts and speech. That God seeks to be known, furthermore, has specific informational content. The essence of Evangelical preaching is to reveal that content and to make known God's gracious offer of salvation, an offer that can only remain hidden apart from evangelistic proclamation. Thus, Henry presents an argument for social concern that is very similar to that of George Sweazey, who describes it as pre-evangelism and post-evangelism, but never as evangelism itself.

Henry's epistemology, despite numerous claims to the contrary, not only fails to hinder a balanced perspective, it is in fact what makes it possible. Post-conservatives who accuse a conservative-propositional approach to theology of fostering a view of Christianity that emphasizes "information over transformation" have simply not read Henry. It is in fact a tremendous embarrassment to post-conservative critics of Henry that their understanding of him has been so far off the mark. Henry is not

Hodge. An Augustinian based, revelation-centered epistemology stands methodologically miles apart from Scottish Common Sense Realism. Had Henry's critics been more careful in their study of him, their critique of a conservative propositional approach would have surely been tempered. At the very least, they would have been reminded that even before McGrath called for an emphasis on *sapientia* over *scientia*, so too did Henry, in particular by standing, again, on the shoulders of Augustine.

Furthermore, critics who are hesitant about Kingdom talk, based on the excesses and errors of others (e.g., the Social Gospel), should learn from Henry the key ingredients of a regenerational approach that keeps Jesus in his unique place, but also faithfully relates Jesus' mission to that of the church in more than an indirect manner. Those who would advocate a strict emphasis on following Paul as the model for the church, would do well to remember that even Paul himself said, to paraphrase, "follow me as I follow Christ" (1 Cor 11:1).

Where to next?

Perhaps it is, as Wright suggests, time to do away with the terms priority and holism, given how heavy laden they are with baggage, and articulate based on Henry's theological foundations a "regeneration model." In contrast to prioritism and holism as designations, a regeneration model regarding the mission of the church offers hope for evangelical unity at a time when new cracks in the veneer seem to appear almost daily. Following Henry, such a model would prioritize evangelism, necessitate social concern, but frame both within the context of God's redemptive purposes, and the present and coming Reign of God. In short, this model would strike out for the biblical center, and thereby retain the hallmarks of Evangelical identity, and especially its evangelistic thrust. It would, as Wright suggests, "ultimize" evangelism, but allow for the church to live in the real world, in contrast to an imagined ideal.

Bibliography

"Agapē." In *Eerdmans Dictionary of the Bible*, edited by David Noel Freedman et al., 27–28. Grand Rapids: Eerdmans, 2000.
Aldrian, William et al., eds. *Engaging Our World: Christian Worlview from Ivory Tower to Global Impact*. Tulsa: Word & Spirit, 2008.
Allen, Diogenes. *Philosophy for Understanding Theology*. Louisville: John Knox, 2007.
Allison, Greg R. *Historical Theology*. Grand Rapids: Zondervan, 2011.
Alsdurf, Phyllis E. "The Founding of *Christianity Today* Magazine and the Construction of an American Evangelical Identity." *Journal of Religious & Theological Information* 9 (2010) 20–43.
Altizer, Thomas J. *The Gospel of Christian Atheism*. Philadelphia: Westminster, 1966.
Anderson, Ray Sherman. *On Being Human: Essays in Theological Anthropology*. Grand Rapids: Eerdmans, 1982.
Arias, Mortimer. *Announcing the Reign of God*. Eugene, OR: Wipf & Stock, 1984.
Atkinson, David J. et al., eds. *New Dictionary of Christian Ethics and Pastoral Theology*. Downers Grove: InterVarsity, 1995.
Austin, Michael W., and Douglas Geivett, eds. *Being Good: Christian Virtues for Everyday Life*. Grand Rapids: Eerdmans, 2012. Kindle.
Baker, Mark D. "Atonement." In *Dictionary of Scripture and Ethic*, edited by Joel B. Green, 81–84. Grand Rapids: Baker Academic, 2011.
Barth, Karl. *Church Dogmatics*. Edited by G. W. Bromiley and Thomas F. Torrance. Edinburgh: T. & T. Clark, 1936–69.
———. *Evangelical Theology: An Introduction*. Translated by Grover Foley. New York: Holt, Rinehart and Winston, 1963.
Basil. *On Social Justice*. Translated by C. Paul Schroeder. Crestwood, NY: St. Vladimir's Seminary Press, 2009.
Batson, David. *The Treasure Chest of the Early Christians*. Grand Rapids: Eerdmans, 2001.
Bebbington, D. W. *Evangelicalism in Modern Britain: A History from the 1730s to the 1980s*. London: Routledge, 1993.
Berg, Thomas C. "Proclaiming Together'? Convergence and Divergence in Mainline and Evangelical Evangelism, 1945–1967." *Religion and American Culture* 5 (1995) 49–76.
Berkhof, Louis. *Systematic Theology*. Grand Rapids: Eerdmans, 1946.
Berkouwer, G. C. *General Revelation*. Grand Rapids: Eerdmans, 1955.
Birch, Bruce C. "Justice." In *Dictionary of Scripture and Ethics*, edited by Joel B. Green, 433–36. Baker Academic, 2011.

Bird, Michael F. *Evangelical Theology: A Biblical and Systematic Introduction*. Grand Rapids: Zondervan, 2013.
Blackburn, W. Ross. *The God Who Makes Himself Known: The Missionary Heart of the Book of Exodus*. Downers Grove: InterVarsity, 2012.
Bloesch, Donald G. *Essentials of Evangelical Theology*. 2 vols. New York: Harper and Row, 1982.
Blomberg, Craig. *Neither Poverty nor Riches*. Downers Grove: InterVarsity, 1999.
Boa, Kenneth, and Robert M. Bowman, Jr., eds. *Faith Has Its Reasons: Integrative Approaches to Defending the Christian Faith*. Downers Grove: InterVarsity, 2005.
Bock, Darrell L. *Luke*. Downers Grove: InterVarsity, 1994.
Bockmuehl, Klaus. *Evangelicals and Social Ethics*. Downers Grove: InterVarsity, 1975.
Boice, James. *Witness and Revelation in the Gospel of John*. Grand Rapids: Zondervan, 1970.
Bonhoeffer, Dietrich. *Christ the Center*. Translated by John Bowden. New York: Harper Row, 1966.
———. *The Cost of Discipleship*. 1st Touchstone ed. New York: Touchstone, 1995.
Bornkamm, Günther. "Mustērion." In *Theological Dictionary of the New Testament*, edited by Gerhard Kittel and Gerhard Friedrich, 4:802–28. Grand Rapids: Eerdmans, 1967.
Bosch, David Jacobus. *Transforming Mission: Paradigm Shifts in Theology of Mission*. American Society of Missiology Series 16. Maryknoll, NY: Orbis, 1995.
Bradley, James E., and Richard A. Muller. *Church History: An Introduction to Research, Reference Works, and Methods*. Grand Rapids: Eerdmans, 1995.
Brand, Chad Owen. "Is Carl Henry a Modernist? Rationalism and Foundationalism in Post-War Evangelical Theology." *Trinity Journal* 20 (1999) 3–21.
Bromiley, Geoffrey W. "Image of God." In *The International Standard Bible Encyclopedia*, edited by Geoffrey W. Bromiley et al., 2:803–5. Grand Rapids: Eerdmans, 1982.
Brown, Colin. *Christainity and Western Thought*. Vol. 1. Downers Grove: InterVarsity, 1990.
Brown, Harold O. "Evangelicals and Social Ethics." In *Evangelical Affirmations*, edited by Kenneth S. Kantzer and Carl F. H. Henry, 257–84. Grand Rapids: Zondervan, 1990.
Bruce, F. F. *The Book of Acts*. New International Commentary on the New Testament. Grand Rapids: Eerdmans, 1988.
Brunner, Emil. *The Christian Doctrine of God*. Philadelphia: Westminster, 1950.
———. *The Divine Imperative: A Study in Christian Ethics*. 1941. Reprint, Cambridge: The Lutterworth Press, 1992.
———. *The Mediator*. Translated by Olive Wyon. Philadelphia: Westminster, 1947.
———. *Natur Und Gnade: Zum Gespräch Mit Karl Barth*. Tübingen: J. C. B. Mohr, 1934.
———. *Revelation and Reason*. Philadelphia: Westminster, 1946.
Brunner, Emil, and Karl Barth. *Natural Theology*. Translated by Peter Fraenkel. Reprint, Eugene, OR: Wipf & Stock, 2002.
Burch, Sharon Peebles. "Tillich on Salvation." *Dialog* 45 (2006) 246–51.
Burgess, Stanley M., and Ed M. Van der Maas. *The New International Dictionary of Pentecostal and Charismatic Movements*. Rev. and expanded ed. Grand Rapids: Zondervan, 2002.

Burridge, Richard A. *Imitating Jesus: An Inclusive Approach to New Testament Ethics*. Grand Rapids: Eerdmans, 2007.
Calvin, John. *The Acts of the Apostles*. Translated by John W. Fraser and J. G. McDonald. Calvin's New Testament Commentaries. Grand Rapids: Eerdmans, 1965.
———. *Commentaries*. Translated by John King et al. Edinburgh: Calvin Translation Society, 1847. Accordance.
Carpenter, Eugene E., and Wayne McCown, eds. *Asbury Bible Commentary*. Grand Rapids: Zondervan, 1992. Accordance.
Carpenter, Joel A. "From Fundamentalism to the New Evangelical Coalition." In *Evangelicalism and Modern America*, edited by George Marsden, 3–16. Grand Rapids: Eerdmans, 1984.
———. "Fundamentalist Institutions and the Rise of Evangelical Protestantism, 1929–1942." *Church History* 49 (1980) 62–75.
———. *Revive Us Again: The Reawakening of American Fundamentalism*. New York: Oxford University Press, 1997.
Carson, D. A. *The Gospel of John*. Pillar New Testament Commentary. Grand Rapids: Eerdmans, 1991. Accordance.
Carson, D. A., and John D. Woodbridge, eds. *God and Culture: Essays in Honor of Carl F.H. Henry*. Grand Rapids: Eerdmans, 1993.
Carswell, Robert Justin. "A Comparative Study of the Religious Epistemology of Carl F. H. Henry and Alvin Plantiga." PhD diss., The Southern Baptist Theological Seminary, 2007.
Carter, Charles W., ed. *A Contemporary Wesleyan Theology*. Vol. 2. Grand Rapids: Zondervan, 1983.
Cerillo, Augustus, Jr., and Murray W. Dempster. "Carl F. H. Henry's Early Apologetic for an Evangelical Social Ethic, 1942–1956." *Journal of the Evangelical Theological Society* 34 (1991) 365–79.
Charles, J. Daryl. *The Unformed Conscience of Evangelicalism*. Downers Grove: InterVarsity, 2002.
Chilcote, Paul Wesley, and Laceye C. Warner, eds. *The Study of Evangelism: Exploring the Missional Practice of the Church*. Grand Rapids: Eerdmans, 2008.
Chilton, Bruce, and J. I. H. McDonald. *Jesus and the Ethics of the Kingdom*. Grand Rapids: Eerdmans, 1987.
Chrysostom, John. "Homily 3 on 1 Corinthians." In *Life and Practice in the Early Church*, edited by Steven A. McKinion. New York: New York University Press, 2001.
Clark, David K. *To Know and Love God: Method for Theology*. Wheaton, IL: Crossway, 2003. Kindle.
Clark, Gordon H. *The Johannine Logos*. Nutley, NJ: Presbyterian and Reformed, 1972.
Collins, Kenneth J. *The Evangelical Moment: The Promise of an American Religion*. Grand Rapids: Baker Academic, 2005.
Corbett, Steve, and Brian Fikkert. *When Helping Hurts*. Chicago: Moody, 2009.
Costas, Orlando. *Christ Outside the Gate*. Maryknoll, NY: Orbis, 1992.
———. *Liberating News: A Theology of Contextual Evangelization*. Grand Rapids: Eerdmans, 1989.
Cowan, Steven B., ed. *Five Views on Apologetics*. Grand Rapids: Zondervan, 2000.
Cox, Harvey. *The Secular City*. New York: Macmillan, 1965.
Craig, William Lane, and J. P. Moreland, eds. *Philosophical Foundations for a Christian Worldview*. Downers Grove: InterVarsity, 2003.

Crouch, Andy. "Emergent Evangelicalism." *Christianity Today* 48, November 2004, 42-43.
Davis, John Jefferson. *Foundations of Evangelical Theology*. Grand Rapids: Baker, 1984.
Dayton, Wilber T. "A Weslyan Note on Election." In *Perspectives on Evangelical Theology*, edited by Kenneth S. Kantzer and Stanley N. Gundry, 95-103. Grand Rapids: Baker, 1979.
Dempster, Murray W. "Pentecostal Social Concern and the Biblical Mandate for Social Justice," *PNEUMA* 9 (1987) 129-53.
———. "The Role of Scripture in the Social Ethical Writings of Carl F. H. Henry." MA thesis, University of Southern California, 1969.
DeYoung, Kevin, and Greg Gilbert. *What Is the Mission of the Church? Making Sense of Social Justice, Shalom, and the Great Commission*. Wheaton, IL: Crossway, 2011.
Dodd, C. H. *The Apostolic Preaching and Its Development*. New York: Harper & Row, 1964.
———. *The Interpretation of the Fourth Gospel*. Cambridge: Cambridge University Press, 1953.
Dollar, George W. *A History of Fundamentalism in America*. Greenville, SC: Bob Jones University Press, 1973.
Douglas, J. D., ed. *Proclaim Christ until He Comes: Calling the Whole Church to Take the Whole Gospel to the Whole World: Lausanne II in Manila*. Minneapolis: World Wide Publications, 1989.
Doyle, G. Wright. *Carl Henry, Theologian for All Seasons: An Introduction and Guide to God, Revelation, and Authority*. Eugene, OR: Pickwick, 2010.
Dulles, Avery. "God, Revelation and Authority 2, Book Review." *Theological Studies* 38 (1977) 773-75.
———. *Models of Revelation*. Maryknoll, NY: Orbis, 1992.
Dyrness, William A. *Let the Earth Rejoice!* Reprint, Eugene, OR: Wipf & Stock, 1998.
Ellingsen, Mark. *The Evangelical Movement*. Minneapolis: Augsburg, 1988.
Elwell, Walter A. *Evangelical Dictionary of Theology*. Grand Rapids: Baker, 1984.
Engelsma, David. "Key '73—What Must We Say About It?" *Standard Bearer* 49 (1973). http://standardbearer.rfpa.org/print/40314.
Erickson, Millard J. *Christian Theology*. 2nd ed. Grand Rapids: Baker, 1998.
Escobar, Samuel. *The New Global Mission*. Downers Grove: InterVarsity, 2003.
Ewing, A. C. "Idealism." In *New Dictionary of Theology*, edited by Sinclair B. Ferguson et al., n.p. Downers Grove: InterVarsity, 1988. Accordance.
Fackre, Gabriel. *The Doctrine of Revelation*. Grand Rapids: Eerdmans, 1997.
Falwell, Jerry, ed. *The Fundamentalist Phenomenon*. New York: Doubleday, 1981.
Fee, Gordon D. "The Kingdom of God." In *Called & Empowered: Global Mission in Pentecostal Perspective*, edited by Murray W. Dempster et al., 7-21. Peabody, MA: Hendrickson, 1991.
Ferguson, Everett. *The Church of Christ: A Biblical Ecclesiology for Today*. Grand Rapids: Eerdmans, 1996.
Ferguson, Sinclair B., et al., eds. *New Dictionary of Theology*. Downers Grove: InterVarsity, 1988.
Field, D. H. "Sermon on the Mount." In *New Dictionary of Christian Ethics and Pastoral Theology*, edited by David J. Atkinson et al., n.p. Downers Grove: InterVarsity, 1995. Kindle.

Flemming, Dean E. *Recovering the Full Mission of God: A Biblical Perspective on Being, Doing, and Telling.* Downers Grove: InterVarsity, 2013.

Ford, David F., and Rachel Muers, eds. *The Modern Theologians: An Introduction to Christian Theology since 1918.* Oxford: Blackwell, 2005.

Frame, Randy. "Modern Evangelicalism Mourns the Loss of One of Its Founding Fathers." *Christianity Today*, March 15, 1985, 34–36.

France, R. T. *The Gospel according to Matthew: An Introduction and Commentary.* Grand Rapids: Eerdmans, 1985.

———. *The Gospel of Matthew.* Grand Rapids: Eerdmans, 2007. Accordance.

Franke, John R. *The Character of Theology: An Introduction to Its Nature, Task, and Purpose.* Grand Rapids: Baker Academic, 2005.

Freedman, David Noel, et al., eds. *Eerdmans Dictionary of the Bible.* Grand Rapids: Eerdmans, 2000.

Frei, Hans W. *The Eclipse of Biblical Narrative: A Study in Eighteenth and Nineteenth Century Hermeneutics.* New Haven: Yale University Press, 1974.

———. *Types of Christian Theology.* New Haven: Yale University Press, 1992.

George, Timothy. "Daddy Evangelical." *Christianity Today*, April 2013, 61.

———. "Inventing Evangelicalism: No One Was More Pivotal to the Emerging Movement Than Carl F H Henry." *Christianity Today*, March 2004, 48–51.

Gill, Athol. "Christian Social Responsibility." In *The New Face of Evangelicalism*, edited by C. René Padilla, 87–102. Downers Grove: InterVarsity, 1976.

Gisel, Pierre, et al., eds. *Albrecht Ritschl: la théologie en modernité: Entre religon, morale et positivé historique.* Stuttgart: Kohlhammer, 1985.

Glasser, Arthur F. *Announcing the Kingdom: The Story of God's Mission in the Bible.* Grand Rapids: Baker Academic, 2003.

Gonzalez, Justo. *A History of Christian Thought: From the Protestant Reformation to the Twentieth Century.* Vol. 3. Nashville: Abingdon, 1987.

Graham, Billy. *Just as I Am: The Autobiography of Billy Graham.* San Francisco: HarperCollins, 1997.

Green, Joel B. ed. *Dictionary of Scripture and Ethics.* Grand Rapids: Baker Academic, 2011.

———."Good News to Whom? Jesus and the 'Poor' in the Gospel of Luke." In *Jesus of Nazareth: Lord and Christ*, edited by Joel B. Green and Max Turner, 59–74. Grand Rapids: Eerdmans, 1994.

———. *The Gospel of Luke.* New International Commentary on the New Testament. Grand Rapids: Eerdmans, 1997. Accordance.

Green, Joel B., and Scot McKnight, eds. *Dictionary of Jesus and the Gospels.* Downers Grove: InterVarsity, 1992.

Green, Michael. *Evangelism in the Early Church.* Grand Rapids: Eerdmans, 2004.

Grenz, Stanley J. "The Deeper Significance of the Millennium Debate." *Southwestern Journal of Theology* 36 (1994) 14–21.

———. *Theology for the Community of God.* Nashville: Broadman and Holman, 1994.

Grenz, Stanley J., and John R. Franke. *Beyond Foundationalism: Shaping Theology in a Postmodern Context.* 1st ed. Louisville: Westminster John Knox, 2001.

Grenz, Stanley J., and Roger Olson. *Twentieth Century Theology: God and the World in a Transitional Age.* Downers Grove: InterVarsity, 1992.

Guder, Darrell L. *The Continuing Conversion of the Church.* Grand Rapids: Eerdmans, 2000.

Gundry, Robert H. *Jesus the Word According to John the Sectarian*. Grand Rapids: Eerdmans, 2002.

Habermas, Gary. "Evidential Apologetics." In *Five Views on Apologetics*, edited by Stephen B. Cowan, chapter 2. Grand Rapids: Zondervan, 2000. Kindle.

Hamilton, Victor P. *Exodus: An Exegetical Commentary*. Grand Rapids: Baker Academic, 2011.

Hardy, Daniel W. "Karl Barth." In *The Modern Theologians*, edited by David F. Ford, 21–42. Oxford: Blackwell, 2005.

Harrison, R. K. "Poor." In *Baker's Dictionary of Christian Ethics*, edited by Carl F. H. Henry, 515–16. Grand Rapids: Baker, 1973.

Hart, Julian N. *Toward a Theology of Evangelism*. New York: Abingdon, 1955.

Hatch, Nathan O., and Mark A. Noll. *The Bible in America: Essays in Cultural History*. New York: Oxford University Press, 1982.

Haykin, Michael A. G., and Kenneth J. Steward, eds. *The Advent of Evangelicalism*. Nashville: B. & H. Academic, 2008.

Hegel, Georg Wilhelm Friedrich. *The Philosophy of History*. Translated by J. Sibree. New York: Dover, 1956.

Heinisch, Paul. *Theology of the Old Testament*. Minneapolis: Liturgical, 1953.

Heldt, Jean-Paul. "Revisiting the 'Whole Gospel': Toward a Biblical Model of Holistic Mission in the 21st Century." *Missiology: An International Review* 32 (2004) 149–67.

Helseth, Paul Kjoss. "Carl F. H. Henry, Old Princeton, and the Right Use of Reason: Continuity or Discontinuity?" *Westminster Theological Journal* 73 (2011) 293–302.

Henry, Carl F. H. "American Evangelicals in a Turning Time." *Christian Century* 97.35 (1980) 1058–62.

———. *Aspects of Christian Social Ethics*. The Payton Lectures. 1964. Reprint, Grand Rapids: Eerdmans, 1980.

———, ed. *Baker's Dictionary of Christian Ethics*. Grand Rapids: Baker, 1973.

———. "The Bible and the Conscience of Our Age." *Journal of the Evangelical Theological Society* 25 (1982) 403–7.

———. *Christian Countermoves in a Decadent Culture*. Portland, OR: Multnomah, 1986.

———, ed. *Christian Faith and Modern Theology*. New York: Channel, 1964.

———. *The Christian Mindset in a Secular Society: Promoting Evangelical Renewal & National Righteousness*. Portland, OR: Multnomah, 1984.

———. *Christian Personal Ethics*. Grand Rapids: Baker, 1957.

———. "Christianity and Resurgent Paganism." *Vital Speeches of the Day* 57 (1990) 87–92.

———. "The Church in the World or the World in the Church: A Review Article." *Journal of the Evangelical Theological Society* 34 (1991) 381–83.

———. "The Concerns and Considerations of Carl Henry." *Christianity Today*, March 13, 1981, 19.

———. *Confessions of a Theologian*. Waco, TX: Word, 1986.

———. *Contemporary Evangelical Thought*. Great Neck, NY: Channel, 1957.

———. *Conversations with Carl Henry: Christianity for Today*. Lewiston, NY: Edwin Mellen, 1986.

———. *Evangelical Responsibility in Contemporary Theology*. Pathway Books; A Series of Contemporary Evangelical Studies. Grand Rapids: Eerdmans, 1957.

———. *Evangelicals at the Brink of Crisis: Significance of the World Congress on Evangelism*. Waco, TX: Word, 1968.

———. "Evangelicals in the Social Struggle." *Christianity Today*, October 8, 1965, 3–11.

———. "Evangelicals: Out of the Closet but Going Nowhere?" *Christianity Today*, January 4, 1980, 16–22.

———. "Facing a New Day in Evangelism." In *One Race, One Gospel, One Task*, edited by Carl F. H. Henry and W. Stanley Mooneyham, 11-18. Minneapolis: World Wide Publications, 1967.

———. *Faith at the Frontiers*. Chicago: Moody, 1969.

———. *Fifty Years of Protestant Theology*. Boston: Wilde, 1950.

———. "Fortunes of the Christian World View." *Trinity Journal* 19 (1998) 163–76.

———. *God, Revelation, and Authority*. 6 vols. 1976–83. Reprint, Wheaton, IL: Crossway, 1999.

———. *The God Who Shows Himself*. Waco, TX: Word, 1966.

———. *Gods of This Age or––God of the Ages?* Nashville: Broadman & Holman, 1994.

———. "Justification: A Doctrine in Crisis." *Journal of the Evangelical Theological Society* 38 (1995) 57–65.

———. "Looking Back at Key 73: A Weathervane of American Protestantism." *Reformed Journal* 24 (1974) 6–12.

———. *New Strides of Faith*. Moody Evangelical Focus. Chicago: Moody, 1972.

———. *Notes on the Doctrine of God*. Boston: Wilde, 1948.

———. *The Pacific Garden Mission: A Doorway to Heaven*. 4th ed. Grand Rapids: Zondervan, 1942.

———. *Personal Idealism and Strong's Theology*. Wheaton, IL: Van Kampen, 1951.

———. *A Plea for Evangelical Demonstration*. Grand Rapids: Baker, 1971.

———. "The Priority of Divine Revelation: A Review Article." *Journal of the Evangelical Theological Society* 27 (1984) 77–92.

———. "Private Sins, Public Office." *Christianity Today*, March 4, 1988, 28.

———. "The Purpose of God." In *The New Face of Evangelicalism*, edited by C. René Padilla, 17–32. Downers Grove: InterVarsity, 1976.

———. "Reflections on the Kingdom of God." *Journal of the Evangelical Theological Society* 35 (1992) 39–49.

———. *Remaking the Modern Mind*. Grand Rapids: Eerdmans, 1946.

———. "The Road to Eternity: A Travel Guide for the '80s." *Christianity Today*, July 17, 1981, 32.

———. "Second Rock Music Church of Boulder." *Christianity Today*, February 11, 1991, 37.

———. "The Spirit and the Written Word." *Bibliotheca Sacra* 111 (1954) 302–16.

———. "Somehow, Let's Get Together." *Christianity Today*, June, 9, 1967.

———. *Successful Church Publicity: A Guidebook for Christian Publicists*. Grand Rapids: Zondervan, 1943.

———. "The Tensions between Evangelism and the Christian Demand for Social Justice." *Fides et Historia* 4 (1972) 3–10.

———. *Toward a Recovery of Christian Belief: The Rutherford Lectures*. Wheaton, IL: Crossway, 1990.

———. *Twilight of a Great Civilization: The Drift toward Neo-Paganism*. Westchester, IL: Crossway, 1988.

———. *The Uneasy Conscience of Modern Fundamentalism*. 1947. Reprint, Grand Rapids: Eerdmans, 2003.

———. "The Uneasy Conscience 45 Years Later." *Vital Speeches of the Day* 58 (1992) 475–80.

———. "A Voice of God." *Criswell Theological Review* 1 (1987) 235–36.

———. "What Is Christianity?" *Bibliotheca Sacra* 123 (1966) 104–14.

———. "What Social Structures?" In *The Best of the Reformed Journal*, edited by James D. Bratt and Ronald A. Wells. Grand Rapids: Eerdmans, 2011.

———. "Who Are the Calvinists?" *Christianity Today*, March 21, 1980.

Henry, Carl F. H., Robert Lincoln Hancock, and Development Assistance Services. *The Ministry of Development in Evangelical Perspective: A Symposium on the Social and Spiritual Mandate*. Pasadena, CA: William Carey Library, 1979.

Henry, Carl F. H., and W. Stanley Mooneyham, eds. *One Race, One Gospel, One Task*. 2 vols. Minneapolis: World Wide Publications, 1966.

Hesselgrave, David J. *Paradigms in Conflict: 10 Key Questions in Christian Missions Today*. Grand Rapids: Kregel, 2005.

Hicks, John. "Pluralism." In *Four Views on Salvation in a Pluralistic World*, edited by Stanley Gundry et al., n.p. Grand Rapids: Zondervan, 1995. Kindle.

Hindson, Ed. "Religion and Politics: Do They Mix?" In *Salt and Light: Evangelical Political Thought in America*, edited by Augustus Cerillo and Murray W. Dempster, 139–43. Grand Rapids: Baker, 1989.

Holmes, Arthur Frank. *The Making of a Christian Mind: A Christian World View and the Academic Enterprise*. Downers Grove: InterVarsity, 1985.

Hoppe, Leslie J. "Poverty and the Poor." In *Dictionary of Scripture and Ethics*, edited by Joel B. Green, 608–11. Grand Rapids: Baker Academic 2011.

Houlden, J. L. *Ethics and the New Testament*. New York: Oxford University Press, 1977.

House, Paul. *Old Testament Theology*. Downers Grove: InterVarsity, 1998.

Hunsinger, George. "What Can Evangelicals and Postliberals Learn from Each Other? The Carl Henry/Hans Frei Exchange Reconsidered." *Pro Ecclesia* 5 (1996) 161–82.

Hunt, Robert A. "The History of the Lausanne Movement, 1974–2010." *International Bulletin of Missionary Research* 35 (2011) 81–84.

Hunter, James Davison. *Evangelicalism: The Coming Generation*. Chicago: University of Chicago Press, 1987.

Hutchens, Steven Mark. "Knowing and Being in the Context of the Fundamentalist Dilemma: A Comparative Study of the Thought of Karl Barth and Carl F. H. Henry." ThD diss., Lutheran School of Theology at Chicago, 1989.

Iosso, Christian. "Social Service, Social Ministry." In *Dictionary of Scripture and Ethics*, edited by Joel B. Green, 739–41. Grand Rapids: Baker Academic, 2011.

Jacob, Edmond. *Theology of the Old Testament*. London: Hodder & Stoughton, 1958.

Jellema, Dirk. "Ethics." In *Contemporary Evangelical Thought*, edited by Carl F. H. Henry, 112–18. Great Neck, NY: Channel, 1957.

Johnson, D. H. "Logos" In *Dictionary of Jesus and the Gospels*, edited by Joel B. Green and Scot McKnight, n.p. Downers Grove: InterVarsity, 1992. Accordance.

Johnston, Arthur P. *The Battle for World Evangelism*. Wheaton, IL: Tyndale House, 1978.

———. *World Evangelism and the Word of God*. Minneapolis: Bethany Fellowship, 1974.

Jones, Kelvin Neal. "Revelation and Reason in the Theology of Carl F. H. Henry, James I. Packer, and Ronald H. Nash." PhD diss., The Southern Baptist Theological Seminary, 1994.

Jones, L. Gregory. "Narrative." In *The Blackwell Encyclopedia of Modern Christian Thought*, edited by Alister McGrath, 395-98. Oxford: Blackwell, 1993.

Just, Arthur A. *Luke 1:1—9:50*. St. Louis: Concordia, 1996.

Kantzer, Kenneth S. "The Carl Henry That Might Have Been." *Christianity Today*, April 5, 1993, 15.

Kantzer, Kenneth S., and Stanley N. Gundry, eds. *Perspectives on Evangelical Theology*. Grand Rapids: Baker, 1979.

Kantzer, Kenneth S., and Carl F. H. Henry, eds. *Evangelical Affirmations*. Grand Rapids: Zondervan, 1990.

Keener, Craig. *Acts*. Vol. 2, *3:1—14:28*. Grand Rapids: Baker Academic, 2013.

———. *Matthew*. Downers Grove: InterVarsity, 1997.

Keller, Timothy J. *Ministries of Mercy*. 2nd ed. Phillipsburg, NJ: P & R, 1997.

King, Kevin, Sr. "The Crisis of Truth and Word in the Revelational Epistemology of Carl F. H. Henry." PhD diss., University of Pretoria, 2008.

Kirk, J. Andrew. *The Good News of the Kingdom Coming: The Marriage of Evangelism and Social Responsibility*. Downers Grove: InterVarsity, 1983.

———. *Liberation Theology: An Evangelical View from the Third World*. Atlanta: John Knox, 1979.

Klooster, Fred H. "Predestination: A Calvinist Note." In *Perspectives on Evangelical Theology*, edited by Kenneth S. Kantzer and Stanley N. Gundry, 82-94. Grand Rapids: Baker, 1979.

Knowles, Michael P. *The Unfolding Mystery of the Divine Name*. Downers Grove: InterVarsity, 2012.

Köstenberger, Andreas J. *The Theology of John's Gospel and Letters*. Biblical Theology of the New Testament. Grand Rapids: Zondervan, 2009.

Kostenberger, Andreas J., and Peter T. O'Brien. *Salvation to the Ends of the Earth: A Biblical Theology of Mission*. Downers Grove: InterVarsity, 2001.

Kvalbein, H. "Poor/Poverty" In *New Dictionary of Biblical Theology*, edited by T. Desmond Alexander and Brian S. Rosner, n.p. Downers Grove: InterVarsity, 2000. Accordance.

Ladd, George Eldon. *The Gospel of the Kingdom: Scriptural Studies in the Kingdom of God*. Grand Rapids: Eerdmans, 1959.

———. *A Theology of the New Testament*. Grand Rapids: Eerdmans, 1974.

Land, Stephen Jack. *Pentecostal Spirituality: A Passion for the Kingdom*. Cleveland, TN: CPT, 2010.

Lapsley, Jacqueline E. "Ten Commandments." In *Dictionary of Scripture and Ethics*, edited by Joel B. Green, 772-74. Grand Rapids: Baker Academic, 2011.

Lausanne Covenant, Article 5, "Christian Social Responsibility." http://www.lausanne.org/en/documents/lausanne-covenant.html.

Leitch, Addison H. "The Primary Task of the Church." *Christianity Today*, October 15, 1956, 11-13, 18.

Lewis, Gordon Russell, and Bruce A. Demarest. *Integrative Theology: Three Volumes in One*. Grand Rapids: Zondervan, 1996.

Lindbeck, George A. *The Nature of Doctrine: Religion and Theology in a Postliberal Age*. 25th anniversary ed. Louisville: Westminster John Knox, 2009.

Lints, Richard. *The Fabric of Theology: A Prolegomenon to Evangelical Theology.* Grand Rapids: Eerdmans, 1993.
Litfin, Duane. *Word Versus Deed: Resetting the Scales to a Biblical Balance.* Wheaton, IL: Crossway, 2012. Kindle.
Little, Christopher R. "Christian Mission Today: Are We on a Slippery Slope? My Response." *International Journal of Frontier Missiology* 25 (2008) 87–92.
———. *Polemic Missiology for the 21st Century: In Memorium of Roland Allen.* Amazon Digital Services, 2013. Kindle.
———. *The Revelation of God among the Unevangelized.* Pasadena, CA: William Carey Library, 2000.
———. "What Makes Mission Christian." *International Journal of Frontier Missiology* 25 (2008) 65–73.
Livingstone, James C. *Modern Christian Thought: The Enlightenment and the Nineteenth Century.* Minneapolis: Fortress, 2006.
Lupton, Robert D. *Toxic Charity.* New York: HarperOne, 2011.
Macchia, Frank. *Baptized in the Spirit: A Global Pentecostal Theology.* Grand Rapids: Zondervan, 2006.
Markham, Paul N. "Conversion." In *Dictionary of Scripture and Ethics*, edited by Joel B. Green, 175–77. Grand Rapids: Baker Academic, 2011.
Marsden, George M. *Evangelicalism and Modern America.* Grand Rapids: Eerdmans, 1984.
———. *Fundamentalism and American Culture.* 2nd ed. New York: Oxford University Press, 2006.
———. *Reforming Fundamentalism: Fuller Seminary and the New Evangelicalism.* Grand Rapids: Eerdmans, 1987.
———. *The Twighlight of the American Enlightenment.* New York: Basic Books, 2014. Kindle.
———. *Understanding Evangelicalism and Fundamentalism.* Grand Rapids: Eerdmans, 1991.
Marshall, I. Howard. *A Concise New Testament Theology.* Downers Grove: IVP Academic, 2008.
Martin, William. *A Prophet without Honor: The Billy Graham Story.* New York: William Morrow, 1991.
McCormick, Bruce, and Clifford B. Anderson. *Karl Barth and American Evangelicalism.* Grand Rapids: Eerdmans, 2011.
McGrath, Alister, ed. *The Blackwell Encyclopedia of Modern Christian Thought.* Oxford: Blackwell, 1993.
———. "Evangelical Theological Method." In *Evangelical Futures: A Conversation on Theological Method*, edited by John Gordon Stackhouse, 15–38. Grand Rapids: Baker, 2000.
———. *Evangelicalism and the Future of Christianity.* Downers Grove: InterVarsity, 1995.
McQuilken, Robert, et al. "Responses to Christopher Little's 'What Makes Mission Christian.'" *International Journal of Frontier Missiology* 25 (2008) 75–85.
Menzies, William W., and Robert P. Menzies. *Spirit and Power: Foundation of Pentecostal Experience: A Call to Evangelical Dialogue.* Grand Rapids: Zondervan, 2000.
Miles, Delos. *Evangelism and Social Involvement.* Nashville: Broadman, 1986.

Moberg, David O. *The Great Reversal: Evangelism Versus Social Concern*. Philadelphia: Lippincott, 1972.

Mohler, R. Albert, Jr. "Carl F. H. Henry." In *Theologians of the Baptist Tradition*, edited by Timothy George and David S. Dockery, 279-96. Nashville: Broadman and Holman, 2001. Kindle.

Moltmann, Jürgen. *God in Creation: A New Theology of Creation and the Spirit of God*. The Gifford Lectures. 1st Fortress Press ed. Minneapolis: Fortress, 1993.

Moo, Douglas J. *The Epistle to the Romans*. New International Commentary on the New Testament. Accordance electronic ed. Grand Rapids: Eerdmans, 1996.

Moore, Russell D. *The Kingdom of Christ: The New Evangelical Perspective*. Wheaton, IL: Crossway, 2004.

———. "Leftward of Scofield: The Eclipse of the Kingdom of God in Post-Conservative Evangelical Theology." *Journal of the Evangelical Theological Society* 47 (2004) 423-40.

———. "The Uneasy Conscience of Modern Fundamentalism." *Journal of the Evangelical Theological Society* 48 (2005) 181-83.

Morris, Leon. *The Gospel of John*. New International Commentary on the New Testament. Grand Rapids: Eerdmans, 1995.

Morrison, John D. "Barth, Barthians, and Evangelicals: Reassessing the Question of the Relation of Holy Scripture and the Word of God." *Trinity Journal* 25 (2004) 187-213.

Mott, Stephen Charles. *Biblical Ethics and Social Change*. New York: Oxford University Press, 1982.

Moyo, Dambisa. *Dead Aid*. New York: Farrar, Straus and Giroux, 2009.

Myers, Bryant. *Walking with the Poor: Principles and Practices of Transformational Development*. Monrovia, CA: World Vision, 1999.

Nash, Ronald H. *The Word of God and the Mind of Man*. Phillipsburg, NJ: Presbyterian and Reformed, 1982.

Neuhaus, Richard John. "A Prophetic Jeremiad." *Christianity Today*, April 7, 1989, 30.

Newbigin, Lesslie. *The Open Secret*. Rev. ed. Grand Rapids: Eerdmans, 1995.

Nichols, Bruce J., ed. *In Word and Deed: Evangelism and Social Responsibility*. Devon: Paternoster, 1985.

Nicole, Roger. "The Nature of Redemption." In *Christian Faith and Modern Theology*, edited by Carl F. H. Henry, 193-222. New York: Channel, 1964.

Niebuhr, Reinhold. *An Interpretation of Christian Ethics*. New York: Harper, 1935.

———. *Moral Man and Immoral Society: A Study in Ethics and Politics*. New York: Scribner, 1960.

Nygren, Anders. *Agape and Eros*. Philadelphia: Westminster, 1953.

Oden, Thomas C. *Classic Christianity: A Systematic Theology: Three Volumes in One*. New York: HarperCollins, 2009. Kindle.

Olson, Roger E. *Against Calvinism*. Grand Rapids: Zondervan, 2011.

———. *Reformed and Always Reforming: The Postconservative Approach to Evangelical Theology*. Grand Rapids: Baker, 2007. Kindle.

———. *The Westminster Handbook to Evangelical Theology*. Louisville: Westminster John Knox, 2004.

"One Race, One Gospel, One Task: Closing Statement of the World Congress on Evangelism." In *One Race, One Gospel, One Task*, edited by Carl F. H. Henry and and W. Stanley Mooneyham, 1:5-6. Minneapolis: World Wide Publications, 1967.

Osborne, Grant R. "Historical Criticism and the Evangelical." *Journal of the Evangelical Theological Society* 42 (1999) 193–210.

Ott, Craig, and Stephen J. Strauss. *Encountering Theology of Mission: Biblical Foundations, Historical Developments, and Contemporary Issues*. Grand Rapids: Baker Academic, 2010.

Padilla, C. René. "Integral Mission and Its Historical Development." In *Justice, Mercy, and Humility: Integral Mission and the Poor*, edited by Tim Chester, 42–58. Waynesboro, GA: Paternoster, 2002.

———. *Mission Between the Times: Essays*. Grand Rapids: Eerdmans, 1985.

———. *The New Face of Evangelicalism*. Downers Grove: InterVarsity, 1976.

Patterson, Bob E. *Carl F. H. Henry*. Makers of the Modern Theological Mind. Peabody, MA: Hendrickson, 1983.

Peachey, Paul. "Aspects of Christian Social Ethics." *Mennonite Quarterly Review* 41 (1967) 174–75.

Pearcey, Nancy. *Total Truth*. Wheaton, IL: Crossway, 2004.

Pierard, R. V. "Evangelicalism." In *Evangelical Dictionary of Theology*, edited by Walter Elwell, 379–82. Grand Rapids: Baker, 1984.

Pinnock, Clark H. "Revelation." In *New Dictionary of Theology*, edited by Sinclair B. Ferguson et al., n.p. Downers Grove: InterVarsity, 1988. Accordance.

Plummer, Robert L. "Paul's Gospel." In *Paul's Missionary Methods*, edited by Robert L. Plummer and John Mark Terry, 44–55. Downers Grove: InterVarsity, 2012.

Pollock, John Charles. *Billy Graham, Evangelist to the World: An Authorized Biography of the Decisive Years*. 1st ed. San Francisco: Harper & Row, 1979.

Porter, Stanley E., ed. *The Messiah in the Old and New Testaments*. Grand Rapids: Eerdmans, 2007.

Preus, Robert. "The Nature of the Bible." In *Christian Faith and Modern Theology*, edited by Carl F. H. Henry et al., 111–28. New York: Channel, 1964.

Purdy, Richard Allan. "Carl Henry and Contemporary Apologetics: An Assessment of the Rational Apologetic Methodology of Carl F. H. Henry in the Context of the Current Impasse between Reformed and Evangelical Apologetics." PhD diss., New York University, 1980.

Quebedeaux, Richard. *The Worldly Evangelical*. San Francisco: Harper & Row, 1978.

———. *The Young Evangelicals: Revolution in Orthodoxy*. 1st ed. New York: Harper & Row, 1974.

Rahner, Karl. *Theological Investigations* Vol. 14. Translated by David Bourke. London: Darton, Longman & Todd, 1976.

Ramsey, Paul. *Basic Christian Ethics*. New York: Scribner, 1950.

Rasmussen, Albert Tervill. "Aspects of Christian Social Ethics." *Review of Religious Research* 6 (1965) 178–79.

Reid, W. S. "Predestination." In *Evangelical Dictionary of Theology*, edited by Walter Elwell, 870–72. Grand Rapids: Baker, 1984.

Reuschling, Wendy Corbin. "Divine Command Theories of Ethics." In *Dictionary of Scripture and Ethics*, edited by Joel B. Green, 242–46. Grand Rapids: Baker Academic, 2011.

Ringe, Sharon H. *Luke*. Louisville: Westminster John Knox, 1995.

Ro, Bong Rin. "The Perspective of Church History from New Testament Times to 1960." In *In Word and Deed: Evangelism and Social Responsibility*, edited by Bruce J. Nichols, 11–40. Exeter: Paternoster, 1985.

Sanders, Jack T. *Ethics in the New Testament: Change and Development*. Philadelphia: Fortress, 1975.
Santa Ana, Julio de. *Good News to the Poor: The Challenge of the Poor in the History of the Church*. Maryknoll, NY: Orbis, 1979.
Schaeffer, Francis. *A Christian Manifesto*. Wheaton, IL: Crossway, 1981.
Schluter, Michael, and John Ashcroft, eds. *Jubilee Manifesto: A Framework, Agenda and Strategy for Christian Social Reform*. Downers Grover: InterVarsity, 2005.
Schmidt, Alvin J. *How Christianity Changed the World*. Grand Rapids: Zondervan, 2004.
Schnucker, R. V. "Neo-orthodoxy." In *Evangelical Dictionary of Theology*, edited by Walter Elwell, 754–56. Grand Rapids, Baker, 1984.
Seifrid, M. A. "Righteousness, Justice and Justification." In *New Dictionary of Biblical Theology*, edited by T. Desmond Alexander and Brian S. Rosner, 740–45. Downers Grove: InterVarsity, 2000.
Sennett, James F., and Douglas Groothuis, eds. *In Defense of Natural Theology: A Post-Humean Assessment*. Downers Grove: InterVarsity, 2005.
Sherman, Steven B. *Revitalizing Theological Epistemology: Holistic Evangelical Approaches to the Knowledge of God*. Eugene, OR: Pickwick, 2008.
Sider, Ron, ed. *The Chicago Declaration*. Carol Stream, IL: Creation House, 1974.
———. *Good News and Good Works*. Grand Rapids: Baker, 1993. Reprint, 2011. Kindle.
———. *I Am Not a Social Activist*. Scottdale, PA: Herald, 2008.
Smalley, S. S. "Mystery." In *New Bible Dictionary*, edited by James D. Douglas, n.p. Grand Rapids: Tyndale, 1962. Accordance.
Smedes, Lewis B. "Evangelicals and the Social Question." In *Salt and Light: Evangelical Political Thought in Modern America*, edited by Augustus Cerillo Jr. and Murray W. Dempster, 40–48. Grand Rapids: Baker, 1989.
Smith, James K. A. *Thinking in Tongues*. Grand Rapids: Eerdmans, 2010.
Soper, David Wesley. "*Remaking the Modern Mind*, by Carl F. H. Henry." *Journal of Bible and Religion* 15 (1947) 184–85.
Spradley, Joseph. "Christian View of the Physical World." In *The Making of a Christian Mind: A Christian World View and the Academic Enterprise*, edited by Arthur Holmes, 55–80. Downers Grove: InterVarsity, 1985.
Stackhouse, John Gordon. *Evangelical Futures: A Conversation on Theological Method*. Grand Rapids: Baker, 2000.
Stassen, Glenn H. "Sermon on the Mount." In *Dictionary of Scripture and Ethics*, edited by Joel B. Green, 715–17. Grand Rapids: Baker Academic, 2011.
Stassen, Glen H., and David P. Gushee. *Kingdom Ethics: Following Jesus in Contemporary Context*. Grand Rapids: InterVarsity, 2003.
Stott, John R. W. *Christian Mission in the Modern World*. IVP Classics. Downers Grove: InterVarsity, 2008.
———. *Christian Mission in the Modern World*. Downers Grove: InterVarsity, 2008b.
———. *The Lausanne Covenant: Complete Text with Study Guide*. Peabody, MA: Henrickson, 2009.
———, ed. *Making Christ Known: Historic Missions Documents from the Lausanne Movement, 1974–1989*. Grand Rapids: Eerdmans, 1996.
Stronstad, Roger. *The Charismatic Theology of St. Luke: Trajectories from the Old Testament to Luke-Acts*. 2nd ed. Grand Rapids: Baker Academic, 2012.

Sugden, Chris. "Evangelicals and Wholistic Evangelism." In *Proclaiming Christ in Christ's Way*, edited by Vinay Samuel and Albrecht Hauser. Oxford: Regnum, 1989.

Swartz, David R. *Moral Minority: The Evangelical Left in an Age of Conservativeism*. Philadelphia: University of Pennsylvania Press, 2012.

Sweazey, George. *The Church as Evangelist*. New York: Harper & Row, 1978.

———. *Preaching the Good News*. Englewood Cliffs, NJ: Prentice-Hall, 1976.

Sweeney, Douglas A. *The American Evangelical Story*. Grand Rapids: Baker Academic, 2005.

Thompson, R. Duane. "Social Involvement: The Responsibility of God's People." In *A Contemporary Wesleyan Theology*, edited by Charles W. Carter, 2:693–732. Grand Rapids: Zondervan, 1983.

Thornbury, Gregory Alan. "Carl F. H. Henry: Heir of Reformation Epistemology." *Southern Baptist Journal of Theology* 8 (2004) 62–72.

———. *Recovering Classic Evangelicalism: Applying the Wisdom and Vision of Carl F. H. Henry*. Wheaton, IL: Crossway, 2013.

Til, Henry R. Van. *Calvinistic Concept of Culture*. 1959. Reprint, Grand Rapids: Baker Academic, 2001.

Tizon, Al. *Transformation after Lausanne: Radical Evangelical Mission in Global-Local Perspective*. Regnum Studies in Mission. Eugene, OR: Wipf & Stock, 2008.

Toon, Peter. *The Development of Doctrine in the Church*. Grand Rapids: Eerdmans, 1979.

Vanhoozer, Kevin J. *The Drama of Doctrine: A Canonical-Linguistic Approach to Christian Theology*. 1st ed. Louisville: Westminster John Knox, 2005.

———. "The Voice and the Actor." In *Evangelical Futures: A Conversation on Theological Method*, edited by John G. Stackhouse, 61–106. Grand Rapids: Baker, 2001.

———. "The World Well Staged?" In *God and Culture: Essays in Honor of Carl F. H. Henry*, edited by D. A. Carson and John D. Woodbridge, 1–30. Grand Rapids: Eerdmans, 1993.

Vempeny, Ishanand. *Inspiration in the Non-Biblical Scriptures*. Bangalore: Theological Publications in India, 1973.

Verhey, Allen. *The Great Reversal: Ethics and the New Testament*. Grand Rapids: Eerdmans, 1984.

Visser 't Hooft, Willem A. *The Background of the Social Gospel in America*. St. Louis: Bethany, 1963.

Vorster, Nico. *Created in the Image of God*. Eugene, OR: Pickwick, 2011.

Wacker, Grant. *Augustus H. Strong and the Dilemma of Historical Consciousness*. Macon, GA: Mercer University Press, 1985.

Wagner, C. Peter. *Church Growth and the Whole Gospel*. San Francisco: Harper & Row, 1981.

Wagner, Travis Mark. "The Revelational Epistemology of Carl F. H. Henry." MA Thesis, University of St. Michael's College, Toronto, 1986.

Waita, Jonathan Mutinda. "Carl F. H. Henry and the Metaphysical Foundations of Epistemology." PhD diss., Dallas Theological Seminary, 2012.

Wallis, Jim. "A Wolf in Sheep's Clothing: The Political Right Invades the Evangelical Fold." In *Salt and Light: Evangelical Political Thought in Modern America*, edited by Augustus Cerillo Jr. and Murray W. Dempster, 132–38. Grand Rapids: Baker, 1989.

Waltermire, Donald E. *The Liberation Christologies of Leonardo Boff and Jon Sobrino.* New York: University Press of America, 1994.

Warner, Laceye C. "Evangelism." In *Dictionary of Scripture and Ethics*, edited by Joel B. Green, 287–88. Grand Rapids: Baker Academic, 2011.

Warrington, Keith. *The Message of the Holy Spirit.* Downers Grove: InterVarsity, 2009.

Weber, Linda J., ed. *Mission Handbook.* 21st Century ed. Wheaton, IL: EMIS, 2010.

Weeks, David L. "Carl F. H. Henry on Public Life." In *Evangelicals in the Public Square*, edited by J. Budziszewksi. Grand Rapids: Baker Academic, 2006.

———. "Carl F. H. Henry's Moral Arguments for Evangelical Political Activism." *Journal of Church & State* 40 (1998) 83–106.

Wells, David. "Evangelical Theology." In *The Modern Theologians*, edited by David F. Ford, chapter 35. Oxford: Blackwell, 2005. Kindle.

———. *No Place for Truth.* Grand Rapids, Eerdmans, 1993.

Werpehowski, William. "Reinhold Niebuhr." In *The Modern Theologians: An Introduction to Christian Theology since 1918*, edited by David F. Ford and Rachel Muers, 204–11. Oxford: Blackwell, 2005.

White, James Emery. *What Is Truth? A Comparative Study of the Positions of Cornelius Van Til, Francis Schaeffer, Carl F.H. Henry, Donald Bloesch, Millard Erickson.* Nashville: Broadman & Holman, 1994.

White, Michael D. "Word and Spirit in the Theological Method of Carl Henry." PhD Diss., Wheaton College, 2012.

Williams, J. R. "Baptism in the Holy Spirit." In *The New International Dictionary of Pentecostal and Charismatic Movements*, edited by Stanley M. Burgess and Ed M. Van der Maas, 354–64. Rev. and expanded ed. Grand Rapids: Zondervan, 2002.

Wirt, Sherwood Eliot. *The Social Conscience of the Evangelical.* New York: Harper & Row, 1968.

Witherington, Ben, III. *The Problem with Evangelical Theology: Testing the Exegetical Foundations of Calvinism, Dispensationalism, and Wesleyanism.* Waco, TX: Baylor University Press, 2005. Kindle.

———. *Work: A Kingdom Perspective on Labor.* Grand Rapids: Eerdmans, 2011.

Wittgenstein, Ludwig. *Philosophical Investigations.* Translated by G. E. M. Anscombe. New York: Macmillan, 1964.

Wogaman, J. Philip. *Christian Ethics: A Historical Introduction.* Louisville: Westminster John Knox, 1993.

Wolterstorff, Nicholas. *Divine Discourse: Philosophical Reflections on the Claim That God Speaks.* Cambridge: Cambridge University Press, 1995.

———. *Journey toward Justice: Personal Encounters in the Global South.* Grand Rapids: Baker Academic, 2013.

Wood, D. R. W., ed. *New Bible Dictionary.* Downers Grove: InterVarsity, 1996.

Wright, Christopher J. H. *The Mission of God: Unlocking the Bible's Grand Narrative.* Downers Grove: IVP Academic, 2006.

———. *Old Testament Ethics for the People of God.* Downers Grove: InterVarsity, 2004.

Wright, N. T. *The Resurrection of the Son of God.* 1st North American ed. Christian Origins and the Question of God 3. Minneapolis: Fortress, 2003.

———. *Surprised by Hope: Rethinking Heaven, the Resurrection, and the Mission of the Church.* New York: HarperOne, 2008.

Yohannan, K. P. *Come Let's Reach the World.* Carrollton, TX: GFA, 2004.

www.ingramcontent.com/pod-product-compliance
Lightning Source LLC
Chambersburg PA
CBHW071017240426
43661CB00073B/2450